Pragmatics in English Language Learning

Written by an international team of experts, this groundbreaking book explores the benefits and challenges of developing pragmatic competence in English as a target language, inside and outside the classroom, and among young and adult learners of English. The chapters present a range of first language (L1) contexts, including China, Germany, Indonesia, Italy, Mexico, and Norway, to provide international perspectives on how different L1s present varying challenges for developing pragmatic awareness in English. The book outlines cutting-edge techniques for investigating spoken and written pragmatic competence, and offers both face-to-face and online practical teaching solutions. It also examines underexplored areas of second language (L2) pragmatics research, such as young learner groups, the effects of textbook materials, study abroad contexts, and technology-mediated instruction and assessment. Innovative and comprehensive, this volume is a unique contribution to the field of L2 pragmatics, and will be essential reading for researchers, course developers, language teachers, and students.

NICOLA HALENKO is a senior lecturer at the University of Central Lancashire, Preston, and has been an English as Foreign Language (EFL) teacher (Europe and Asia), teacher-trainer, and researcher for over twenty-five years. Her main areas of interest are L2 pragmatics, intercultural communication, and teacher pedagogy. Her recent publications include *Teaching Pragmatics and Instructed Second Language Acquisition* (Bloomsbury, 2021) and *Successful Spoken English* (co-authored, Routledge, 2018).

JIAYI WANG is an associate professor at De Montfort University, UK. Her research interests include pragmatics and intercultural communication. Recent publications include a co-edited journal special issue *Second Language Pragmatics* (with N. Halenko, 2019) for *East Asian Pragmatics* and the article 'Culture, context, and concerns about face: Synergistic insights from pragmatics and social psychology' for the *Journal of Language and Social Psychology* (with H. Spencer-Oatey, 2020).

T0384497

Pragmatics in English Language Learning

Edited by

Nicola Halenko
University of Central Lancashire, Preston

Jiayi Wang
De Montfort University, Leicester

CAMBRIDGE
UNIVERSITY PRESS

CAMBRIDGE
UNIVERSITY PRESS

Shaftesbury Road, Cambridge CB2 8EA, United Kingdom

One Liberty Plaza, 20th Floor, New York, NY 10006, USA

477 Williamstown Road, Port Melbourne, VIC 3207, Australia

314–321, 3rd Floor, Plot 3, Splendor Forum, Jasola District Centre, New Delhi – 110025, India

103 Penang Road, #05–06/07, Visioncrest Commercial, Singapore 238467

Cambridge University Press is part of Cambridge University Press & Assessment, a department of the University of Cambridge.

We share the University's mission to contribute to society through the pursuit of education, learning and research at the highest international levels of excellence.

www.cambridge.org
Information on this title: www.cambridge.org/9781108794930

DOI: 10.1017/9781108894241

First published 2022
First paperback edition 2024

A catalogue record for this publication is available from the British Library

Library of Congress Cataloging-in-Publication data
Names: Halenko, Nicola, editor. | Wang, Jiayi, editor.
Title: Pragmatics in English language learning / edited by
Nicola Halenko, Jiayi Wang.
Description: Cambridge, United Kingdom; New York, NY: Cambridge University
Press, 2022. | Includes bibliographical references and index.
Identifiers: LCCN 2022020708 | ISBN 9781108841528 (hardback) |
ISBN 9781108894241 (ebook)
Subjects: LCSH: English language – Study and teaching – Foreign speakers. |
Pragmatics – Study and teaching. | BISAC: LANGUAGE ARTS & DISCIPLINES /
Linguistics / General | LCGFT: Essays.
Classification: LCC PE1128.A2 P6934 2022 | DDC 428.0071–dc23/eng/20220608
LC record available at https://lccn.loc.gov/2022020708

ISBN   978-1-108-84152-8   Hardback
ISBN   978-1-108-79493-0   Paperback

Contents

Figures

Tables

Contributors

MARIA ECONOMIDOU-KOGETSIDIS (University of Nicosia, Cyprus) is Professor of English and Applied Linguistics at the Department of Languages and Literature. Her current research interests include interlanguage and intercultural pragmatics, email pragmatics, and developmental pragmatics, especially in relation to speech acts and young learners. She has recently co-edited (with M. Savić and N. Halenko) *Email Pragmatics and Second Language Learners* (John Benjamins, 2021).

ELIZABETH FLORES-SALGADO (Meritorious Autonomous University of Puebla, Mexico) is a full-time professor/researcher at the language school of this university. She has delivered multiple papers at international level and published several articles and book chapters. Her research interests include computer-mediated communication, cross-cultural pragmatics, and interlanguage pragmatics.

SARA GESUATO (University of Padua, Italy) is Associate Professor at the Department of Linguistic and Literary Studies, where she teaches English Language and Linguistics. Her research fields include pragmatics, genre analysis, and corpus linguistics. Her most recent research has investigated pedagogical applications of the qualitative-quantitative analysis of speech acts. She has organised various conferences and published over ninety works.

NICOLA HALENKO (University of Central Lancashire, UK) is a senior lecturer in Teaching English to Speakers of Other Languages (TESOL) and Applied Linguistics. She has been involved in English language teaching for over twenty-five years in Europe, Australia, and East Asia, as a teacher, teacher-trainer, and researcher. She has a recently published (2021) monograph by Bloomsbury, *Teaching Pragmatics and Instructed Second Language Learning.*

ANANDA MUHAMMAD (Iowa State University, USA) is a PhD student in Applied Linguistics and Technology. She has taught English as a foreign/second language in Indonesia and the USA respectively for seven years. Her research interests include L2 pragmatics teaching and assessment, as well as teacher professional development.

ANDERS MYRSET (University of Stavanger, Norway) is a doctoral research fellow in English at the Department of Education and Sports Science, Faculty of Arts and Education. His research interests are (meta)pragmatic development, second/foreign language teaching, and research with children.

MILICA SAVIĆ (University of Stavanger, Norway) is Associate Professor at the Department of Teacher Education and Sports Science, where she teaches courses in linguistics and developmental pragmatics for pre- and in-service EFL teachers. Her research interests include interlanguage and intercultural pragmatics, especially (meta)pragmatic development in young L2 learners, and relational practices in institutional email communication.

GILA A. SCHAUER (University of Erfurt, Germany) is Professor of English and Applied Linguistics in the Department of Linguistics. She has authored two monographs: *Interlanguage Pragmatic Development: The Study Abroad Context* (Continuum/Bloomsbury, 2009) and *Teaching and Learning English in the Primary School: Interlanguage Pragmatics in the EFL Context* (Springer, 2019).

NAOKO TAGUCHI (Northern Arizona University, USA) is a professor in the English Department where she teaches courses in applied linguistics. Her research interests include L2 pragmatics, intercultural competence, technology-assisted learning, and English-medium education. She recently edited *The Routledge Handbook of Second Language Acquisition and Pragmatics* (Routledge, 2019). She is the co-editor of the journal *Applied Pragmatics* (John Benjamins).

JIAYI WANG (De Montfort University, UK) is an associate professor. Her research interests include pragmatics, intercultural communication, and language education. Recent publications include a co-edited journal special issue *Learning and Teaching Second Language Pragmatics* (with N. Halenko, 2022) for *The Language Learning Journal* and the article 'Culture, Context, and Concerns about Face: Synergistic Insights from Pragmatics and Social Psychology' for the *Journal of Language and Social Psychology* (with H. Spencer-Oatey, 2020).

Foreword

The reader of this edited volume has a real treasure chest in hand. Now, before the reader quickly leafs through this Foreword – quite right, this is an endorsement any foreword is supposed to make – I would like to emphasise that my previous sentence is not a standard marketing opening. This book *is* a particularly thought-provoking collection of studies, and in this Foreword I aim to point out why this is the case, hopefully without revealing too much about the actual content of the book – a task that is due to be left to the editors.

When it comes to the pragmatics of language teaching and learning, one can consider two particular problems. Firstly, L2 pragmaticians rarely work with oft-fetishised 'naturally occurring' types data, such as naturally occurring audio-recordings. As Edmondson et al. (2022) argue, a language classroom is a typical ritual space, in which rights and obligations are strictly determined, and while these rights and obligations may change in language games, such changes do not make the ritual space of the classroom disappear. The participants of any classroom interaction are aware of their status and use and interpret language accordingly. Thus, the very setting in which the L2 pragmatician collects data precludes certain 'naturalistic' features that characterise other types of pragmatic data such as a phone call made between friends. Furthermore, in pragmatic research on language teaching and learning one simply cannot limit oneself to the study of audio- and video-recorded data: there is a rich variety of methodologies through which language is taught and language learning is assessed, and all these methodologies are invaluable sources for data collection and study.

Secondly, the types of data that one can collect in classrooms have methodological implications: many conventional L2 pragmatic methodologies may appear to be rather pedestrian 'applications' of more 'mainstream' pragmatic research. That is, L2 pragmaticians often appear to engage in replicating and fine-tuning the parameters of well-established research methodologies such as discourse completion tests (DCTs). Such fine-tuning is, of course, anything but pedestrian: the L2 pragmatician working with groups of real learners needs to consider many practical issues, perhaps even more than their colleagues working in other areas. However, such methodological considerations may appear to outsiders to this area as 'applied' in the literary sense of the word.

In the following, I consider these two issues: the seeming lack of 'naturally occurring-ness' of data in L2 pragmatics, and the related seeming methodological pedestrian character of the field. As regards the first of these issues, 'naturally occurring' has indeed become a fetish in pragmatics: in pragmatic studies influenced by conversation analysis and so-called discursive research, the only data with real appeal is often one that the researcher audio- and video-records. A particularly well-known critique of elicited data in pragmatics is Eelen (2001), who, in his criticism of politeness theories, heavily lashed out against the seminal work of Blum-Kulka et al. (1989), a framework that created the foundations of interlanguage and L2 pragmatics. The essence of discursive criticisms such as Eelen's is that in all data elicitation methodologies the researcher projects his a priori knowledge about the data. Convincing as this criticism may sound, there is a beautiful glitch in it, as the seminal work of House (2018) pointed out: in practically any audio- or video-recording William Labov's 'Observer Paradox' cannot be overcome, and so the 'natural occurring-ness' of our data is always merely a matter of degree. Furthermore, as Marquez Reiter (2018) demonstrated, even if one accepts that 'naturally occurring' data is somehow the *non plus ultra* of datatypes in pragmatic research – a claim that one can rightly question – some seemingly non-naturalistic datatypes such as ethnographic interviews may turn out to be as much 'naturally occurring' as 'proper' audio-recorded interactions, because in such data the subjects often forget that they are participating in a guided game and start to build interpersonal relationships with the researcher who records the data. This implies that many datatypes that L2 pragmaticians have used, spanning role play, DCT, and guided learner conversations are close to what one may call naturally occurring. Furthermore, such data may provide insight into a wealth of pragmatic phenomena, not least because in the ritual frame of a classroom the participants unavoidably reveal a lot about the pragmatic conventions of their own native tongues. The present book provides first-hand evidence for this: the authors of the book provide the reader with richly diverse data, drawn from both formal and informal learning settings, from learners of different age groups, sociocultural backgrounds and learning goals, and from learners of different competence.

Regarding the second of the above-mentioned issues, L2 pragmatic research has shown that experts often do much more than simply substantiate their results with existing research methodologies. As House and Kádár (2021) have pointed out in their recent study, in any cross-cultural pragmatic research – including L2 pragmatics, which is a key subfield of cross-cultural pragmatic research – one is well advised to mutually use a basic analysis and supplement it with an ancillary approach. Such an ancillary approach may either precede or follow the main approach. For example, one may conduct interviews (ancillary research) to set the parameters of the main pragmatic enquiry, or, the other way around, the outcomes of the main analysis may be tested with the aid of ancillary research. Irrespective of how one designs particular research, an essential point to bear in mind is that in L2 settings one unavoidably works with cross-cultural data, and so any research outcome needs to be meticulously cross-tested. Accepting this logic implies that cutting-edge L2 pragmatic research is methodologically *not* pedestrian at all – on the contrary, as the contributions of the present volume also insightfully show, it provides a fertile ground for methodological innovation.

I believe that, after reading this book, the reader will also agree with me that this book is a *must read*, not only for experts of pragmatics and other areas of linguistics, but also for practitioners with interest in cutting-edge research on language teaching and learning.

DÁNIEL Z. KÁDÁR

Dalian University of Foreign Languages, China and
Hungarian Academy of Sciences Momentum Interactional
Rituals Research Group, Hungary

References

Blum-Kulka, S., House, J., & Kasper, G. (eds.) (1989). *Cross-Cultural Pragmatics: Requests and Apologies*. Norwood, NJ: Ablex.

Edmondson, W., House, J., & Kadar, D. Z. (2022). *Speech Acts, Discourse, and Interaction: An Integrative Pedagogic Grammar of English*. Cambridge: Cambridge University Press.

Eelen, G. (2001). *A Critique of Politeness Theories*. Manchester: St Jerome.

House, J. (2018). Authentic versus elicited data and qualitative versus quantitative research methods in pragmatics: Overcoming two non-fruitful dichotomies. *System*, 75, 4–11.

House, J., & Kadar, D. Z. (2021). *Cross-Cultural Pragmatics*. Cambridge: Cambridge University Press.

Márquez Reiter, R. (2018). Interviews as sites of ideological work. *Spanish in Context*, 15(1), 54–76.

Acknowledgements

We hope this volume will be as much of a pleasure to read as it has been to work with all its contributors, who have worked hard to deliver a collection of high-quality chapters in challenging world circumstances. We owe a great deal of thanks and appreciation to all who have been involved in this collaborative effort and to Cambridge University Press for seeing the potential of the volume. We are especially grateful to Rebecca Taylor and Isabel Collins for their clear and timely guidance throughout this process.

Finally, on a personal note, we would like to thank our family, friends, colleagues, and students for their unwavering support throughout.

Introduction

Nicola Halenko and Jiayi Wang

This edited volume showcases a series of unique and thought-provoking investigations which track the interlanguage challenges and benefits of developing pragmatic competence for successful interaction in English as a target language of study. As existing reviews indicate (Jeon & Kaya, 2006; Plonsky & Zhuang, 2019; Taguchi, 2015), English as a target language dominates second language (L2) pragmatics inquiry but, regrettably, no such collection which draws on such a wide range of learners from European and East Asian backgrounds has been produced. This original and comprehensive volume offers an overview of very recent efforts to update researchers, course developers, and language teachers on significant advances in the field when investigating spoken and written pragmatic competence with English language learners in either the at-home (EFL) or study abroad (ESL) learning contexts. The studies included in the volume change the scope of methodological and pedagogical approaches to L2 pragmatics research, so readers can be sure of accessing some cutting-edge techniques in these areas. This introductory chapter will briefly outline the place for pragmatic competence in language learning, highlight the volume's innovations and readership appeal, and then go on to summarise each chapter's contribution. This Introduction sets the scene for a more comprehensive conceptual and theoretical overview of the L2 pragmatics field presented in Chapter 1.

Being a successful language user is not just about knowing how to convey your message in a well-structured manner. Knowing the right words to choose for the right social situation is just as important. Making appropriate linguistic choices can be the making or breaking of successful communication. As a simple example, this means we might ask a favour of a close friend in quite a different way than we would of a superior. This notion of making socially appropriate linguistic choices is known as *pragmatic competence.*

As Taguchi (Chapter 1) points out, developing pragmatic competence is not at all straightforward and a number of challenges exist. Language learners must overcome L1 to L2 form-function-context mapping, in addition to then applying this knowledge in real-time interaction. Since no pragmatic rule books exist and language textbooks often lack any helpful or meaningful direction for receptive or productive pragmatic use, it is often the case that when we communicate in a foreign language, we are left to our own devices to work the pragmatics out for ourselves. While some pragmatic rules can be transferred successfully across language systems, this is not always the case. Where cross-cultural norms vary and influence language production and comprehension in different ways, is often the point at which learners come unstuck trying to convey their pragmatic intentions. Learners and instructors therefore need guidance on developing pragmatic competency which is still under construction during the language learning process (House, 2011). *Pragmatics in English Language Learning* offers readers this helping hand.

About this Volume

The reader will find the empirical studies are all forward-thinking in terms of addressing gaps in current L2 pragmatics research. Firstly, much existing pragmatics research offers an American perspective by way of sampling American study abroad (SA) foreign language learners themselves or using L1 American data for direct comparison to foreign language users' pragmatic abilities in English. This collection expands pragmatics insights with learners from diverse international backgrounds to see how pragmatic development in English language learning is tracked and researched amongst different L1 communities. Each of the original empirical investigations in this volume employs participants across several continents based in either the at-home learning experience or during a SA stay. This exclusive focus on English language learning helps to identify links between different first language pragmalinguistic and sociopragmatic challenges, such as linguistic interference or cross-cultural differences, and how these impact the development of pragmatic competence in one target language. The range of English language learning contexts included in the volume (China, Cyprus, Germany, Indonesia, Italy, Mexico, Norway) gives the volume its international focus and wide readership appeal.

Secondly, the varied speech act studies (requests, apologies, refusals, dis/agreements, thanks) address a number of methodological concerns which are in greater need of attention. Each study focusses on either underexplored participant groups (e.g., young or adolescent English language learners, advanced-level postgraduate students), underexplored factors which influence pragmatic development (e.g., perlocutionary effects on the interlocutor, textbook materials), or underexplored contexts for learning and teaching (e.g., SA, technology-mediated instruction). This volume is an essential read for researchers and practitioners. It brings together a much-needed collection of empirical investigations on pragmatics in English language learning, undertaken by world-leading scholars and upcoming researchers.

Organisation of this Volume

To help the reader navigate this collection of studies, the chapters have been organised thematically. Taguchi's Chapter 1 provides a useful and insightful starting point to situate the subsequent empirical contributions in this volume. The chapter charts the evolution of theoretical and contextual developments in L2 pragmatics research from its early beginning in the 1980s to the current landscape in the post-2000s, acknowledging the influences of global and technological developments within the field. The chapter concludes with recommendations for future directions which include diversifying our conceptual and methodological approaches to L2 pragmatics research and considering the advantages of cross-disciplinary perspectives to better understand the complexities of pragmatic competence moving forward.

Following this state-of-the-art overview, the remainder of the volume is organised into two main sections. Part I, Pragmatics in Action, introduces studies which monitor the development of pragmatic ability in EFL learning in the absence of targeted instruction. Each chapter innovates or refreshes existing methodological approaches and techniques when examining spoken and written pragmatic competency. Beginning with Chapter 2, Wang and Halenko examine L2 pragmatic development during SA by tracking Chinese postgraduate students' evolving asymmetrical email communication with academic staff. Using 170 authentic L2 emails in comparison to a reference corpus of 162 authentic L1 emails, this study identifies distinct features of the Chinese learners' L2 email requests to faculty: significant directness and limited choices of conventional indirectness, extensive external modification and relative limited internal modification, and heavy reliance on the request perspectives of 'you' and 'I'. Participant interviews reveal learner agency played a key role in pragmatic learning and unlearning, the latter of which refers to the process by which learners, after acquiring the target forms, actively dissociate from L2 norms when conflicts with the L1 systems arise, implying that L2 pragmatic development is fluid. The inclusion of learner testimonials is typically exceptional in empirical studies, and the in-depth reflections presented in this study allow for a more nuanced understanding of the affective and cognitive processes involved in pragmatics decision-making and some of the struggles learners experience.

Moving to the EFL context, Economidou-Kogetsidis's cross-sectional study in Chapter 3 examines Greek learners' interlanguage pragmatic performance, shedding light on their L2 pragmatic development. Using interactive role plays, this study analyses and compares learners' request production across three proficiency levels and examines whether learners who receive classroom instruction in a FL context show pragmalinguistic development in making requests as their English language proficiency improves. The scope of proficiency levels investigated provides important insights for language trainers. Results suggest that despite signs of pragmatic development with increasing proficiency, the advanced learners' performance still lagged far behind in the pragmatic areas examined. She calls for more systematic studies to investigate the role of L1 and native culture. In this way, trainers may be better equipped to deal with the L1-based challenges of pragmatic development in foreign language settings when access to the target community is limited or non-existent. Tackling this issue of access to the L2 as an authentic intercultural resource remains an important priority for EFL pragmatics training.

Gesuato's study in Chapter 4 is also university-based but shifts the focus from EFL learners to English language teachers' perceptions and evaluations. The study explores how native English-speaking university lecturers perceive the communicative in/adequacy of Italian EFL learners' gratitude emails. She defines adequacy as accuracy and appropriateness, meaning successful achievement of interactional goals in a way that is efficient and acceptable to the addressee and the situation. Using small-scale surveys with open-ended questions and scalar ratings of elicited written texts, this study contributes to the underexplored research on the assessment of learners' ability to produce extended discourse beyond the single utterance. Moreover, it adds to a limited number of studies focussing on the perlocutionary effects of language use.

In Chapter 5, Savić and Myrset's study is also perception-based but uses a series of task-based data collection techniques to investigate how a group of 9–13-year-old Norwegian learners of English appraised and reflected on different types of request strategies in English that they themselves had produced. Greater attention to linguistic request behaviour was observed in all the age groups, with contextual considerations first appearing among the older learners. This study advances methodological techniques which can be used in young learner investigations. Adopting visual and kinaesthetic collaborative tasks, which activate young-learner interest and engagement when eliciting pragmatic reflections, holds much promise for further research in this underexplored EFL age group.

Part II of the volume, Instructed L2 Pragmatics, includes a set of distinct investigations which have undertaken some form of planned pedagogical action to address shortfalls in pragmatic knowledge, with or without the use of technology to enhance the instructional input. Schauer's study in Chapter 6 links instructional input with German EFL learners' output in relation to the speech acts of agreement and disagreement. This is the second study in the volume focussing on young learners (see also Chapter 5, this volume). Specifically, the investigation examines the link between input materials (EFL textbooks and audio material) and intermediate secondary school learners' pragmatic output, elicited via an illustrated discourse completion task. The pragmatic output consists of an illustrated discourse completion task completed by two groups of EFL learners around 14 to 15 years old, who were attending grades 8 and 10 respectively. The study's unique contribution of furthering our understanding of pragmatic input and output, and in an underrepresented secondary school setting, sets the benchmark for future investigations of this kind.

In Chapter 7, Flores-Salgado and Halenko's study offers several innovative features in their investigation of the efficacy of explicit instruction to enhance pragmatic learning. Firstly, the study focusses on the relatively underexplored speech act of refusals, situated within an underrepresented participant group of Mexican EFL learners. A further original feature is the (classroom-based) technology-mediated instruction used alongside the virtual role plays for evaluating pragmatic performance. The study also demonstrates the benefits of using film clips as an authentic and contextually rich audiovisual resource. Finally, the study is another good example of data triangulation whereby linguistic output is investigated alongside learner interview data to gain a greater understanding of the connection between cognitive and linguistic processes when conveying pragmatic intentions.

The final empirical chapter has great potential to resolve some of the key concerns of language trainers when undertaking pragmatics training: classroom time, teacher knowledge and skills, and pragmatics resources. In Chapter 8, Muhammad's study on the efficacy of self-access learning materials to advance pragmatic development contributes much to the value and development of open-source learning platforms (in this case, Moodle) for pragmatics training. The self-paced modular course was able to increase the Indonesian EFL learners' linguistic and sociocultural pragmatic awareness of spoken and written (email) requests after following the training for approximately one month. While the pragmatics training here was designed to facilitate future academic socialisation into graduate programmes in the US, it is clear to see the possible scope for further application of self-access materials to a wide range of learning contexts which could substitute or enhance the time-limited classroom experience, for instance. In an increasingly interconnected world, this chapter seems a fitting final contribution by offering an insight into how pragmatics teaching and learning may develop in the coming years.

We end this volume by drawing together some common threads emerging from this collection of chapters across the different countries as well as the various modes and contexts of learning. The synthesis also points out directions for future research and pedagogical action. We hope this book will stimulate the reader to undertake their own L2 pragmatic explorations to continue advancing our understanding of this important field.

References

House, J. (2011). What is an intercultural speaker? In E. Alcón Soler & M. P. Safont Jordà (eds.), *Intercultural Language Use and Language Learning*. Dordrecht Springer, pp. 7–21.

Jeon, E. H., & Kaya, T. (2006). Effects of L2 instruction on interlanguage pragmatic development: A meta-analysis. In J. M. Morris & L. Ortega (eds.), *Synthesizing Research on Language Learning and Teaching*. Amsterdam: John Benjamins, pp. 165–211.

Plonsky, L., & Zhuang, J. (2019). A meta-analysis of L2 pragmatics instruction. In N. Taguchi (ed.), *The Routledge Handbook of SLA and Pragmatics*, pp. 297–307.

Taguchi, N. (2015). Instructed pragmatics at a glance: Where instructional studies were, are, and should be going. *Language Teaching*, 48, 1–50.

1 Second Language Pragmatics
A Historical Overview and Future Directions

Naoko Taguchi

1.1 Introduction

Second language (L2) pragmatics, a field of second language acquisition (SLA), investigates L2 learners' ability to communicate meaning in a socially appropriate manner and how such ability develops over time. The field started in the 1980s, owing, in part, to the concept of *pragmatic failure,* introduced by Jenny Thomas (1983) in her seminal paper. This concept reinforced the idea that learners can be perfect in grammar and vocabulary but still fail in communication due to a lack of understanding of social conventions or rules of communication. Following this, Kasper and Dahl (1991) presented the term *interlanguage pragmatics* (ILP) as a field that studies non-native speakers' knowledge of pragmatics. Although the definition of ILP and pragmatic competence has gone through several reiterations (Bardovi-Harlig, 2010; Kasper & Rose, 2002; Taguchi & Roever, 2017), the area of primary interest remains the same – L2 learners' knowledge and use of language in a social context.

Since its inception the field has grown rapidly, as seen in the steep increase in the scope and number of empirical studies since the 1980s. These developments can also be seen in the over fifty books now available on the topic of L2 pragmatics (for a review, see Taguchi & Roever, 2017). Some of these books are research monographs documenting pragmatic competence of particular individuals and groups. Others are edited volumes with specific themes, including cross-cultural pragmatics; speech act production, instruction, and assessment; pragmatics in institutional discourse; pragmatic variation; technology-enhanced pragmatics learning; and contexts of pragmatics learning. Others still are teachers' guides and resource books with ready-made lesson plans and tips for teaching pragmatics. Handbooks and review books have presented a comprehensive treatment of key topics in ILP. Collectively, these books have highlighted the significance of pragmatics in L2 learning, as well as in a broader discourse of multiculturalism and intercultural communication.

Keeping in mind various changes that have occurred in the last few decades, this chapter surveys historical developments of L2 pragmatics research from the 1980s up to now. Section 1.2 presents the historical sketch in three time

7

periods: (1) the 1980s–1990s, (2) the 1990s–2000s, and (3) the 2000s–present. The section discusses major trends and milestone events characterising each period. It is important to note that these events and trends may not be fixed within the time period; more often, certain instances that occurred in the specific time period were carried over to the next time period and expanded further with more research.

1.2   The 1980s–1990s

1.2.1   *Defining the Construct of Pragmatic Competence*

The fundamental question in L2 pragmatics research is what makes someone pragmatically competent. The early phase of the field was characterised by researchers' efforts to define the construct of pragmatic competence – what elements were involved in the construct and how they interact with each other. The original definition goes back to theoretical models of communicative competence, which situated pragmatic competence as a fundamental and distinct component of L2 ability (Bachman & Palmer, 1996; Canale & Swain, 1980). According to these models, pragmatic competence involves two types of knowledge: functional knowledge and sociolinguistic knowledge. The former involves the knowledge of linguistic forms for performing a communicative function (e.g., saying 'Talk to you later' when ending a phone call), while the latter involves selecting appropriate forms to use in a specific context (e.g., how to end a phone call with a friend vs how to end a call with a customer). These two dimensions are also illustrated in Thomas's (1983) distinction of *pragmalinguistics* and *sociopragmatics*. The former refers to linguistic resources for performing a communicative act, while the latter involves knowledge of sociocultural norms associated with the act.

1.2.2   *Comparative, Cross-Sectional Research of Speech Acts*

In the 1980s–1990s, comparative studies of speech acts across languages dominated the research practice of L2 pragmatics. The popularity of speech acts research was probably because the concepts of locution, illocution, and perlocution in speech acts present a clear connection among form, function, and context of use. Based on the assumption that different languages have different linguistic means for conveying illocutionary force, a large body of studies compared speech act strategies across different first language (L1) and L2 groups. Drawing on speech act theory (Austin, 1962; Seale, 1969) and politeness theory (Brown & Levinson, 1987), studies analysed linguistic strategies (positive and negative politeness strategies) used to perform speech acts (e.g., request, refusal). Specifically, those studies examined variations in speech act strategies across languages, and the influence of contextual parameters (e.g., interlocutors' power relationship, social distance, and degree of imposition) on people's selection of the strategies.

A milestone project that served as the foundation of L2 pragmatics research is Cross-Cultural Speech Act Project (CCSARP) initiated by Blum-Kulka et al. (1989). The goal of the project was to examine variations in speech act strategies across seven languages (German, Hebrew, French, Danish, and three varieties of English). Using a discourse completion task (DCT), the project elicited speech acts of request and apology from native and non-native speakers of respective languages. By categorising speech act strategies across languages using a uniform coding framework, the researchers were able to document how many speech act strategies exist in a language, which strategies are direct or indirect, and how those strategies vary across situations involving different speaker relationships and social distance. The coding framework and DCT instrument facilitated a large number of replication studies, which provided empirical descriptions of speech act patterns across language groups. The use of DCTs and coding frameworks for speech act analysis is still a trend today. Nguyen's (2019) review of 246 empirical studies published from 1979 to 2017 showed that eighty-nine studies (36 per cent) used DCTs, making it the most common data collection method.

Following the CCSARP, in the same period, the comparative analysis of speech act strategies expanded to include cross-sectional studies of L2 learner groups at different proficiency levels, lengths of formal study, and duration of residence in the target language country. The cross-sectional studies analysed speech act data collected from two or more L2 groups based on different proficiency levels or lengths of study. Findings regarding the role of proficiency and length of study in L2 speech act performance are largely mixed and inconclusive. Some studies revealed a positive influence of proficiency and length of study on increased pragmatic competence, while others did not, suggesting that pragmatic competence is a complex construct influenced by a number of factors simultaneously.

1.3   The 1990s–2000s

1.3.1   Teaching Pragmatics

After the comparative, cross-sectional research phase, research in the 1990s increasingly focussed on instruction and assessment of pragmatic competence. Moving away from the dominance of morpho-syntax studies in instructed SLA, researchers started to explore how formal instruction can be applied to develop sociocultural aspects of language use (Kasper, 1997). Since then, about 100 instructional studies have emerged in the field, which were surveyed in several review articles. Jeon and Kaya's (2006) meta-analysis examined thirty-four instructional studies, while Takahashi (2010) reviewed forty-nine studies. Taguchi's (2015b) paper synthesised findings from fifty-eight studies. The most recent meta-analysis by Plonsky and Zhang (2019) examined fifty studies. These reviews generally confirmed that pragmatics is certainly teachable; instructed groups, particularly those who have received explicit metapragmatic information, tend to outperform their non-instructed counterpart.

One notable trend that emerged in Taguchi's (2015b) review is the dominance of English as a target language. Of fifty-eight studies, thirty-eight involve teaching English pragmatics. Other languages, such as Japanese, German, French, Chinese, and Spanish, are seriously underrepresented (two to eight studies for each language group). The scope of pragmatic targets is skewed towards speech acts, with the request being most popular. Besides speech acts, studies have targeted address forms, discourse organisational skills (e.g., small talk), and interactional devices (e.g., discourse markers, hedging, and response forms). Taguchi concluded the generalisations about effective teaching as follows (2015b, pp. 35–36):

(1) Effects of instruction vary depending on the pragmatic targets. Pragmatic targets that are structurally simple (e.g., routines) or pragmatic rules that are systematic are learned more easily.
(2) Explicit teaching is generally more effective than implicit teaching, particularly when it involves direct metapragmatic information followed by production practice.
(3) Implicit teaching can be as effective as explicit teaching if it promotes noticing of the target form-function-context mappings and deeper-level processing of the mappings. Effective teaching is closely related to the quality of processing depth. Learners who receive direct metapragmatic information, or learners who are guided to deduce pragmatic rules, can process the input at a deeper level.

Parallel to the growth of instructional research, a variety of materials and activities has been developed to teach pragmatics. Those materials are designed to address the elements specific to pragmatics – sociocultural language use, context, and interaction. Dozens of teachers' guides and resource books demonstrated how these elements can be incorporated into instructional activities (e.g., Bardovi-Harlig & Mahan-Taylor, 2003; Houck & Tatsuki, 2011; Ishihara & Cohen, 2010). Cohen and Ishihara (2013) outline several guidelines for materials development. They emphasise that materials need to be designed to raise learners' awareness of pragmatics-related language use, have learners engage in pragmatic-focussed communication, and guide learners' discovery and understanding of pragmatic rules. These resource books and teachers' guides also provide tips on how to adapt or supplement existing materials for the purpose of improving students' pragmatic knowledge (Tatsuki, 2019).

Supplementary materials can often rectify problems the formal classroom setting poses for pragmatics learning. The classroom is considered noticeably limited in terms of learning opportunities for pragmatics because of the lack of contextualised, real-life language use in classroom discourse. In a classroom, learners do not typically interact with speakers in diverse social roles and situations or experience real-life consequences of their pragmatic behaviours (Taguchi, 2015a). Classroom materials and textbooks often lack pragmatics-focussed information and activities, limiting learners' exposure to authentic samples of pragmatics (Ren & Han, 2016; see also Chapter 6). Furthermore, studies comparing textbook dialogues and naturalistic dialogues revealed a discrepancy between the two (e.g., Gilmore, 2004). Given these limitations of a classroom, teachers' guides and resource books are useful in supplementing classroom practices for pragmatics-learning opportunities.

1.3.2 Assessing Pragmatic Competence

While the teaching of pragmatics has grown rapidly since the 1990s, during the same period, research in the assessment of pragmatic competence has also increased multi-fold (for a review, see Roever, 2011; Youn & Bogorevich, 2019). Researchers have engaged in typical assessment practices, including construct definition and operationalisation, measurement design, validity argument, and reliability estimates, to develop a valid, reliable battery for assessing pragmatic competence. Hudson et al. (1995) initiated this trend by adopting the multi-trait, multi-method approach to the assessment of pragmatics. They showed how different measures (e.g., DCTs, role plays, multiple-choice questions, self-assessment) can be designed to evaluate speech acts of requests, apologies, and refusals. Roever (2005) moved this practice forward with technology applications, developing a web-based test battery that assessed speech acts, implicature, and routines in L2 English.

Existing methods for collecting and assessing language samples are diverse and include written and spoken DCTs (see Chapter 7, this volume), role plays (Chapter 3, this volume), self-assessment surveys, interviews (Chapters 2 and 7, this volume), think-aloud protocols, and multiple-choice tests (for a review, see Nguyen, 2019). Analyses of learners' test performance have generated SLA-related insights such as learners' developmental stages and relationship between general proficiency and pragmatic competence. Research has also generated pedagogy-related insights into curricula decisions and materials developments. More recently, the testing of L2 pragmatics shifted from assessing knowledge of isolated speech acts (requests, compliments) to inter-actional competence and participation in extended discourse (Roever, 2021; Youn, 2015).

1.3.3   Longitudinal Investigation into Pragmatic Development

In the period when teaching and assessment started to receive attention, the field also moved away from the traditional practice of cross-sectional inves-tigation and instead expanded the body of longitudinal studies. Longitudinal design is suitable for studying pragmatics because the acquisition of pragmatic competence is a long-term process. To become pragmatically competent, learners need linguistic resources, as well as the ability to evaluate layers of contextual information, select appropriate resources, and use them effectively. Given the complexity of pragmatic competence, longitudinal lenses, which allow researchers to track learners over time, can provide fuller insights into learners' changing pragmatic abilities.

Despite the value of longitudinal investigation, early research mainly focused on pragmatics language use, rather than development. This was origi-nally noted in Kasper and Schmidt's (1996) seminal paper, which stated that the majority of studies investigate how L2 learners' pragmalinguistic and sociopragmatic knowledge differs from that of native speakers, rather than investigating learners' acquisition patterns of the knowledge. This observation was repeated in subsequent seminal publications (e.g., Bardovi-Harlig, 2000; Kasper & Rose, 1999), all of which underscored the need for more longitudinal studies. Although their call did not immediately lead to a substantial expan-sion of longitudinal studies, the number of studies focused on development gradually increased over time. There were only nine longitudinal studies in Kasper and Rose's (1999) early review, but the number increased to about a dozen in Bardovi-Harlig's (2000) paper. More recently, Taguchi's (2010) review located twenty-one longitudinal studies. This trend clearly indicates a growing interest in the longitudinal perspective towards L2 pragmatics (see also Chapter 2, this volume).

Existing longitudinal studies have documented changing pragmatic abili-ties in a variety of features, ranging from traditional constructs of speech acts, implicature, and routines, to interactional features that facilitate learners' participation in a communicative act (e.g., acknowledgement and alignment expressions). Findings point to several generalisations about patterns of prag-matic development. Research in the area of *pragmatic comprehension* found that learners typically progress from the stage where meaning is marked via conventional linguistic cues or discourse patterns, to the stage where meaning does not involve those cues and thus requires extensive inferencing (Bouton, 1994; Taguchi, 2007).

In the area of *pragmatic production*, learners usually show an initial tendency of sticking to one-to-one correspondence between form and function, often symbolised by the overgeneralisation of a few pragmalinguistic forms over a range of functions or the use of routine formulae (e.g., Hassall, 2006; Ohta, 2001; Shively, 2011). Learners gradually expand their pragmalinguistic repertoire by adopting a new form-function association into their systems. This process is slow, but feedback and modelling from community members can facilitate the process (e.g., Hassall, 2006).

In the area of *pragmatic interaction*, development is often characterised as learners' diversification of interactional resources and ability to adapt the resources to the specific interactional context. Taguchi and Roever (2017) outlined three stages of development in interactional-pragmatic competence. In the initial *egocentric stage*, learners focus on getting their meaning across and achieving the communicative goal with little attention to establishing shared understanding or maintaining social solidarity. This stage is followed by a stage of *basic mutuality* where learners begin to use some interactional resources (e.g., making a dispreferred social action such as a refusal) but still focus on efficiency of communication. In the last stage of *shared understandings*, learners organise their linguistic behaviours based on their interlocutor's displayed understanding of the behaviours; they also start adapting their behaviours to the specific interlocutor and interactional context.

Previous studies also found developmental variation across pragmatic targets; some aspects of pragmatics show faster developmental pace than others. For instance, learners' use of pragmalinguistic forms (e.g., hedges, lexical and syntactic mitigations) tend to take a longer time to develop than semantic strategies and tactics used to organise a speech act (e.g., use of small talk to build solidarity, expressions of considerations) (e.g., Félix-Brasdefer & Hasler-Barker, 2015; Ren, 2012).

1.3.4   Pragmatic Development in a Study Abroad Setting

In Taguchi's (2010) review of longitudinal studies in L2 pragmatics, sixteen out of twenty-one studies were conducted in a second language (SL) context where the target language is spoken (e.g., study abroad [SA] settings), while the rest took place in a foreign language (FL) environment (e.g., domestic classroom settings). The pattern is reversed in instructional intervention studies: more studies were conducted in a FL rather than SL context. This lopsided pattern suggests that naturalistic pragmatic development is best observed in a SL context where sociocultural input and practice are readily available. Lacking such input, learners in a FL context can benefit more from direct teaching of pragmatics.

These generalisations are largely confirmed in findings related to the benefits of SL contexts, particularly SA settings, for pragmatic development. Research revealed that L2 learners generally improve their pragmatic competence after participating in a SA program. As Vidal-Perez and Shively (2019) claim, 'a key affordance of a study abroad (SA) experience is the potential to use and be exposed to the L2 in a variety of settings and situations, which involve different interlocutors, topics, registers, and interactional norms' (p. 355). These opportunities unique to SA settings are likely to boost pragmatic development while abroad.

However, existing findings also show that SA is not a uniform experience for all L2 learners. Learners' pragmatic development is affected by a complex set of factors, both personal and contextual, which in turn lead to a great individual variation in the size and rate of pragmatic development (for a review, see Vidal-Perez & Shively, 2019). In pursuing a more nuanced analysis of the context-learning connection, a number of studies have addressed what contextual features in the SA – nature, type, and intensity of social contact and experience – lead to linguistic achievement. Particularly notable in this trend is a line of studies that adapted the language socialisation approach to reveal learners' community involvement and pragmatic development. Language socialisation views learning as a process in which novices become competent members in a society through interaction with expert members in that society (Schieffelin & Ochs, 1986). Adopting this framework, several studies conducted a microgeneric analysis of learners' interaction with local members to reveal how pragmatics learning occurs in situated social activities. For example, on the investigation of Japanese speech styles, Cook (2008) documented numerous instances where host family members explicitly and implicitly socialised learners into target-like uses of the plain and polite forms. Shively (2011) examined service encounter transactions among learners of Spanish in Spain. She found that some learners acquired the speech act of request for service by observing other customers, while others learned it through feedback from their host families. Focusing on a college dorm as a place for socialisation, Diao (2016) analysed conversations between L2 Chinese learners and their Chinese roommates. She revealed the participants' use of sentence-final particles and their discussion about the social meaning of sexuality and gender that the particles project. These studies illustrate how social experiences built around local networks present a community into which learners integrate themselves. Socialisation occurred when learners entered the new community, took up a new role as a host family member or a customer, and participated in the role in recurrent practices of social interaction. Pragmatic development was the by-product of this socialisation process.

Yet, a positive socialisation process does not always happen in these situations, because there is no guarantee that learners can successfully establish a membership in a local community. Learners' success often depends on their agency, as shown in Kinginger's (2008) study that examined L2 French learners' awareness of sociolinguistic forms during a semester abroad. Interview data revealed how learners negotiated their membership in the community. For example, one learner had a host family who preferred a quiet environment at home. To compensate for the lack of conversation at home, he actively developed a social network outside the home by talking to his peers in French and participating in volunteer activities. These findings reiterate how learner agency can reshape the context and learning opportunities available during SA.

1.4   The 2000s and Beyond

1.4.1   Application of Diverse SLA Theories to L2 Pragmatics Research

The first two decades of the twenty-first century have seen a continuing development of instructional and longitudinal research, characterised by a more explicit application of mainstream SLA theories to L2 pragmatics. Instructional and longitudinal research essentially address the same question: what mechanisms drive pragmatic development, pushing learners from the current state to a higher level of pragmatic competence? To address this question, longitudinal studies investigate, on the one hand, naturalistic changes in learners' pragmatic systems with the goal of revealing factors – both individual and contextual – that contribute to those changes. On the other hand, instructional studies consider direct teaching as the sole factor affecting pragmatic development. Hence, instructional studies typically control extraneous factors (e.g., individual characteristics, contextual factors) so researchers can attribute the observed development (or non-development) directly to instruction. Because instruction is carried out with the sole goal of producing learning, any change found from the pre- to post-instruction phase is considered an anticipated change.

Whether longitudinal or instructional, the role of SLA theories is critical because theories provide a guiding framework for tracing change in longitudinal research or developing instructional methods. The last few decades have seen an increasing diversity in theoretical frameworks that guide pragmatics research. Although Schmidt's (1993) noticing hypothesis has dominated the literature since the 1990s, the field has recently expanded this scope by adding new guiding frameworks for longitudinal and instructional investigations. This shift is summarised in Section 1.4.2.

Rooted in the cognitivist approach, the noticing hypothesis (Schmidt, 1993) emphasises L2 learners' attention to form as a necessary condition for learning. Schmidt contends that input becomes intake and leads to acquisition only if learners notice the input. In pragmatics, noticing involves attention to linguistic forms, functional meanings, and relevant contextual features. To my knowledge, no longitudinal studies have applied the noticing hypothesis as a priori theory or tested its predictive validity in pragmatics learning. Instead, the noticing hypothesis has offered post hoc explanations for pragmatic development in many studies, illustrating how pragmatics learning occurred in a particular moment, in a particular learner (e.g., Hassall, 2006).

In the 2000s, researchers started to adopt skill acquisition theories (Anderson et al., 2004) as another cognitivist paradigm in L2 pragmatics research. While the noticing hypothesis focuses on the initial conditions of attention to input, skill acquisition theories focus on stages of acquisition in progression. These theories explain how practice helps learners move beyond the initial stage of conscious learning of rules, to the end point of skill acquisition where they can use rules fluently. Several studies adopted this theoretical paradigm to illustrate how pragmatic development occurs as a function of practice (e.g., Li, 2012; Li & Taguchi, 2014).

Another cognitive theory that has recently advanced the field is Robinson's (2011) Cognition Hypothesis. Unlike the noticing hypothesis or skill acquisition theories, the Cognition Hypothesis focuses on how features of an instructional task impact learners' processing of pragmatics information and its subsequent learning. The hypothesis claims that more complex tasks promote more interaction, leading to more development of targeted linguistic features. Several studies have confirmed this hypothesis in pragmatics learning. Kim and Taguchi (2016) showed that a cognitively complex task generated a greater amount of interaction among learners as they were completing a task of request-making. There was also a positive effect of task complexity on the retention of knowledge of request-making forms (Kim & Taguchi, 2015).

More recently, the field has expanded its scope with the addition of socially oriented theories that view learning as a socially situated activity. Swain and Lapkin's (1998) concept of collaborative dialogue is one exemplary approach that views language knowledge as jointly constructed in interaction. In this view, verbalising target pragmatic features in a collaborative task is considered to promote a deeper-level understanding of the features. Adopting this theoretical claim, Taguchi and Kim (2016) investigated whether a collaborative dialogue designed to focus learners' attention on pragmatic features can actually promote learning of the features in L2 English. They found that learners negotiated and co-constructed their knowledge of request-making forms while completing a goal-oriented task. Another theory grounded on verbalisation and interaction is sociocultural theory (Lantolf & Thorne, 2006). Based on the Vygotskyan principle of language as a cognitive tool, van Compernolle (2014) used concept diagrams as a semiotic tool and taught social meanings of French pronouns *tu* and *vous* by having learners verbalise their understanding of the pronoun distinction.

Finally, language socialisation theory is a long-term player in L2 pragmatics research, as seen in several classic studies that appeared in the 1990s (e.g., Kanagy, 1999). Language socialisation theory attests that linguistic and sociocultural knowledge develop simultaneously through participation in a local community (Schieffelin & Ochs, 1986). The learning-through-participation framework has been documented in a number of studies (see Section 1.3.4).

As illustrated, the connection between SLA and L2 pragmatics has become fortified through a growing number of SLA theories that have been applied to examining pragmatic development. Despite different epistemologies and assumptions, these theories are similar in that they all explicate how pragmatic knowledge becomes consolidated. While the noticing hypothesis emphasises attention as a primary state, skill acquisition theories view repeated practice as a force for the consolidation of pragmatic knowledge. Collaborative dialogue and sociocultural theory consider verbalisation as a means for externalising understanding of pragmatics, which in turn facilitates internalisation of pragmatic knowledge. Under the language socialisation paradigm, pragmatic knowledge becomes consolidated through participation in routine social activities with competent members. Critically, these different theories – and essentially different research methods used under different theories – have jointly enriched understanding of pragmatic development since the 2000s.

1.4.2   Technology-Mediated Pragmatics Teaching and Assessment

Another trend characterising the 2000s and beyond is the application of technology to teaching and assessing pragmatic competence (see Chapters 7 and 8, this volume). This trend is seen in the growing popularity of social media, virtual environments, digital games, and mobile devices for examining learners' pragmatics language use (González-Lloret, 2018; Taguchi & Sykes, 2013). The most obvious benefit of technology is the contextualisation of learning made available via technology. For example, computer-mediated communication (CMC) tools (e.g., SMS, chat, blogs, and video conferencing) can offer space for learners to directly interact with users of the target language across distance (for a review, see Cunningham, 2019). Digital games can provide an interactive environment where learners simulate different roles in diverse social settings (for a review, see Sykes & Dubreil, 2019). Immersive virtual reality (VR) can promote authentic simulations of real-life through a 360° view of the computer-generated world (Taguchi, 2022, in press).

Researchers have started to critically explore the potential of technology-mediated environments by examining whether those environments can actually lead to pragmatics learning. Particularly notable in this trend are a growing number of studies exploring the benefits of game-based pragmatics learning. Studies by Sykes (2009, 2013) and Holden and Sykes (2013) are the forerunner of this trend. Sykes (2009, 2013) developed a 3D immersive space *Croquelandia* in which learners of Spanish can navigate a series of request and apology interactions with built-in characters. Although Sykes found only minimal to moderate improvements on making requests and issuing apologies after playing the game, interview data did show learners' growth in their metapragmatic awareness.

Clear learning outcomes resulting from a gameplay were documented in Tang's (2019) dissertation research. She used the platform Unity to develop a scenario-based digital game *Questaurant* to teach twenty-five formulaic expressions in L2 Chinese. In the game, the player/learner took the role of a robot who works in a restaurant in China and runs quests by interacting with built-in characters using formulaic expressions. The game incorporated key gaming attributes, including *context (representation), goal, feedback*, and *interactivity*. Results showed that learners made significant gains in their receptive and productive knowledge of target formulaic expressions, and maintained these gains two weeks later at the delayed post-test. Although their gains were comparable to those of the comparison group who were exposed to the same materials in a regular computer-assisted language learning (CALL) environment, the game-based learning group showed significantly greater motivation. Interview data showed that the gaming attributes of *context, goals*, and *interactivity* were particularly motivating and engaging for the participants, while *feedback* directly contributed to their learning.

While still small in volume, existing studies point to the potential of using games for pragmatics learning. More studies are needed to directly test benefits of games (Taguchi, forthcoming), which are promising for pragmatics learning because they can provide an immersive environment where learners take on a variety of roles and interact in diverse social situations. To leverage the use of digital games in L2 pragmatics, it is important to understand the affordances and challenges of different gaming attributes on pragmatics learning.

1.4.3   Lingua Franca Framework in L2 Pragmatics Research

Another important change that is currently underway is the influence of globalisation in L2 pragmatics research (Taguchi & Roever, 2017; Taguchi, 2021b). The change is most notable in growing research in the areas of intercultural pragmatics (Kecskes, 2014), pragmatics in lingua franca communication (Cogo & House, 2017; Walkinshaw, 2022), multilingual pragmatic competence (Alcón-Soler, 2013), and heritage learner pragmatics (for a review, see Xiao-Desai, 2019). These areas have transformed the traditional practice of L2 pragmatics research in a number of ways. Most notably, in the area of English as a lingua franca (ELF), the concept of pragmatics extends beyond traditional notions of politeness and appropriateness in speech acts. Instead, ELF research commits to discourse and interaction-based analysis, looking at speakers' negotiation of meaning, interactional management, and use of multilingual resources (Cogo & House, 2017). This tendency indicates that ELF pragmatics research focuses on how L2 speakers co-construct mutual understanding and establish common ground in intercultural communication.

In addition, ELF research has helped us realise the problem of using native speaker norms in assessing L2 pragmatic competence. A generalisation emerging in the ELF literature is that intercultural speakers use English not to identify with native English speakers, but to achieve mutual understanding with other intercultural speakers (Jenkins, 2015; Seidlfofer, 2011). Because ELF speakers focus on mutual understanding over native speaker correctness, native speaker norms should not serve as a yardstick against which L2 performance is assessed. Socially appropriate language use needs to be conceptualised according to local norms rather than idealised native speaker norms. To gauge local norms, we should start with needs analyses so we can identify the purpose of language use shared among local members (Ishihara & Cohen, 2010). Seidlhofer (2011) claims that appropriateness in ELF refers to the 'legitimate appropriation of the English language by its majority expanding circle users, together with whatever diversity and hybridity suited their own purposes rather than the purposes of inner circle speakers' (p. 149). The notion of 'legitimate appropriation' has become a useful resource for researchers as they reconceptualise appropriateness from the local community viewpoint.

Indeed, Taguchi and Ishihara's (2018) recent review has illustrated these new considerations emerging from the ELF literature and their impact on L2 pragmatics research. They synthesised findings of twenty-seven empirical studies that examined pragmatics-related language use among ELF speakers (e.g., face-threatening acts, rapport-building, and use of discourse markers and communication strategies). Those twenty-seven studies largely fall into three categories of investigation: (1) speech acts as a goal-oriented interactional achievement, (2) strategies for communicative effectiveness, and (3) strategies for accommodation and rapport-building. These findings suggest that pragmatics research in ELF extends beyond the traditional scope of pragmalinguistics and sociopragmatics, to incorporate a wider domain of analysis, including communicative effectiveness, negotiation of meaning, interactional management, and common-ground seeking.

1.5   Conclusion and Future Directions

This chapter provided a historical sketch of L2 pragmatics as a field by surveying research trends since the 1980s. I have illustrated the dominance of cross-linguistic, cross-sectional investigations in the 1980s and 1990s, and then described how the research foci in the 1990s shifted to the instruction, assessment, and development of L2 pragmatics. After the turn of the twenty-first century, the field has seen a further expansion of these research strands, as characterised by the application of a broader range of SLA theories, as well as the use of technology in pragmatics teaching and assessment. As the field moves into the next decade, new research agendas have emerged. For example, pragmatic strategies used to achieve mutual understanding have been highlighted in lingua franca communication, which have encouraged researchers to reconsider the commonplace practice of using native speaker norms when analysing L2 pragmatic behaviours.

Building on these shifts and developments witnessed since the 1980s, several directions for future research are in order. One important direction is the re-configuration of the construct of pragmatic competence and the development of appropriate tools for assessing the construct. As I summarised in this chapter, in the early period, pragmatic competence was mainly defined as the knowledge of form-function-context mappings – which forms to use for what communicative functions in what social contexts. While this early definition had a lasting impact in the field, we have also witnessed a shift in the definition over time, corresponding to the changing epistemology in the larger field of SLA. Specifically, in the rise of discursive pragmatics (Kasper, 2006) and interactional competence (Young, 2011), the view of pragmatic competence has shifted from the knowledge of form-function-context mappings alone, to the ability to use knowledge in a flexible, adaptive manner in interaction. In addition, the concept of learner agency (LoCastro, 2003) has also influenced our understanding of pragmatic competence. The knowledge of form-function-context mappings is part of pragmatic knowledge, but deciding whether or not to actually use this knowledge is the learners' own choice. Based on their beliefs and values, learners make their own linguistic choices even when their choices do not conform to the normative form-function-context mappings widely practised in the local community. Hence, agency and subjectivity are important considerations when defining the construct of pragmatic competence. Considering these recent developments, new assessment methods encompassing three dimensions – knowledge of form-function-context mappings, adaptability, and agency – are necessary in the future.

Another future direction involves a closer alignment of L2 pragmatics to research in the lingua franca framework and intercultural communication. L2 pragmatics is no longer understood in the comparison between native and non-native speakers' performance, as envisaged in the early time of the field. In the current era, L2 pragmatics is situated within the frameworks of interactional pragmatics and intercultural pragmatics where L2 speakers are valued in their ability to collaboratively construct meaning with other L2 speakers in intercultural communication. As such, some of the traditional assumptions about norms of communication and the concept of pragmatic competence need to be re-evaluated. For example, pragmatic competence needs to be determined based on how L2 speakers can skilfully navigate communicative demands by using strategies while maintaining their identities. Future research should fine-tune available methods for analysing intercultural communication by attending to how speakers negotiate pragmatic meanings using available resources. We also need to move away from the traditional practice of using native speaker models, and instead explore alternative instructional and assessment models under the lingua franca framework.

Related to these new agendas emerging from the lingua franca communication, multilingual pragmatic competence is an important topic to address under the influence of globalisation in L2 pragmatics research. Globalisation has led to a transnational society where people grow up being exposed to multiple languages for different functions (e.g., home language, school language, and societal language). The growing population of heritage language learners and multilingual speakers is indicative of this trend. Because of the simultaneous exposure to multiple language systems and mundane transitions among them, multilingual speakers develop a hybrid pragmatic competence by blending pragmatic systems of several languages and cultures. This situation has made us realise that the traditional framework of native vs. FL speakers is no longer useful when analysing pragmatics of multilingual speakers. Instead, researchers need to cultivate ways of analysing multilingual influence on pragmatics behaviours.

Finally, L2 pragmatics research in the next decade should firmly embrace the interdisciplinary stance in terms of theoretical frameworks and research methods (for a review the interdisciplinary approaches, see Taguchi, 2019). Empirical practice based on existing theories such as cognitive approaches, language socialisation, and sociocultural theory can be enriched with recent theoretical paradigms of usage-based approaches, complex, dynamic systems approaches, and task-based language teaching (TBLT). Similarly, research methods coming from the field of corpus linguistics, systemic functional linguistics, and psycholinguistics can help us explore new ways of investigating the construct of pragmatic competence and its development. Since research findings under these new theories and research methods are still nascent in both quantity and quality, inclusion of these areas will add to the methodological and conceptual diversity of L2 pragmatics as the field continues to grow in the next decade.

References

Alcón-Soler, E. (2013). Teachability and bilingual effects on third language knowledge of refusals. *Intercultural Pragmatics*, 9, 511–541.

Anderson, J. R., Bothell, D., Byrne, M. D., Douglass, S., Lebiere, C., & Qin, Y. (2004). An integrated theory of the mind. *Psychological Review*, 111, 1036–1060.

Austin, J. L. (1962). *How to Do Things with Words*. Oxford: Oxford University Press.

Bachman, L. F., & Palmer, A. S. (1996). *Language Testing in Practice*. Oxford: Oxford University Press.

Bardovi-Harlig, K. (2000). Pragmatics and second language acquisition. In R. B. Kaplan (ed.), *Oxford Handbook of Applied Linguistics*. Oxford: Oxford University Press, pp. 182–192.

Bardovi-Harlig, K. (2010). Exploring the pragmatics of interlanguage pragmatics: Definition by design. In A. Trosborg (ed.), *Handbook of Pragmatics: Pragmatics across Languages and Cultures*. Berlin: Mouton de Gruyter, pp. 219–260.

Bardovi-Harlig, K., & Mahan-Taylor, R. (2003). *Teaching Pragmatics*. Washington, DC: Office of English Programs, US Department of State.

Blum-Kulka, S., House, J., & Kasper, G. (1989). *Cross-Cultural Pragmatics: Requests and Apologies*. Norwood, NJ: Ablex.

Bouton, L. (1994). Conversational implicature in the second language: Learned slowly when not deliberately taught. *Journal of Pragmatics*, 22, 157–167.

Brown, P., & Levinson, S. D. (1987). *Politeness: Some Universals in Language Usage* (2nd ed.). Cambridge: Cambridge University Press.

Canale, M., & Swain, M. (1980). Theoretical aspects of communicative approaches to second language teaching and testing. *Applied Linguistics*, 1, 1–47.

Cogo, A., & House, J. (2017). Intercultural pragmatics. In A. Barron, Y. Gu, & G. Steen (eds.), *Routledge Handbook of Pragmatics*. London and New York: Routledge, pp. 168–183.

Cohen, A., & Ishihara, N. (2013). Pragmatics. In B. Tomlinson (ed.), *Applied Linguistics and Materials Development*. Huntingdon: Bloomsbury Academic, pp. 113–126.

Cook, H. (2008). *Socializing Identities through Speech Style*. New York and Bristol: Multilingual Matters.

Cunningham, J. D. (2019). L2 pragmatics learning in computer-mediated communication. In N. Taguchi (ed.), *The Routledge Handbook of Second Language Acquisition and Pragmatics*. New York: Routledge, pp. 372–386.

Diao, W. (2016). Peer socialization into gendered Mandarin practices in a study abroad context: Talk in the dorm. *Applied Linguistics*, 37(5), 599–620.

Félix-Brasdefer, J. C., & Hasler-Barker, M. (2015). Complimenting in Spanish in a short-term study abroad context. In E. Alcón-Soler & L. Yates (eds.), *Pragmatic Learning across Contexts. Special issue. System*, 48, 75–85.

Gilmore, A. (2004). A comparison of textbooks and authentic interactions. *ELT Journal*, 58, 362–374.

González-Lloret, M. (2018). Pragmatics in technology-mediated contexts. In A. Sanchez-Hernández & A. Herraiz-Martínez (eds.) *Learning Second Language Pragmatics beyond Traditional Contexts*. Berlin: Peter Lang, pp. 17–48.

Hassall, T. (2006). Learning to take leave in social conversations: A diary study. In M. DuFon & E. Churchill (eds.), *Language Learners in Study Abroad Contexts*. Clevedon: Multilingual Matters, pp. 31–58.

Holden, C., & Sykes, J. M. (2013). Complex L2 pragmatic feedback via place-based mobile games. In N. Taguchi & J. M. Sykes (eds.), *Technology in Interlanguage Pragmatics Research and Teaching* (pp. 155–184). Amsterdam and Philadelphia: John Benjamins.

Houck, N., & Tatsuki, D. (2011). *Pragmatics from Research to Practice: New Directions*. Alexandria, VA: TESOL.

Hudson, T., Detmer, E., & Brown, J. D. (1995). *Developing Prototypic Measures of Cross-Cultural Pragmatics* (Technical Report No. 7). Honolulu: University of Hawai'i at Manoa, Second Language Teaching and Curriculum Center.

Ishihara, N., & Cohen, A. (2010). *Teaching and Learning Pragmatics: Where Language and Culture Meet*. Harlow: Pearson Longman.

Jenkins, J. (2015). *Global Englishes* (3rd ed.). London: Routledge.

Jeon, E.-H., & Kaya, T. (2006). Effects of L2 instruction on interlanguage pragmatic development. In N. John & L. Ortega (eds.), *Synthesizing Research on Language Learning and Teaching*. Philadelphia, PA: John Benjamins, pp. 165–211.

Kanagy, R. (1999). Interactional routines as a mechanism for L2 acquisition and socialization in an immersion context. *Journal of Pragmatics*, 31, 1467–1492.

Kasper, G. (1997). Can pragmatic competence be taught? (Net Work #6) [HTML document]. Honolulu: University of Hawai'i, Second Language Teaching & Curriculum Center. www.nflrc.hawaii.edu/networks/NW06/.

Kasper, G. (2006). Introduction. *Multilingua*, 25, 243–248.

Kasper, G., & Dahl, M. (1991). Research methods in interlanguage pragmatics. *Studies in Second Language Acquisition*, 13, 215–247.

Kasper, G., & Rose, K. (1999). Pragmatics and SLA. *Annual Review of Applied Linguistics*, 19, 81–104.

Kasper, G., & Rose, K. (2002). *Pragmatic Development in a Second Language*. Oxford: Blackwell.

Kasper, G., & Schmidt, R. (1996). Developmental issues in interlanguage pragmatics. *Studies in Second Language Acquisition*, 18, 149–169.

Kecskes, I. (2014). *Intercultural Pragmatics*. New York: Oxford University Press.

Kim, Y., & Taguchi, N. (2015). Promoting task-based pragmatics instruction in EFL classroom context: The role of task complexity. *Modern Language Journal*, 99, 656–677.

Kim, Y., & Taguchi, N. (2016). Learner–learner interaction during collaborative pragmatic tasks: The role of cognitive and pragmatic task demands. *Foreign Language Annals*, 49, 42–57.

Kinginger, C. (2008). Language learning in study abroad: Case studies of Americans in France. *Modern Language Journal*, 92, Supplement SI.

Lantolf, J. P., & Thorne, S. L. (2006). *Sociocultural Theory and the Genesis of L2 Development*. Oxford: Oxford University Press.

Li, S. (2012). The effects of input-based practice on pragmatic development of requests in L2 Chinese. *Language Learning*, 62, 403–438.

Li, S., & Taguchi, N. (2014). The effect of practice modality on the development of pragmatic performance in L2 Chinese. *Modern Language Journal*, 98, 794–812.

LoCastro, V. (2003). *An Introduction to Pragmatics: Social Action for Language Teachers*. Ann Arbor: University of Michigan Press.

Nguyen, T. T. M. (2019). Data collection methods in L2 pragmatics research: An overview. In N. Taguchi (ed.), *The Routledge Handbook of SLA and Pragmatics*. New York: Routledge, pp. 195–211.

Ohta, A. (2001). *Second Language Acquisition Processes in the Classroom: Learning Japanese*. Mahwah, NJ: Lawrence Erlbaum.

Pérez-Vidal, C., & Shively, R. (2019). L2 pragmatic development in study abroad settings. In N. Taguchi (ed.), *The Routledge Handbook of SLA and Pragmatics*. New York: Routledge, pp. 355–371.

Plonsky, L., & Zhuang, J. (2019). A meta-analysis of L2 pragmatics instruction. In N. Taguchi (ed.), *The Routledge Handbook of SLA and Pragmatics*. New York: Routledge, pp. 287–307.

Ren, W. (2012). Pragmatic development in Chinese speakers' L2 English refusals. *EUROSLA Yearbook*, 12, 63–87.

Ren, W., & Han, Z. (2016). The representation of pragmatic knowledge in recent ELT textbooks. *ELT Journal*, 70, 424–434.

Robinson, P. (2011). Task-based language learning: A review of issues. *Language Learning*, 61, 1–36.

Roever, C. (2005). *Testing ESL Pragmatics*. Frankfurt: Peter Lang.

Roever, C. (2011). Tests of second language pragmatics: past and future. *Language Testing*, 28, 463–481.

Roever, C. (2021). *Teaching and Testing Second Language Pragmatics*. Abingdon: Routledge.

Schmidt, R. (1993). Consciousness, learning and interlanguage pragmatics. In G. Kasper & S. Blum-Kulka (eds.), *Interlanguage Pragmatics*. New York: Oxford University Press, pp. 43–57.

Schieffelin, B., & Ochs, E. (1986). Language socialization. *Annual Review of Anthropology*, 15, 163–191.

Searle, J. R. (1969). *Speech Acts: An Essay in the Philosophy of Language*. Cambridge: Cambridge University Press.

Seidlhofer, B. (2011). *Understanding English as a Lingua Franca*. Oxford: Oxford University Press.

Shively, R. L. (2011). L2 pragmatic development in study abroad: A longitudinal study of Spanish service encounters. *Journal of Pragmatics*, 43(6), 1818–1835.

Swain, M., & Lapkin, S. (1998). Interaction and second language learning: Two adolescent French immersion students working together. *Modern Language Journal*, 82, 320–337.

Sykes, J. M. (2009). Learner request in Spanish: Examining the potential of multiuser virtual environments for L2 pragmatics acquisition. In L. Lomika & G. Lord (eds.), *The Second Generation: Online Collaboration and Social Networking in CALL*. CALICO Monograph. San Marcos, TX: CALICO, 199–234.

Sykes, J. M. (2013). Multiuser virtual environments: Apologies in Spanish. In N. Taguchi & J. M. Sykes (eds.), *Technology in Interlanguage Pragmatics Research and Teaching*. Amsterdam and Philadelphia: John Benjamins, pp. 71–100.

Sykes, J. M., & Dubreil, S. (2019). Pragmatics learning in digital games and virtual environments. In N. Taguchi (ed.), *The Routledge Handbook of SLA and Pragmatics*. New York: Routledge, pp. 387–399.

Sykes, J. M., & Reinhardt, J. (2012). *Language at Play: Digital Games in Second and Foreign Language Teaching and Learning*. New York: Pearson-Prentice Hall.

Taguchi, N. (2007). Development of speed and accuracy in pragmatic comprehension in English as a foreign language. *TESOL Quarterly*, 41(2), 313–338.

Taguchi, N. (2010). Longitudinal studies in interlanguage pragmatics. In A. Trosborg (ed.), *Handbook of Pragmatics, Vol. 7*. Berlin: Mouton de Gruyter, pp. 333–361.

Taguchi, N. (2015a). 'Contextually' speaking: A survey of pragmatics learning abroad, in class and online. In E. Alcón-Soler & L. Yates (eds.), *Pragmatic Learning across Contexts*. Special issue, *System*, 48, 3–20.

Taguchi, N. (2015b). Instructed pragmatics at a glance: Where instructional studies were, are, and should be going. *Language Teaching*, 48, 1–50.

Taguchi, N. (2019). *The Routledge Handbook of SLA and Pragmatics*. New York: Routledge.

Taguchi, N. (2021a). Application of immersive virtual reality (VR) to pragmatics data collection methods: Insights from interviews. *CALICO Journal*, 38(2), 181–201.

Taguchi, N. (2021b). Learning and teaching pragmatics in the globalized world. *Modern Language Journal*, 105(3) Special Issue.

Taguchi, N. (2022). Immersive virtual reality for pragmatics task development. *TESOL Quarterly*, 56(1), 308–335.

Taguchi, N. (in press). Dispreferred speech acts in virtual reality: Analysis of tone choices and hesitations. *System*.

Taguchi, N. (forthcoming). Game-based pragmatics learning: Learning request-making through perlocutionary effects. *Language Learning & Technology*.

Taguchi, N., & Ishihara, N. (2018). The pragmatics of English as a lingua franca: Research and pedagogy in the era of globalization. *Annual Review of Applied Linguistics*, 38, 80–101.

Taguchi, N., & Kim, Y. (2016). Collaborative dialogue in learning pragmatics: Pragmatics-related episodes as an opportunity for learning request-making. *Applied Linguistics*, 37, 416–437.

Taguchi, N., & Roever, C. (2017). *Second Language Pragmatics*. New York: Oxford University Press.

Taguchi, N., & Sykes, J. M. (2013). *Technology in Interlanguage Pragmatics Research and Teaching*. Amsterdam and Philadelphia: John Benjamins.

Takahashi, S. (2010). Assessing learnability in second language pragmatics. In A. Trosborg (ed.), *Handbook of Pragmatics, Vol. 7*. Berlin: Mouton de Gruyter, pp. 391–421.

Tang, X. (2019). Digital Game-Based Learning for L2 Chinese Formulaic Expressions. Unpublished doctoral dissertation. Pittsburgh, PA: Carnegie Mellon University.

Tatsuki, D. (2019). Instructional material development in L2 pragmatics. In N. Taguchi (ed.), *The Routledge Handbook of SLA and Pragmatics*. New York: Routledge, pp. 322–337.

Thomas, J. (1983). Cross-cultural pragmatic failure. *Applied Linguistics*, 4, 91–111.

Van Compernolle, R. A. (2014). *Sociocultural Theory and Instructed L2 Pragmatics*. Bristol and New York: Multilingual Matters.

Walkinshaw, I. (2022). *Pragmatics in English as a Lingua Franca*. Berlin: Mouton de Gruyter.

Xiao-Desai, Y. (2019). Heritage learner pragmatics. In N. Taguchi (ed.), *The Routledge Handbook of SLA and Pragmatics*. New York: Routledge, pp. 462–478.

Youn, S. J. (2015). Validity argument for assessing L2 pragmatics in interaction using mixed methods. *Language Testing*, 32(2), 199–225.

Young, S. J., & Bogorevich, V. (2019). Assessment in L2 pragmatics. In N. Taguchi (ed.), *The Routledge Handbook of SLA and Pragmatics*. New York: Routledge, pp. 308–321.

Young, R. (2011). Interactional competence in language learning, teaching, and testing. In H. Hinkel (ed.), *Handbook of Research in Language Learning and Teaching*. New York: Routledge, pp. 426–443.

Part I

Pragmatics in Action

2 'Mind Your Language'
L2 English Email Requests during Study Abroad

Jiayi Wang and Nicola Halenko

2.1 Introduction

Interaction between faculty and students in institutional settings now predominantly unfolds through online spaces, with email being one of the most familiar and viable options. In addition to being effective and convenient for carrying out academic matters, email serves an equally important social function for co-creating relationships and building rapport. Success in utilising this hybrid form of oral and written communication requires a particular set of skills. It is likely the case, however, that socialisation into email practices is more often than not cultivated through experience rather than direction, which leaves L2 language users in a vulnerable position. This is partly due to the lack of explicit guidance available for learners (Biesenbach-Lucas, 2007; Bou-Franch, 2011) and partly perpetuated by the broader lack of agreed conventions on appropriate email behaviour (Bjørge, 2007; Chen, 2006).

This gap between the need for and provision of explicit guidance regarding email writing presents pragmatic challenges for L2 students on international study programmes. One of the most challenging tasks in L2 email writing is simultaneously managing three specific pragmatic aspects: L2 language, L2 (institutional and local) cultural norms, and adequate knowledge of L2 email conventions (Chen, 2006). L2 English emails are often reportedly flawed with a variety of linguistic and non-linguistic pragmatic devices. Faculty reports of being 'disturbed' (Biesenbach-Lucas, 2007), 'irritated' (Lewin-Jones & Mason, 2014), or 'annoyed' (Economidou-Kogetsidis, 2011) by inappropriate emails are common.

Relying on the study abroad context for guidance on these issues may not be the solution. Despite increased access to information on contextualised, local pragmatics norms and increased opportunities to engage in real-time interaction in the L2, research suggests that a positive association between the SA experience and improved pragmatic development cannot always be made (e.g., Schauer, 2009; Taguchi, 2015; Ren, 2015). Studies typically report variability in both pragmatic comprehension and production, while aspects of non-target-like features often remain. Such non-linear trajectories are well documented in a range of L2 SA investigations (e.g., Barron, 2003; Li, 2014; Ren, 2015; Schauer, 2009; Woodfield, 2012).

This study follows the pragmatic development of one group of postgraduate international students from China as they tackle these two issues of managing email interaction within an SA programme in the UK. The data provide evidence of the learners' evolving email requests to staff over two semesters (ten months), using the following research questions to guide the study:

1. What are the distinctive linguistic features of L2 email requests?
2. How do the L2 learners perceive diachronic change in their request emails?

2.2   Review of Existing Research

2.2.1   The Study Abroad Context

Collentine and Freed (2004) consider the value of both the in-class and out-of-class learning experiences in their definition of SA as 'a hybrid communicative-learning context' (p. 156). This view is particularly useful as it encapsulates the aspect of formal learning and the social dimension of SA. As with much SA literature, the present study focusses on the more traditional conceptualisation of SA in that there is a time-limited duration spent in the L2 context, with students then returning to their home institution to continue formal study (Barron, 2019).

The SA context is known to offer a unique set of features that appears to mediate varying degrees of pragmatic growth. These include opportunities to observe interaction at a localised level, gain contextualised pragmatic practice and feedback, experience the positive and negative consequences of pragmatic behaviour, and be exposed to a diversity of communicative contexts and styles (Taguchi, 2015). At the same time, these advantages are known to be affected by other variables that may stifle pragmatic growth. Factors reported to impact the variability of pragmatic gains include quantity and quality of L2 contact, length of stay, and individual characteristics such as proficiency, motivation, age, and identity (Pérez-Vidal & Shively, 2019).

Longitudinal investigations of pragmatic development are still underrepresented in SA literature. Taguchi (2012) found only twenty-three studies covering comprehension of implicature, perception/recognition of pragmatic features, and production of pragmatic functions. In relation to the latter group, in which the present study fits, development of L2 pragmalinguistic forms was found to be slow overall and broadly characterised by an initial overgeneralisation of a few forms to a gradual but slow expansion of forms as time passed.

As example investigations, Barron (2003) and Cole and Anderson (2001) traced SA pragmatic gains, using variables similar to the present study (an extended SA period of ten months and the acquisition of request language). Since there are presently no longitudinal email investigations of this kind, it is important to note that these findings draw on oral data elicited via a written mode (Discourse Completion Tasks). First, Barron's study tracked thirty-three Irish learners of German and their pragmatic development of three speech acts that included request routines. Data were elicited three times over the course of a ten-month stay in Germany and compared to L2 German and L1 Irish responses to assess overall gains. The findings evidenced mixed successes. On the one hand increases in L2-like use of downgraders, revised L2-like positioning of 'please' and decreases in non-target-like translations from the learners' L1, e.g., 'I wonder if …' were reported. On the other hand, aspects of non-linear development were recorded in the lack of syntactic downgrading and inappropriate sociopragmatic use of 'I wanted to ask if/whether …'.

In Cole and Anderson's study (2001), Japanese learners of English showed considerable developmental changes from their pre-SA use of direct requests + 'please' to post-SA use of conventionally indirect requests with modals, following their ten-month homestays in New Zealand and Canada. Other target-like features acquired included an increase in the variety and frequency of downgraders within the request. Although not a conclusion offered by the authors, it is likely the immersive homestay environment with daily access, exposure to the L2, and frequent opportunities to interact, helped facilitate the gains recorded. The takeaway points from both studies are that L2 immersion can have some facilitative effects but these are generally limited. Barron notes that 'noticing' the pragmatic gap and use of the L2 are some of the important prerequisites for the development of L2 pragmatic competence (2003: 247).

In short, the impact of SA stays is not at all straightforward and teasing apart the variables is an important step to better understand the complexities that enhance or constrain pragmatic development. The present study is a further attempt to take on this effort from a longitudinal perspective and focus on pragmatic growth in email interaction, as discussed in Section 2.2.2.

2.2.2   *Developing Email Literacy in L2 English*

The email data in this study is examined on two levels: the content moves of the request emails and learners' underlying thought processes of email writing. This section focusses on current research related to these two aspects.

Beginning with existing research on content moves of request emails, L1 and L2 users are known to vary the style, structure, and content in a number of ways. Despite the potential of the pragmatic-rich L2 environment, students from a range of first language backgrounds reportedly struggle to demonstrate appropriate L2 linguistic moves and appropriate sociocultural knowledge of academic norms in their emails: Chinese (Chen, 2015; Chen, Rau, &

Rau 2016), Dutch (Hendriks, 2010), Greek (Economidou-Kogetsidis, 2011, 2018), Norwegian (Savić, 2018), Spanish (Alcón-Soler, 2015; Bou-Franch, 2011) and mixed East Asian L1s (Biesenbach-Lucas, 2006, 2007 covered Korean, Japanese, Taiwanese, and Thai). As recent examples, Savić (2018) captured lecturer perceptions of (im)politeness and (in)appropriateness in Norwegian EFL students' request emails. Lecturers' negative evaluations of emails included insufficiently mitigated direct requests, use of imperatives, and offering non-negotiable timelines to get the job done. Similarly, Economidou-Kogetsidis (2018) reported that her Greek learners mostly opted for high degrees of directness in their emails. Evidence of directness even in high imposition requests, and those where learners began the email with a formal address term, suggested the EFL learners lacked the necessary pragmatic skills to manage emails successfully. L1 interference and resistance to change, as well as broader issues with lack of agreed email conventions and familiarity with L2 norms, are commonly cited causes of this seemingly pervasive inability to interact appropriately in L2 email communication.

Turning to the second part of this study, focussing on the cognitive aspects, data captured from participant interviews has proven fruitful for capturing a more holistic understanding of the underlying thought processes behind pragmatic choices. Employing mixed-methods research in this way, which enables triangulation of both quantitative and qualitative data, provides important insights that may account for any variability found when measuring pragmatic outcomes (Taguchi, 2015). Mixed-methods approaches are, therefore, a particularly suitable method for studies tracking learning over an extended period of time (e.g., Barron, 2003; Sánchez-Hernández, 2018; Schauer, 2009).

In the context of Chinese L2 learners of English, Chen (2006) conducted several face-to-face and online interviews across key time points during her Taiwanese student's two-and-a-half-year doctoral study in the US. The student's emails, combined with interviews, shed light on how her L1 cultural values interacted with her L2 knowledge and perceptions. The interviews provided in-depth testimony regarding choice of linguistic features, the email writing process, and sociocultural practice at institution and societal levels, as the student described her evolving email practices with both peers and professors. The study also offers a sense that these periodic reflections were instrumental to stimulating the student's own awareness-raising and longer-term socialisation into the academic community.

Tseng's (2016) interview data from at-home EFL learners also provides valuable insights into learners' linguistic and pragmatic choices after completing experimental email writing tasks. Here, the interview data allows an understanding of the varied challenges faced by different proficiency groups when managing email writing. Higher-level learners described combining clarity and politeness as challenging, so often resorted to adopting more elaborate external supportive moves to compensate for their uncertainty. Lower-level learners recognised their limited linguistic abilities and recalled opting for safer linguistic options in the form of direct strategies, especially since the Chinese equivalents of these (e.g., 'Dear Teacher, I want a reference') are not considered impolite.

What the interviews in both email studies reveal is that regardless of proficiency, L1 pragmatics remains a strong influence on L2 performance. Learners' testimonials seem to mark them as being fundamentally risk-averse L2 users who intentionally or unintentionally draw on 'the Chinese way' (Tseng, 2016) of doing politeness as a result. We also seek to exploit the information-rich potential of interviews to gain learner perspectives on email writing. Email studies that include interview data are exceptional, but it is through these mechanisms that issues such as identity, agency, and culture-specific ideologies surface. It is for these reasons that participant interviews were included in the present study.

2.2.3   Requests in L2 Emails

As the following studies show, composing L2 email requests can be challenging in a number of ways. First, status-unequal emails are reportedly demanding for Chinese learners of English on a linguistic level. Empirical findings from naturally occurring (Chen, 2006; Lee, 2010) and elicited (Chen, 2015; Li, 2018; Tseng, 2016; Zhu, 2012) email data highlight the following as common features in Chinese ESL email requests: wrong terms of address, student/ self-oriented, weak reasons/justifications, lengthy emails, delayed request, and favouring directness, which is assumed to be mitigated by external modification.

Internal modifiers are those that form part of the request head act and include *downtoners* 'possibly' and *hedges* 'some/any'. External modifiers surround the head act and include *grounders* that provide explanations or reasons and *apologies*. Chinese speakers are known to exploit external rather than internal modifications (Li, 2018; Wang, 2011). They have also shown divergence from L1 practices from the request perspective. For example, the learners in Zhu's study (2012) relied heavily on the request perspectives of 'you' and 'I', whereas the two other options 'we' and 'impersonal' were absent in his data. In the majority of studies (e.g., Chen, 2006; Chen, 2015; Lee, 2010; Li, 2018; Tseng, 2016; Wang, 2011; Zhu, 2012), first language transfer is reported to be accountable for much of the aforementioned variation when analysed against L1 email practices.

Second, status-unequal emails may also be demanding in terms of understanding local norms and values. As Bjørge (2007) outlines, the choice of expressions is often dictated by how students see their relationships with academic staff, and to what extent these vary according to the student's L1 background and host culture's L2 norms. Challenges arise where cross-cultural variations exist along these dimensions. In the case of Chinese ESL learners, central features like relationship-building and positive politeness strategies that would not be expected in L2 correspondence may appear in emails (Bjørge, 2007). Such evidence, demonstrated through excessive use of personal and irrelevant details and other external supportive moves such as small talk, is a trend found in Chinese ESL studies (Chen, 2006; Li, 2018; Tseng, 2016). The influence of cultural misunderstandings on email practice also surfaced in other studies too: conflating one's rights as a student, raising the expectation of a teacher's moral obligations to help, failing to appropriately acknowledge imposition, and proposing unrealistic timescales to underscore urgency (Chen, 2006; Chen, 2015; Li, 2018; Wang, forthcoming; Zhu, 2012).

Finally, status-unequal emails are also demanding in terms of negotiating existing linguistic or cultural norms which may conflict with those of the host culture. In such cases learners may demonstrate resistance to change and exercise their own agency, described as 'people's ability to make choices, take control, self-regulate and thereby pursue their goals as individuals' (Duff, 2012: 417). In the context of conflicting norms illustrated here, agency enables learners to actively resist local behaviours and practices if feelings of annoyance or discomfort are triggered. For instance, Chen's (2006) doctoral student structured her email requests with a reason + request sequence throughout her overseas stay regardless of evolving understanding that this was a non-target-like strategy. She viewed this inductive structure of delaying her request statement as a signal of both indirectness and politeness, even though this was likely to be seen as ineffective by her professors. Only in a few cases is learner resistance and agency examined as a central theme in L2 pragmatics (e.g., Davies, 2007; Eslami et al., 2014; Ishihara, 2019; Ishihara & Tarone, 2009), so this study aims to contribute to this underexplored area.

2.3   Methodology

2.3.1   Data and Participants

The L2 dataset consisted of (1) 170 authentic emails to faculty sent by fifteen L2 users of English during their ten-month study abroad in England, (2) two retrospective focus group interviews, one at the end of each semester, (3) five one-to-one retrospective interviews at the end of the academic year to reflect on the development of their L2 email practices, and (4) twenty-nine cross cultural record sheets as supplementary data. In order to identify the distinct

Table 2.1 *Profile of the L1 and L2 email corpora*

Type of email requests	L2 data	L1 data
Requests for meetings	29%	31%
Requests for information	34%	37%
Requests for action	37%	32%

features of the L2 emails, we also compared the L2 data with an L1 email data-set (Halenko & Winder, 2021) collected by one of the authors of this study, which comprised 162 authentic emails to faculty by L1 users of English who were final-year British students on a TESOL programme at the same British university. The two corpora are comparable, especially in terms of profiles of the email users (age range 20–28 years old), corpus size and request type (Table 2.1).

The study participants were fifteen L2 English users on a postgraduate programme in England, falling within the age range of 22–28. They were L1 Chinese students who had completed a bachelor's degree in China, mostly in English/TESOL, and eleven of them came from a partner university in Shanghai having already completed one year of master's studies there. None of them had studied abroad before. The Chinese students' L2 English proficiency level could be described as upper-intermediate to advanced (B2–C1 on the Common European Framework of Reference for Languages, CEFR) since this is the English language requirement to join the programme. All the partici-pants gave consent to the use of the emails that they shared with or sent to the researchers over the course of an academic year.

Emails that were self-contained requests, that is, not part of longer chains of messages such as follow-up requests (Economidou-Kogetsidis, 2011), and did not include any sensitive or personal information, were included in the corpus. At the end of each semester, a retrospective focus group inter-view of approximately one hour was conducted to discuss the emails gath-ered thus far and all the emails shared were anonymised. The focus group interviews were video recorded. At the end of the academic year, all the participants were invited to a one-to-one interview to reflect on the develop-ment of their L2 email practices over their period abroad. Five accepted the invitation and the interviews were video recorded, too. The average length of the individual interviews was around twenty minutes. Additionally, all fifteen participants were asked to fill in a cross-cultural record sheet to describe emails which they sent or received that had a positive or negative impact on them as a visitor in England. Twenty-nine record sheets were received. Informed consent was given by all the participants for each type of data collected.

2.3.2   Data Analysis

To answer the first research question 'What are the distinctive linguistic features of L2 email requests?', the data were analysed on three levels: (in) directness; internal and external modification; and request perspective. The coding schemes categorising the data were adopted from existing studies of email requests for comparability purposes (e.g., Biesenbach-Lucas, 2007; Blum-Kulka, House, & Kasper 1989; Economidou-Kogetsidis, 2011; Woodfield 2012; Zhu 2012). The classification for request strategies (direct, indirect or hints) draws on several studies (Biesenbach-Lucas, 2007; Economidou-Kogetsidis, 2011; Zhu, 2012) to capture the range identified in the L2 English email dataset. Direct strategies typically state the illocutionary point of the utterance via performative verbs such as 'I want you to help', and because they fail to offer the hearer any options, they tend to be considered the most coercive. Indirect strategies, on the other hand, do not take compliance for granted but instead offer a means to opt out by questioning the ability or willingness of the hearer to comply, for example, 'Could you help?' Hints require that the hearer's intention matches that of the speaker since the request is typically covertly embedded into a question or statement, for example, 'These bags are really heavy.' Hints tend to be regarded as the least coercive option.

Regarding lexical modification devices, which act as mitigators to the request head act, Chinese speakers are known to employ more external than internal modification (Li, 2018; Wang, 2011; Wang, forthcoming), so exploring to the extent of behavioural change of both these aspects over the academic year was considered a valuable exercise. The coding used for internal modification in this study is an adaptation of Biesenbach-Lucas (2007) and Economidou-Kogetsidis (2011), and the coding for external modification drew on Woodfield's (2012) comprehensive analysis. Blum-Kulka, House, and Kasper (1989), Biesenbach-Lucas (2007), and Zhu (2012)'s categories were used to examine the L2 and L1 use of request perspectives in this study.

Addressing the second research question 'How do L2 users perceive diachronic change in their request emails?' relied on thematically analysing the interview data, email data, and cross-cultural record sheets in NVivo for the participants' personal insights into the linguistic content, style, and structure of their email requests. Two common themes emerged from the L2 users' perceptions of their changing email practice during study abroad: pragmatic learning and pragmatic unlearning, cutting across the categories of forms, norms, and beliefs regarding features of English request emails to faculty (e.g., email length, small talk, and sequencing). All data were anonymised by giving each participant a code (P1 = Participant 1).

2.4   Findings

*2.4.1   Distinctive Linguistic Features of L2 English
User Request Emails (RQ1)*

Marked contrasts between L1 and L2 users are evident in all three areas of focus: in/directness strategies, internal and external modification, and request perspectives. Each of these areas is examined in the following sections.

2.4.1.1   In/Direct Request Strategies   Three distinct features of L2 users' in/direct request strategies were identified in the email data: (1) more frequent employment of direct strategies; (2) relatively limited use of conventionally indirect strategies (concentrating on the modals *can* and *could* and not using possibility statements very often); and (3) exclusive use of hints. Table 2.2 describes choices of request strategy for both groups.

First, the L2 users employed significantly more direct strategies (forty-three instances) to realise email requests than the L1 users (only three instances recorded). Several strategies including imperatives (e.g., Please just give me one more week), need statements (e.g., I need a transcript by next Monday), want statements (e.g., I want to borrow your book for two weeks), and expectation statements (e.g., I really hope you can look at it and give me some suggestions) were exclusive to the L2 group. It is worth pointing out that even when L1 users did employ directness, which was rare, the requests were heavily mitigated internally, whereas the L2 learners tended to place a strong emphasis on their own personal wants and needs without much internal modification.

The differences are visually presented in Figure 2.1.

Nevertheless, examining the email texts beyond the request head acts, the Chinese L2 learners of English preferred to use external modification rather than internal modifiers as a mitigator. Several participants identified pre-request small talk as one of the most important modifiers, as shown by the example below.

I have received my marks, which I am very satisfied with, because I am a non-English major student, so I am weaker than others. You have always encouraged me patiently and have given me huge support. I am unable to make such huge progress without you. I have finished the book I borrowed from you, and I want to return it to you. When are you in your office?

In this example, the student did not initiate his request until the end of the email and the section in italics prior to the request seemed irrelevant. However, 'having some phatic talk before saying "I want you to help me to

Table 2.2 *Preferred choice of request strategy for L1 and L2 users*

Directness levels	Request strategy	L1 users	L2 users	L2 example
Direct	Imperatives	0	3 (7%)	Please send me an electronic copy of the timetable.
	Performatives	2 (67%)	19 (44%)	I am writing to ask for an extension.
	Direct questions	1 (33%)	9 (21%)	What do I do next?
	Want statements	0	5 (12%)	I want 1 ticket for myself.
	Need statements	0	3 (7%)	I need your signature as the module leader.
	Expectation statements	0	4 (9%)	I hope to have a meeting with you next Thursday.
Totals		**3**	**43**	
Conventionally Indirect	Query preparatory Ability (can)	6 (4%)	36 (30%)	Can I have a reference from you?
	Ability (could)	33 (21%)	58 (48%)	Could we rearrange our meeting?
	Ability (would)	19 (12%)	14 (12%)	Would you please send your ppt to me?
	Possibility statement	61 (39%)	8 (7%)	Would it be possible for me to bring my research questions to you sometime later this week?
	Query: permission	1 (1%)	5 (4%)	May I ask you a question about it?
	Query: no modals	39 (25%)	0	(L1 example: I was wondering how long it will take?)
Totals		**159**	**121**	
Non-conditionally Indirect	Strong/mild hints	0	6 (100%)	I have got appointments with Barclays Bank to open an account, so it's better for me to have the tutorial next week.
Totals		**0**	**6**	
Grand total L1/L2 emails		**162**	**170**	

do something'" is prevalent in the Chinese language/culture and it plays a key role to 'build rapport and express politeness' (P4), highlighting the importance of relationship building to the Chinese participants (Spencer-Oatey & Wang, 2019, 2020; Wang, forthcoming; Wang & Spencer-Oatey, 2015). A more detailed examination of internal and external modifiers will be discussed in the Section 2.4.1.2.

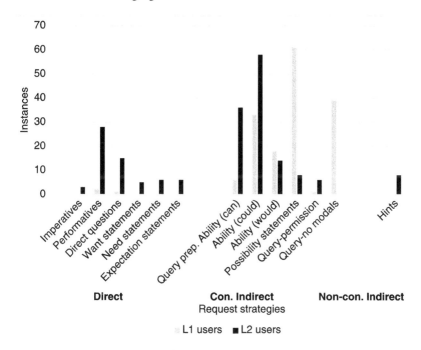

Figure 2.1 A comparison of L2 and L1 users' in/direct request strategies

Second, when it comes to conventionally indirect strategies, the L2 users demonstrated a strong preference for the modals *could* (48 per cent) (e.g., Could you give me an extension) and *can* (30 per cent) (e.g., Can I come to see you tomorrow) versus the L1 users' strong preference for possibility statements (39 per cent) (e.g., Will it be possible to see you before Thursday this week). Third, the use of hints, strong or mild (e.g., I have some doubts), were exclusive to the L2 users, too.

In retrospective interviews, the participants attributed these features identified above to their native influence. The variations largely correspond to the broad tendencies of differentiations between native Chinese requests and native English requests (e.g., Chen, 2006, 2015; Chen et al., 2016; Li, 2018; Zhu, 2012). Direct strategies such as 'want statements' (e.g., I want a reference letter) are relatively common in L1 Chinese but not in L1 English (Lin, 2009). A similar trend was observed in our Chinese ESL data. The results echo the findings of prior research that ESL/EFL learners tend to vary from native speakers and the variations seem to be partly due to native influence and therefore to pragmalinguistic and socio-pragmatic transfer (Economidou-Kogetsidis, 2008; Li, 2018; Woodfield, 2012).

Table 2.3 *Preferred choice of internal lexical modifiers between L1 and L2 users*

Internal modifier	L1 users	Totals	L2 users	Totals
Please	27	27 (12%)	21	21 (36%)
Downtoners	2 (maybe) 4 (possibly)	6 (3%)	1 (maybe)	1 (2%)
Understaters	30 (just)	30 (14%)	1 (just) 1 (a bit)	2 (3%)
Subjectivisers	86 (I was wondering)	86 (39%)	6 (I was/I am/I'm wondering/I wonder)	6 (10%)
Consultative devices	54 (would it be possible) 2 (is there a chance)	56 (26%)	3 (would it be possible/is it possible)	3 (5%)
Hedges	8 (some) 5 (any)	13 (6%)	26 (some)	26 (44%)
Totals		**218**		**59**

2.4.1.2 Internal and External Modification   Clear contrasts in internal and external modification also existed between L2 and L1 users. The L2 learners used considerably fewer internal modifiers and many more external modifiers than the L1 users. In fact, the L1 users' emails recorded nearly three times more internal modifiers (218 instances) than the L2 users (59 instances). Table 2.3 illustrates the distribution of internal modifiers across the two groups.

Only hedges featured more prominently in the L2 data than in the L1 dataset and the most commonly used hedge by L2 learners was *some* (44 per cent) as in 'Could you give me *some* suggestions?'. Apart from that, L2 learners used all the other internal lexical modifiers less frequently, including *please* (12 per cent), consultative devices (e.g., *Would it be possible*) (5 per cent), subjectivisers (e.g., *I was wondering*) (10 per cent), understaters (e.g., *a bit* in 'I would need *a bit* more time for the proposal') (3 per cent), and downtoners (e.g., *maybe* in "can I use one booth on my own, *maybe* not sharing it with others this time") (2 per cent). By contrast, L1 users used these specific internal modifiers much more often with the subjectiviser *I was wondering* (39 per cent) and the consultative device *Would it be/is it possible* (25 per cent) consistently being the L1 speakers' go-to mitigators, as shown by Figure 2.2.

This broad trend of internal lexical use was identified by a few participants in their retrospective interviews. They mentioned that they noted native speakers of English preferred to use internal modification within the request utterance

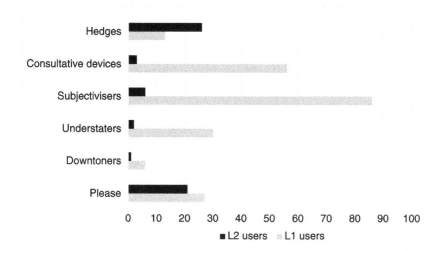

Figure 2.2 A comparison of L2 and L1 users' internal modifiers

to 'decorate it', but they still preferred external modification, especially pre-request small talk to create warmth and build rapport (P4, P12, P15), as the following quote shows:

I must say that I have learned a lot by carefully observing the emails I received. For example, English people like to say 'I was just wondering if you could help me' to express politeness, but for me, my native Chinese mindset tells me to just put some phatic exchanges before raising a request. I think that's uncommon in English, but the function is the same—to express politeness. So in almost all my emails, I put my request at the end of email. I remember a professor once missed my request completely. When I spoke to her and showed my email to her on my mobile phone, she laughed and said I hid my question towards the end of my long email. (P15, retrospective interview)

Indeed, L2 users' email requests contained more than two times as many external modifiers (299 instances recorded) as L1 users (130 instances recorded). Table 2.4 describes the distribution of external modifiers across the two groups.

While *grounders* and *small talk* were the top two preferred external modifiers for both L1 and L2 students, the L2 users employed significantly more *grounders* (113 instances in 170 L2 emails versus 76 instances in 162 L1 emails), *small talk* (101 instances in L2 versus 26 instances in L1), *appreciators* (fifty-five instances in L2 versus twelve in L1) and *discourse orientation moves* (twenty-three instances in L2 versus two in L1), as shown in Figure 2.3.

Table 2.4 *Preferred choice of external modifiers between L1 and L2 users*

External modifier	L1 users	L2 users	L2 example
Grounder	76 (58%)	113 (38%)	*I am applying for a graduate job at Goldman Sachs.*
Disarmer	2 (2%)	2 (0.7%)	*I guess you must be busy with marking our essays. But …*
Getting a precommitment	1 (1%)	1 (0.3%)	*Could you do me a favour?*
Promise	1 (1%)	1 (0.3%)	*I will do my best to do as much work as possible from now on.*
Imposition minimiser	4 (3%)	1 (0.3%)	*I hope you can understand.* Please delete me from your name list of the court visit.
Apology	6 (5%)	2 (0.7%)	*I want to apologise* that I have to postpone our meeting next week.
Discourse orientation move	2 (2%)	23 (8%)	*I have read about Nationwide Building Society in some news several times and I am quite interested in it. What I want to know is that …*
Small talk	26 (20%)	101 (34%)	*My classmates and I went to Liverpool during the weekend and we all love Liverpool! Thank you for recommending the museums in Liverpool. We like them very much! … Can I send my draft to you later this week?*
Appreciator	12 (9%)	55 (18%)	*Thank you for considering my request.*
Totals	**130**	**299**	

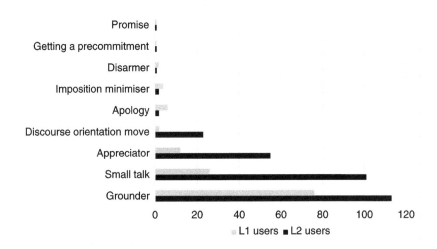

Figure 2.3 A comparison of L2 and L1 users' external modifiers

Example 1 *A Typical Example of L2 Email Requests*

Dear [First Name]	Opener	
I have learned so much about English language and culture since I came to England. I'm very happy that I seized the opportunity of study abroad.	**Small talk**	External modification 1
I've heard my British classmates talking about an organised visit to the Crown Court for the master's students of our programme. I have never been to a court before, let alone an English court.	**Grounder**	External modification 2
Could I book a place for this visit?	**Request head act**	
Many thanks.	**Appreciator**	External modification 3
Best regards,	**Closer**	

Example 2 *A Typical Example of L1 Email Requests*

Hi [First Name]	Opener	
I was just wondering who is helping me with my Korean dissertation?	**Request head act**	
Because I don't think I know who I'm supposed to ask for help.	**Grounder**	External modification 1
Kind regards,	**Closer**	

The most frequently recurring structure of the L2 learners' emails tended to contain three external modifiers: *small talk* (34 per cent), *grounder* (38 per cent), and *appreciator* (18 per cent) surrounding the request, as shown by Example 1.

Example 1 describes the typical L2 email composition. A conventional opener such as 'Dear/Hi [Addressee]' is followed by two external modifiers, that is, *small talk,* which is intended to establish a positive atmosphere and rapport (Schauer, 2006; Woodfield, 2012), and a *grounder* which gives reasons, explanations, or justifications for the request. Then, the request is made and it is subsequently reinforced by an *appreciator* before the email closes with a conventional closer, such as 'Best regards'. It is worth pointing out that the lengthy pre-request supportive moves, like the small talk in the example above, were not always relevant to the request. This is in sharp contrast to the typical structure of our L1 emails, as illustrated in Example 2.

Clearly firstly, the typical L2 example is about twice as long as the typical L1 example. Secondly, the L2 email contains the external modifiers of *small talk* and *appreciator* which are absent in the typical L1 structure. Finally, the request itself is placed towards the end of the L2 email whereas it is located near the beginning of the L1 email. In fact, these differences epitomise the distinctive features of the Chinese ESL learners' email practices. In our dataset, L2 emails (seventy-six words per email on average) were typically longer than L1 emails (forty-five words per email on average), and the L2 users employed significantly more external modifiers and fewer internal modifiers. While the main purpose of the emails was to make a request to faculty, they tended to place the request itself towards the end of an email rather than getting straight to the point. The participants attributed the distinct features to the information sequencing in their native language/culture, as the following excerpt illustrates.

Excerpt from the second focus-group interview
P15: The Chinese logic is BECAUSE SO. The English logic is SO BECAUSE, the other way around.
P2:   Indeed. We need to explain the situation first and then we can say 'Professor, I need your help'.
P3:   These paragraphs [*small talk* or *discourse orientation moves* prior to a request in the L2 data presented to all the participants] are very important. They make us sound politer, less cold and utilitarian. It shows we respect you, care about you and want to build a good relationship with you.
      …
P5:   I know the topic-comment construction in Chinese is also unique to the Chinese language. We tend to bring up a topic first, describe the background, and then we express our views. What we really think comes last.

In this excerpt taken from the L2 users' retrospective focus group interviews, they stated that they felt that the background information and/or the reason of the request had to be provided first, following the generic Chinese sequencing of BECAUSE THEREFORE and the Chinese topic-comment construction, and that having some small talk first and delaying the request in the email meant politeness (P2, P3, P5, P7, P8, P9, P10, P11, P12, P15). Although they seemed to be aware of the cross-linguistic and cross-cultural variations, their native influence on their L2 email construction remained prominent.

2.4.1.3 Request Perspectives   Finally, the results demonstrate different group preferences for request perspective, as illustrated by Table 2.5.

Second language users displayed a strong preference for the perspective options 'you' (46 per cent) and 'I' (45 per cent) over 'we' (6 per cent) and 'impersonal' (2 per cent). The latter two options, which appear to be less coercive because they specifically avoid assigning an agent, dominated the L1 data (accounting for 86 per cent), but were rarely used by L2 learners (8 per cent). Figure 2.4 depicts the contrast visually.

In short, the distinctive features of L2 email requests lie in in/direct request strategies, internal and external modification and request perspectives. Let us

Table 2.5 *Preferred choice of perspective between L1 and L2 users*

Request perspective	L1 users	L2 users
Impersonal	61 (38%)	4 (2%)
I	6 (4%)	77 (45%)
We	77 (48%)	10 (6%)
You	18 (11%)	79 (46%)

Note: Total emails: L1 = 162; L2 = 170

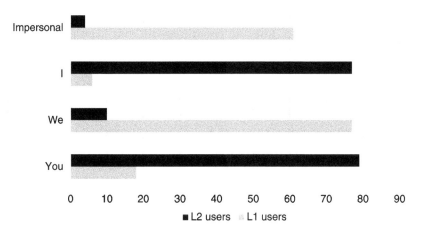

Figure 2.4 A comparison of L2 and L1 users' request perspectives

now shift our focus to the second research question regarding the diachronic change of the L2 users' email practices during their study abroad.

2.4.2   *How Do L2 Users Perceive Diachronic Change in their Request Emails? (RQ2)*

The definition of pragmatic competence is evolving. In a recent iteration, Taguchi (2019) contends that linguistic and sociolinguistic knowledge (i.e., form-function-context mappings), interactional abilities (i.e., for using the aforementioned knowledge adaptively according to changing contexts), and agency (i.e., choice of whether to demonstrate the aforementioned knowledge in a community) are key components. This definition captures well the importance of these tripartite elements, as identified in the participant interview data and examined further in this section.

The results show that more sophisticated pragmatic structures such as internal modification remained largely unacquired, but the participants showed progress in other aspects. They developed their L2 pragmatic competence during the period abroad mainly through observation, engineered peer discussion and, occasionally, through faculty's feedback. First, all of them observed patterns of different L2 email practices, most notably email openings and closings, in the emails they received during their SA. Take the form of address as an example. They quickly learned that it was generally fine to address professors by their first name in an email in the UK and gradually started to do so over time (P6, P10, P14, P15). Second, at the beginning of each week, all the participants were asked to reflect on email writing and discuss their thoughts in a group. Although this meeting was pre-arranged for the group, the researchers distanced themselves from the discussions, allowing students to further their own learning through peer talk. Most of the participants found the peer discussion helpful in terms of sharing newly acquired pragmatic knowledge and experiences (P1, P2, P5, P6, P7, P8, P10, P11, P12, P15). For instance, P3 recalled adopting the formulaic expression 'I would appreciate' as a result of the weekly discussion with his peers (P3, retrospective interview).

Additionally, the learners reported that faculty's feedback on their emails also contributed to their pragmatic learning, but this occurred less frequently. Participants found it difficult to gauge the level of politeness of their emails perceived by the recipients, because 'professors rarely tell international students that they feel the students' emails are inappropriate' (P7, retrospective interview). There were a few exceptions in the data. For example, P2 wrote the following email to her professor to ask for a ticket.

Dear Professor [First Name]
I am [First Name Last Name] and my English name is [First Name]. I am a Master student. I have seen your email that you have free tickets available for the performance in the music hall. I like live performances. I want 1 ticket for myself. Can I collect it from your office this afternoon?
Best regards

The professor, who did not know P2 personally, replied that 'It's fine but mind your language'. P2 was stunned by his response, because she did not think her email was rude and 'his words rang an alarm-bell' for her (P2, cross-cultural record sheet).

'Mind your language!' Oh my god! I have never thought my email could be seen as very impolite by professors. To be frank, I was extremely shocked, confused and embarrassed by his reply, but I didn't dare to ask him why. I've approached a few good English friends and you for help. His incisive criticism was an important moment of revelation for me. From then on, I became more careful about my email language. For example, do not say 'I want' to my English professors. (P2, retrospective interview)

The excerpt above illustrates pragmatic learning. More intriguingly, however, an intentional process, which we term 'pragmatic unlearning', was identified among some of the participants, and it is particularly pertinent to the agency component of pragmatic competence. Pragmatic unlearning refers to the process by which learners actively disassociate from L2 norms when conflicts with the L1 systems arise. In these cases, L2 users might choose not to deploy the active L2 norms, or there might be initial uptake, which is later intentionally dropped, due to various concerns and considerations. These kinds of pragmatic unlearning were primarily reflected in two interrelated features of L2 English emails: pre-request small talk and length of emails, as examined below.

During their year abroad, all the participants seemed to realise that L1 English emails tended to be shorter and more concise, with requesters tending to bypass pre-request small talk and going straight to the request. Some participants, such as P12, did initially align to these L2 norms but, later, they intentionally reverted back to their L1 practices, because they regarded shorter emails as 'cold and impolite' (P5). For some of our participants, getting rid of the lengthy pre-request small talk, which might be irrelevant to the request, equated to 'saying that I don't want to build rapport with you' and 'I don't care about politeness', despite their awareness of different L2 norms (P12). The learners intentionally opted out of the L2 practices after a period of time and attributed it to the stickiness of their L1 norms in English language learning (P1, P2, P4, P11, P12). The outcome of this changing practice consequently affected the overall length of emails over time, as depicted in Figure 2.5 from one of the learners (P12).

Over a period of one semester, P12 shared one request email she sent each week. As can be seen from Figure 2.5, the length of her emails reduced considerably at first and then bounced back. The examples below are her longest email sent in Week 1 and her shortest email in Week 5.

P12's Email 1

Dear Professor
I hope you are doing well. My groupmates and I met several times to discuss our group project. It was a new experience for me. I have never done group projects like this before, whereas Lucy and Matthew have. They taught me how to conceptualise and implement such projects. However, we disagree with a few fundamental concepts. We all reviewed the assignment brief and the marking criteria, but we struggled to agree on a few key points. Since this assignment accounts for 30% of the final grade, we have to be cautious. *Can you meet with us and let us know whether we are going in the right direction?*

Many thanks.
Best regards

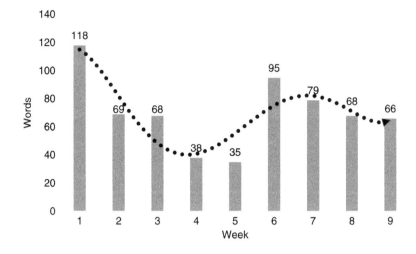

Figure 2.5 The word count of P12's request emails over a semester

P12's Email 5

Dear [First Name]
I hope you are well. *I would appreciate it if I could take a draft of my essay to you, and you give me some advice.* Is that OK?

Many thanks.
Best regards

The sections in italics mark the request head act. Lengthy pre-request supportive moves, including the external modifier of small talk, which could be irrelevant to the request made, featured prominently in P12's longer emails, but reduced considerably in Week 4 and 5. In her interview, she was asked to chronologically examine all nine emails she had shared with the researchers and reflect on how her emails had changed since the beginning of the semester. She immediately identified length as a trend and, while reflecting, unpacked her journey of learning and unlearning processes (the segment in italics in the excerpt below refers to the outcomes of exercising agency).

I didn't use English emails before I came to the UK. My professors and I used WeChat or QQ all the time. To me, email communication is very formal. This is a new learning experience for me. Not long after I started my studies in the UK, I've noted that the English emails sent by my English classmates, friends, and professors are much shorter … and they don't do much phatic talk and directly raise their requests, [like] 'Could you help me with this?' … In my mother tongue, the longer the phatic talk before you make a request, the politer you are. But this is not the case in English. Initially, I did start to follow English habits, deleting a lot of the phatic talk before I raised my requests and asked my questions, but *I just felt very uncomfortable. I felt I was being cold and impolite to my British professors, so even though I knew it was not necessarily in line with the English habits, I must switch back to the way I feel comfortable with.* (P12, retrospective interview)

This excerpt captured well the tug-of-war between evolving L1 and L2 norms in the learners' pragmatic development when the two systems conflict. The italics in the excerpt highlight the emotional reaction and the agency of the L2 user as an intercultural speaker who is making choices dynamically. Arguably, the learners' pragmatic choices reflected how they constructed their identity through the use of L2, as they consciously diverged from L2 to maintain their L1 sociocultural identity (Ren, 2017; Wang, forthcoming). These choices were based on their understandings of broader cultural values underlying target pragmatic behaviours (Ishihara, 2019; Wang & Halenko, 2022; Yates 2010). This subtle process of pragmatic learning and unlearning, including pragmatic resistance, was also identified by several other participants (P1, P3, P4, P6, P15). Learners may not be willing to actively adopt certain L2 pragmatics practices despite an ability to do so (Wang & Halenko, 2019a: 3), and more importantly, their willingness is fluid.

2.5   Discussion

Not all roads lead to Rome. To achieve politeness, L1 and L2 request practices may vary and when L1 and L2 pragmatics norms conflict, proficient L2 users, even when they possess the L2 knowledge, may demonstrate a strong native influence of their L1. This is reflected in the answers to both research questions.

Regarding the first research question, the distinctive linguistic features of L2 emails largely echo the findings of prior request research of Chinese, Asian, and Greek ESL/EFL learners of English (Chen, 2006; Chen, 2015; Economidou-Kogetsidis, 2011; Lin, 2009; Lee, 2010; Li, 2018; Tseng, 2016; Woodfield, 2012; Zhu, 2012). In making status-unequal requests, first, the L2 learners in our study, who were proficient English users, still used considerably more direct strategies and fewer conventionally indirect strategies than L1 users (Chen, 2006; Chen, 2015; Economidou-Kogetsidis, 2011; Lin, 2009; Woodfield, 2012). In line with Zhang (1995), the cultural preference for directness, which is economical, clear and explicit, seems to be corroborated by our findings. When the L2 learners did employ strategies of conventional indirectness, their preferences were much narrower, mainly limited to *could* and *can*, whereas L1 users adopted a wider range of request strategies and their choices were dominated by more sophisticated structures such as *possibility statements* ('would it be possible'). This series of findings is congruent with previous research (Economidou-Kogetsidis, 2011; Li, 2018; Lin, 2009; Zhu, 2012). For instance, Li's (2018) higher-proficiency EFL learners also showed an underuse of more complex downgraders such as past tense (I wondered if …) and continuous aspect (I was wondering if …) in their upward request emails. The author largely attributed this feature to L1 interference and the lack of practice and familiarity with these forms, which may have also been the case in the present study.

Such findings also relate to the third identified feature of L2 emails with respect to request perspective. The L2 users favoured the perspective options of 'you' and 'I' which often collocate with the modals of *could* and *can*. Their reliance on speaker and hearer perspectives could likely be transferred from L1 linguistic practices or the broader Chinese sociopragmatic view of rights and obligations between teachers and students. In Chinese societies, students often draw on the teachers' moral obligations to help and take for granted their rights to appeal directly for this help (Chen, 2006). Meanwhile, L1 users tended to opt for the 'we' and 'impersonal' perspectives to distance themselves from the request and make it appear less coercive, as reported elsewhere (Biesenbach-Lucas, 2007; Merrison et al., 2012; Zhu, 2012).

Another distinctive feature of L2 emails lies in internal and external modification. Underusing internal modifiers often leaves L2 learners open to pragmatic failure, as their emails may be perceived as overly direct and assertive. Li (2018), whose email study also featured low levels of internal modifiers, speculated that the cause may be linked to a lack of equivalent English internal modifiers in Chinese (e.g., past tense inflection, biclausals), the unavailability of Chinese internal modifiers in English (e.g., particles and honorific pronouns), L1 interference, or the processing complexity of internal modification. By contrast, the L2 learners used considerably more external modifiers than L1 users to express politeness and build rapport. The use of small talk, which may be lengthy, and even irrelevant to the request at hand, appeared to be the most favoured type of modifier and is a trend consistent with other email studies (e.g., Chen, 2006; Li, 2018; Wang, forthcoming). As suggested by our L2 participants, the importance of relationship building cannot be underestimated (Spencer-Oatey & Wang, 2019, 2020; Wang & Spencer-Oatey, 2015). Priming a request with small talk is about building rapport and conveying concern and appreciation for the addressee. In doing so, 'a reputable and respectable image (face) that the addressee wants to claim for him/herself from the public is thus enhanced' (Li, 2018: 204).

Regarding the second research question about the L2 learners' diachronic change during their study abroad, our participants experienced interesting processes of pragmatic learning and unlearning in developing their L2 pragmatic competence in email requests. Drawing on implicit input for pragmatic guidance on appropriate email behaviour was limited. Explicit feedback from faculty proved useful but was rarely offered. The second language users did benefit from observing L1 users' email practices to some extent. For instance, the L2 group seemed to be able to quickly acquire certain simple, formulaic framing moves, such as openers and closers. This finding agrees with Chen (2006), whose learner also adopted similar features from emails received and used this strategy to advance her email knowledge and practice. Chen (2015) also found the formulaicity of email openers and closers to be particularly amenable to explicit instruction, supporting the ease with which the learners in our study were able to adopt these features from implicit input alone.

More advanced elements such as internal modification, however, remained largely unacquired, for the reasons discussed previously. Stylistic features such as keeping emails brief and concise, out of consideration for faculty's limited time (Chen, 2006), were even resisted in some cases. Regarding message length, L2 users realised that L1 English emails are generally shorter and often go straight to the request, but this seemed to contradict their native L1 values. In line with Chen (2006), Li (2018), and Tseng (2016), the Chinese students in our study tended to consider longer emails as markers of politeness and shorter emails to be impolite. Due to their strong native influence, they deemed lengthy pre-request supportive moves, especially small talk, an important politeness strategy to build rapport and create warmth. Eliminating this feature from emails was considered a step too far for some of the ESL learners in this study. An initial reduction of this strategy, in line with L2 expectations, was later reversed, providing the strongest evidence for pragmatic unlearning, and revealing development may not always follow a one-way linear trajectory. In her study of five American learners of Japanese during a year abroad, Iwasaki (2011) found similar evidence of learner agency when examining the acquisition of polite and casual speech styles. Interview data revealed the learners' dilemma of knowing the appropriate (more formal) speech to use, but struggling to adopt it due to a desire to maintain their identity and use a preferred casual style. Iwasaki's finding also resonates with the interview data in the present study. Learners resisted or diverged from L2 to maintain their L1 sociocultural identity (Ishihara, 2019; Ren, 2017; Wang & Halenko, 2022; Yates 2010).

Pedagogically, the findings have some important implications. When it comes to email requests, it may be hard even for advanced L2 learners to acquire certain pragmatic knowledge implicitly in an L2 environment. Explicit feedback and instruction before or during study abroad would be beneficial (e.g., Alcón-Soler, 2015; Chen, 2015; Halenko & Jones, 2011, 2017; Wang & Halenko, 2019a, 2019b, 2022), but this raises the questions of what to teach and how. As Kecskes (2003) pointed out, formulaic expressions could be easy to learn but hard to understand. Learner agency matters, and helping L2 learners develop L2 pragmatic competence is more than imparting linguistic and sociolinguistic knowledge. Moreover, competence development is fluid and does not necessarily follow a linear fashion. Second language learners may be constantly negotiating L1 and L2 norms, especially when they contradict each other. Unpacking the deeper layers of beliefs may help learners to better attend to the *affective* and *cognitive* aspects of pragmatic competence development (Wang, forthcoming; Wang & Halenko, 2022).

It also further underlines that the students' pragmatic successes, failures and general growth rates are all individual, influenced by many factors and in many ways. On a methodological note, and as implicitly observed in Chen's (2006) findings, the postgraduate students in this study also seemed to profit from the staged reflections on their own pragmatic growth in unexpected ways. The frequent opportunities set up to elicit the data in the present study (group interviews, one-to-one interviews, and cross-cultural record sheets) gave the students ample and specific cause to consider their pragmatic journeys with respect to email communication throughout the SA stay. We believe these provided useful outlets for students as they negotiated their way through some of the pragmatic challenges they faced. Although it is likely that this approach was more successful because of the extended timeframe of the investigation, future studies would do well to also adopt some form of 'cause and pause' approach, where both a purposeful opportunity for reflection and time to share views are offered. In this way, reciprocity for both the researcher and participant is also ensured (Creswell & Plano Clark, 2010).

2.6   Conclusion

To summarise, the Chinese learners' L2 email requests to faculty are characterised by (1) significant directness and limited choices of conventional indirectness, (2) significant external modification and relative limited internal modification, and (3) strong preference for the request perspectives of 'you' and 'I' and relative lack of use of distancing options of 'impersonal' and 'we'. The L2 learners showed relatively limited change in email practices during their SA in England. It seemed hard for them to implicitly acquire more sophisticated pragmatic structures. This is perhaps partly because they rarely received feedback on the perceived level of politeness by the recipient of the request, and partly because their L1 influence remained strong.

Moreover, the L2 users' retrospective interviews revealed intriguing processes of pragmatic learning and unlearning including pragmatic resistance, implying that L2 pragmatic competence development is fluid. Learner' agency plays an important role as L2 users seem to be constantly negotiating L1 and L2 norms, beliefs, and identities. When L1 and L2 norms and beliefs conflict, they tend to fall back on the safety net of L1 practices even when they possess the L2 knowledge. How to address this through teaching warrants further research, for example, on repeated feedback unpacking the deeper layers of beliefs (Wang & Halenko, 2022) and explicit instruction on English email requests before and/or during study abroad.

When in Rome, do as the Romans do – but do we? There is an established consensus among ESL/EFL researchers and educators that even proficient English language users do not necessarily show concomitant pragmatic development, even after a long period of residence abroad. Yet there is still a comparative dearth of studies of how to address this through teaching, especially ones that analyse not only the L2 email discourse but also the perspectives and interpretations of the participants themselves. Much more research of this kind is needed, along with appropriate theorising.

References

Alcón-Soler, E. (2015). *Learning How to Request in an Instructed Learning Context.* Bern: Peter Lang.

Barron, A. (2003). *Acquisition in Interlanguage Pragmatics: Learning How to Do Things with Words in a Study Abroad Context.* Amsterdam: John Benjamins.

Barron, A. (2019). Pragmatic development and stay abroad. *Journal of Pragmatics,* 146, 43–53.

Biesenbach-Lucas, S. (2006). Making requests in e-mail: do cyber-consultations entail directness? Toward conventions in a new medium. In K. Bardovi-Harlig, C. Félix-Brasdefer, & A. Omar, eds., *Pragmatics Language Learning,* Vol. 11, Honolulu, HI: University of Hawaii Press, pp. 81–107.

Biesenbach-Lucas, S. (2007). Students writing e-mails to faculty: An examination of e-politeness among native and non-native speakers of English. *Language Learning and Technology,* 11(2), 59–81.

Bjørge, A. K. (2007). Power distance in English lingua franca email communication. *International Journal of Applied Linguistics,* 17(1), 60–80.

Blum-Kulka, S., House, J., & Kasper, G. (1989). *Cross-Cultural Pragmatics: Requests and Apologies,* Vol. 31. Norwood, NJ: Ablex Pub.

Bou-Franch, P. (2011). Openings and closings in Spanish email conversations. *Journal of Pragmatics,* 43(6), 1772–1785.

Chen, C-F E. (2006). The development of e-mail literacy: From writing to peers to writing to authority figures. *Language Learning and Technology,* 10(2), 35–55.

Chen, Y-S. (2015). Developing Chinese EFL learners' email literacy through requests to faculty. *Journal of Pragmatics,* 75, 131–149.

Chen, Y-S., Rau, D-H.V., & Rau, G. (2016). *Email Discourse among Chinese Using English as a Lingua Franca.* Singapore: Springer.

Cole, S., & Anderson, A. (2001). Requests by young Japanese: A longitudinal study. *The Language Teacher,* 25(8), 7–11.

Collentine, J., & Freed, B. F. (2004). Learning context and its effects on second language acquisition. *Studies in Second Language Acquisition,* 26, 153–171.

Creswell, J. W., & Plano Clark, V. L. (2010). *Designing and Conducting Mixed Methods Research* (2nd ed.). Thousand Oaks, CA: Sage Publications.

Davies, J. M. (2007). Resistance to L2 pragmatics in the Australian ESL context. *Language Learning,* 57(4), 611–649.

Duff, P. A. (2012). Identity, agency, and second language acquisition. In S. M. Gass & A. Mackey (eds.) *The Routledge Handbook of Second Language Acquisition.* London: Routledge, pp. 410–426.

Economidou-Kogetsidis, M. (2008). Internal and external mitigation in interlanguage request production: The case of Greek learners of English. *Journal of Politeness Research*, 4(1), 111–137.

Economidou-Kogetsidis, M. (2011). 'Please answer me as soon as possible': Pragmatic failure in non-native speakers' e-mail requests to faculty. *Journal of Pragmatics*, 43(13), 3193–3215.

Economidou-Kogetsidis, M. (2018). 'Mr Paul, please inform me accordingly': Address forms, directness and degree of imposition in L2 emails. *Pragmatics*, 28(4), 489–515.

Eslami, Z. R., Kim, H., Wright, K. L., & Burlbaw, L. M. (2014). The role of learner subjectivity in Korean English language learners' pragmatic choices. *Lodz Papers in Pragmatics*, 10(1), 117–146.

Halenko, N., & Jones, C. (2011). Teaching pragmatic awareness of spoken requests to Chinese EAP learners in the UK: Is explicit instruction effective? *System*, 39 (2), 240–250.

Halenko, N., & Jones, C. (2017). Explicit instruction of spoken requests: an examination of pre-departure instruction and the study abroad environment. *System*, 68, 26–37.

Halenko, N., & Winder, L. (2021). Experts and novices: Examining academic email requests to faculty and developmental change during study abroad. In M. Economidou-Kogetsidis, M. Savic and N. Halenko (eds.), *Email Pragmatics and Second Language Learners*. Amsterdam: John Benjamins, pp. 101–128.

Hendriks, B. (2010). An experimental study of native speaker perceptions of non-native request modification in emails in English. *Intercultural Pragmatics*, 7(2), 221–255.

Ishihara, N. (2019). Understanding English language learners' pragmatic resistance. In X. Gao (ed.), *Second Handbook of English Language Teaching*. Cham: Springer, pp. 621–641.

Ishihara, N., & Tarone, E. (2009). Subjectivity and pragmatic choice in L2 Japanese: emulating and resisting pragmatic norms. In N. Taguchi (ed.), *Pragmatic Competence*. Berlin: Mouton de Gruyter, pp. 101–128.

Iwasaki, N. (2011). Learning L2 Japanese 'politeness' and 'impoliteness': Young American men's dilemmas during study abroad. *Japanese Language and Literature*, 45, 67–106.

Kecskes, I. (2003). *Situation-bound Utterances in L1 and L2*. Studies on Language Acquisition, Vol. 19. Berlin: Mouton De Gruyter.

Lee, C. F. K. (2010). Written requests in emails sent by adult Chinese learners of English. *Language, Culture and Curriculum*, 17(1), 58–72.

Lewin-Jones, J., & Mason, V. (2014). Understanding style, language and etiquette in email communication in higher education: A survey. *Research in Post-Compulsory Education*, 19(1), 75–90.

Li, S. (2014). The effects of different levels of linguistic proficiency on the development of L2 Chinese request production during study abroad. *System*, 45, 103–116.

Li, W. (2018). *Pragmatic Transfer and Development: Evidence from EFL Learners in China*. Amsterdam and Philadelphia: John Benjamins.

Lin, Y-H. (2009). Query preparatory modals: Cross-linguistic and cross-situational variations in request modification. *Journal of Pragmatics*, 41(8), 1636–1656.

Merrison, A. J., Wilson, J., Davies, B., & Haugh, M. (2012). Getting stuff done: Comparing e-mail requests from students in higher education in Britain and Australia. *Journal of Pragmatics*, 44, 1077–1098.

Pérez-Vidal, C., & Shively, R. (2019). L2 pragmatic development in study abroad settings. In N. Taguchi (ed.), *The Routledge Handbook of Second Language Acquisition and Pragmatics*. Abingdon and New York: Routledge, pp. 355–371.

Ren, W. (2015). *L2 Pragmatic Development in Study Abroad Contexts*. Bern: Peter Lang.

Ren, W. (2017). Pragmatics and politeness in Chinese graduate students' gratitude emails in English. In Z. Xu & D. He (eds.), *Researching Chinese English: The State of the Art*. Singapore: Springer, pp. 109–124.

Sánchez-Hernández, A. (2018). A mixed-methods study of the impact of sociocultural adaptation on the development of pragmatic production. *System*, 75, 93–105.

Savić, M. (2018). Lecturer perceptions of im/politeness and in/appropriateness in student e-mail requests: A Norwegian perspective. *Journal of Pragmatics*, 124, 52–72.

Schauer, G. A. (2006). Pragmatic awareness in ESL and EFL contexts: Contrast and development. *Language Learning*, 56(2), 269–318.

Schauer, G. A. (2009). *Interlanguage Pragmatic Development: The Study Abroad Context*. London: Continuum.

Spencer-Oatey, H., & Wang, J. (2019). Culture, context, and concerns about face: Synergistic insights from pragmatics and social psychology. *Journal of Language and Social Psychology*, 38(4), 423–440.

Spencer-Oatey, H., & Wang, J. (2020). Establishing professional intercultural relations: Chinese perceptions of behavioural success in a Sino-American exchange visit. *Journal of Intercultural Communication Research*, 49(6), 499–519.

Taguchi, N. (2012). *Context, Individual Differences and Pragmatic Competence*. New York and Bristol: Multilingual Matters.

Taguchi, N. (2015). 'Contextually' speaking: A survey of pragmatic learning abroad, in class and online. *System*, 48, 3–20.

Taguchi, N. (2019). Second language acquisition and pragmatics: An overview. In N. Taguchi (ed.), *The Routledge Handbook of Second Language Acquisition and Pragmatics*. London: Routledge, pp. 1–14.

Tseng, C-T H. (2016). *An Interlanguage Pragmatic Study on Taiwanese EFL Learners' Email Request*. The Asian Conference on Language Learning 2016 Official Conference Proceedings, Aichi, Japan: pp. 41–57.

Wang, J. (forthcoming). Rapport management and evaluation in intercultural email communication. In P. Hinton & T. McConachy (eds.), *Negotiating Intercultural Relations*. London: Bloomsbury.

Wang, J., & Halenko, N. (2019a). Second language pragmatics. *A Special Issue of East Asian Pragmatics*, 4(1), 1–9.

Wang, J., & Halenko, N. (2019b). Longitudinal benefits of pre-departure pragmatics instruction for study abroad: Chinese as a second/foreign language. *East Asian Pragmatics*, 4(1), 87–111.

Wang, J., & Halenko, N. (2022). Developing formulaic competence for study abroad: A targeted instructional intervention. *The Language Learning Journal*.

Wang, J., & Spencer-Oatey, H. (2015). The gains and losses of face in ongoing intercultural interaction: A case study of Chinese participant perspectives. *Journal of Pragmatics*, 89, 50–65.

Wang, V. X. (2011). *Making Requests by Chinese EFL Learners*. Amsterdam: John Benjamins.

Woodfield, H. (2012). 'I think maybe I want to lend the notes from you.' Development of request modification in graduate learners. In M. Economidou-Kogetsidis & H. Woodfield (eds.), *Interlanguage Request Modification*. Amsterdam: John Benjamins, pp. 9–49.

Yates, L. (2010). Pragmatic challenges for second language learners. In A. Trosborg (ed.), *Pragmatics across Languages and Cultures*. Berlin: Mouton De Gruyter, pp. 287–308.

Zhang, Y. (1995). Indirectness in Chinese requesting. In G. Kasper (ed.), *Pragmatics of Chinese as Native and Target Language*. Honolulu, HI: University of Hawai'i Press, pp. 69–118.

Zhu, W. (2012). Polite requestive strategies in emails: An investigation of pragmatic competence of Chinese EFL learners. *RELC Journal*, 43(2), 217–238.

3 Pragmatic Development in Request Performance

A Cross-Sectional Study of Greek EFL Learners

Maria Economidou-Kogetsidis

3.1 Introduction

Research on L2 acquisitional pragmatics and on the developmental aspects of speech acts is a field which is still emerging at a slow pace (Bardovi-Harlig, 1999, 2006; Kasper & Rose, 2002), being noticeably neglected in the 1980s and 1990s, with the exception of a few longitudinal studies (e.g., Achiba, 2003 Ellis, 1992; Schmidt, 1983). Despite the need for a systematic study of the acquisition of pragmatic abilities by L2 learners, the body of research is heavily weighted towards studies that investigate the learners' pragmatic production rather than development (Kasper & Rose, 2002).

Research on the acquisition of L2 pragmatics in the foreign language (FL) classroom has been systematically investigated even less. Yet, a careful analysis of interlanguage learner data across proficiency levels may serve to improve our understanding of L2 pragmatic development (Félix-Brasdefer, 2007). Such an analysis of interlanguage data across different proficiency levels may also shed more light into the relationship between learners' pragmatic ability and grammatical competence. It is now widely accepted and well-documented that 'high levels of grammatical competence do not guarantee concomitant high levels of pragmatic competence' (Bardovi-Harlig, 1999: 686), and early work in language testing (reviewed by Canale & Swain, 1980) shows that performance on measures of grammatical ability (e.g., TOEFL, Michigan Test of English Language Performance) does not predict performance on communicative tasks (Kasper & Rose, 2002: 163). However, the exact nature of the relationship between grammatical and pragmatic competence is still unclear (Barron, 2003: 46) although it is likely that grammatical competence can greatly constrain the development of pragmatic competence (Hassall, 1997: 286).

Kasper and Rose (2002) present two different debates: (1) pragmatics precedes grammar, and (2) grammar precedes pragmatics. Even though there is evidence which supports both of these contradictory tendencies in adults' development, Kasper and Rose (2002: 190), in reviewing the empirical evidence, conclude that pragmatics precedes grammar in the early stages of pragmatic development (i.e., 'learners accomplish actions in a pregrammaticalised fashion by relying on situational and discourse context in conjunction with whatever L2 knowledge they have available'), while the reverse seems to be true for advanced learners. The authors explain that three possible scenarios might be found. First, learners may demonstrate the grammatical knowledge of a specific structure 'but do not use it to express or modify illocutionary force' (Kasper & Rose, 2002:190). A second scenario is that learners demonstrate the grammatical knowledge of a specific structure but use it to express pragmalinguistic functions that are not conventional in the target language (TL). Finally, learners might demonstrate knowledge of specific grammatical structures and their pragmalinguistic functions, yet they use this knowledge for non-target-like sociopragmatic use (Kasper & Rose, 2002: 190). Importantly, however, as Bardovi-Harlig (2013: 78–79) insightfully puts it, 'studying the development of grammar and lexicon in pragmatics is not a question of determining whether pragmatics or grammar develops first, but rather of explaining how the emergent systems interact, and how one supports the other'.

The present study aims to shed more light on L2 pragmatic development of EFL learners' request strategies and internal modification. It uses a cross-sectional design in order to examine the extent to which pragmatic competence develops in conjunction with language proficiency. More specifically, it analyses and compares Greek Cypriot learners' request strategies, internal modification, and request perspective across different proficiency levels, and examines whether learners who receive classroom instruction in an EFL context and are not exposed to pragmatic instruction or to the target language culture, show pragmalinguistic development in making requests as their English language proficiency improves. The data is collected through interactive role plays and comes from three learner groups of three different proficiency levels (B1 level in the Common European Framework Reference for Languages (CEFR) (Lower Intermediate), B2 (Higher Intermediate), C1 (Advanced)), and one native-speaker group (American NSs), which provides the baseline data.

More specifically, the research questions are:

1. How do Greek EFL learners' request strategies and request perspective develop across proficiency levels?
2. How does Greek EFL learners' internal request modification develop across proficiency levels? Is there evidence of pragmalinguistic development across the three groups?
3. To what extent does the learners' pragmatic development approximate NS use?

The chapter begins with a review of the relevant research and the theoretical background (Section 3.2) and continues with the presentation of the methods and procedures used in the study (Section 3.3). Section 3.4 presents the main findings of the study, and Section 3.5 offers a discussion of these findings in light of the relevant literature. Finally, Section 3.6 presents the conclusions and the limitations of the investigation.

3.2 Background: Pragmatic Development of L2 Requests

3.2.1 Longitudinal Studies and Stages of Pragmatic Development

Both cross-sectional and longitudinal studies have been used to analyse the pragmatic development of requests by adult and young learners (e.g., Achiba, 2003; Ellis, 1992; Félix-Brasdefer, 2007; Trosborg, 1995). While cross-sectional studies examine synchronic states of language performance or knowledge in different learner groups of different proficiency levels, longitudinal studies follow the same participants over a period of time and analyse change at an individual/micro level (i.e., as their L2 proficiency develops) (Cohen & Worrison, 2000: 178). Ellis's (1992) and Achiba's (2003) investigations are perhaps the most well-known longitudinal studies which focussed on the development of requests and 'documented staged development of pragmatic competence in accordance to grammatical maturity' (Taguchi, 2012: 43). Their studies have identified specific stages in the development of L2 requests that coincide in several respects.

Ellis's study (1992) investigated the development of requests in two young ESL learners in a classroom setting over a period of two years. He found that, although considerable development took place over this period, the learners did not fully develop their range of request types. Direct requests predominated throughout, mostly in the form of imperatives, and they relied on a restricted range of internal and external downgraders ('please', grounders). Overall, the learners exhibited limited development of request modification. Importantly, Ellis (1992) identified a three-stage developmental sequence: in the first stage (the pre-basic stage), the children conveyed requestive intent by relying on highly context-dependent realisations that had no syntax and no relational goals, for example, 'Me no blue' (Kasper & Rose, 2002: 140). In the second stage (the formulaic stage), children's requests were expressed with unanalysed routines and imperatives, for example, 'Don't look'. In the third stage (the unpacking stage), the requests began to exhibit conventional indirectness and other routine formulas.

A similar analysis was provided by Achiba's (2003) study, which examined the pragmatic development of her 7-year-old Japanese daughter, Yao, during her stay in Australia. Unlike Ellis's (1992) participants, Yao doubled the proportion of lexical/phrasal downgraders she used in her requests, showed a fast decrease in the number of imperatives employed, and a shift to conventional indirectness. One noteworthy finding was Yao's use of conventional indirectness and hints. By the last stage, conventional indirectness had become the most frequently used strategy, while the use of hints doubled with each stage. Achiba's (2003) analysis presents four stages of development but her first stage is more reminiscent of Ellis's second stage, while her second stage is equivalent to Ellis's (1992) third stage. This was because her participant, Yao, was more than an absolute beginner when the observation began. Achiba's (2003) additional stages of pragmatic development are 'pragmatic expansion' and 'fine tuning'. In the 'pragmatic expansion' stage, Yao's pragmalinguistic repertoire included many new forms, a shift in modality (from 'can' to 'could'), more complex syntax, and more frequent use of mitigation (especially supportive moves). In the 'fine tuning' stage, Yao's requests became even more refined.

To sum up, five stages of pragmatic development of requests therefore arise from Ellis's (1992) and Achiba's (2003) studies, as summarised by Kasper and Rose (2002): (1) the pre-basic stage characterised by highly context-dependent realisations that have no syntax and no relational goal, (2) the formulaic stage, characterised by imperatives and unanalysed formulas (i.e., routines that cannot be analysed by the learners' grammar at this stage), (3) the unpacking stage which is characterised by a shift to conventional indirectness and formulas that are incorporated into productive language use, (4) the pragmatic expansion stage which is characterised by the addition of new forms, an increased mitigation and more complex syntactic structures, and (5) the fine-tuning stage which involves the fine-tuning of requests according to participants, goals, and contexts (Kasper & Rose, 2002: 140).

3.2.2   *Longitudinal Studies and Pragmatic Development in Requests*

A number of longitudinal studies, mainly study-abroad (SA) investigations, have examined learners' request development and often compared it to NS production in order to establish the existence of any developmental patterns (e.g., Cole & Anderson, 2001; Schauer, 2004, 2006, 2009; Woodfield, 2012; see also Chapter 2, this volume). Such studies have examined the development of pragmatic features such as learners' development of request strategies, and/or internal and/or external request modification in a SA context. As the present study examines learners' request strategies and internal rather than external modification development, the discussion will limit itself to only these two aspects.

Using oral role plays, Woodfield (2012) examined the development of request modification strategies in eight graduate students at a UK university over a period of eight months. Her study found that the NS group internally modified their requests with greater frequency than the learner group, a finding which agreed with other developmental studies (Goy et al., 2012; Otçu & Zeyrek, 2008; Trosborg, 1995). Moreover, the learner group decreased their use of internal modifiers across the three phrases (Woodfield, 2012: 21), a finding similar to that of Cole and Anderson's (2001) study.

Cole and Anderson's (2001) longitudinal investigation found that, although towards the end of their stay in New Zealand and Canada their Japanese learners' pragmatic development included more than two downgraders per request, they used overall slightly fewer downgraders post-SA. Syntactic modifiers were also employed more extensively by the end of the learners' sojourn. At the same time, Cole and Anderson's (2001) participants moved from a direct style to conventionally indirect in all ten situations on the discourse completion task (DCT) at the end of their stay in the target language community, a strategy that the authors explained through an approach of playing it safe and attaching a politeness marker to everything. This development confirmed the findings of Ellis's study (1992), which showed that learners follow a developmental pattern from direct to conventionally indirect request strategies.

Schauer (2004, 2009) examined the interlanguage pragmatic development of nine German learners of English at a British university over the course of a year using a multimedia elicitation task and compared their production with British English NSs. Unlike Woodfield's (2012) Japanese participants, Schauer's (2004, 2009) German participants increased their repertoire of internal modifiers during their SA time. However, several internal modifiers such as consultative devices (e.g., 'Would you mind'), and imposition minimisers (e.g., 'a bit') were used less frequently than NSs and they remained overall underdeveloped. Schauer (2004) also found that politeness markers ('please'), downtowners, past tense modals, consultative devices and understaters were acquired or transferred from the L1 in most learners at the beginning of their stay. Schauer's (2009) study further indicated that conventionally indirect requests were employed by the highest number of learners and NSs, arguing that this strategy seems to be a very routinised request form. Hints (nonconventionally indirect requests) were more extensively used by NSs than by SA learners. This was a finding which contrasted Trosborg's (1995) results which revealed an equal number of hints in her least proficient learners and her NSs. Overall, Schauer's study (2009) found that the SA learners employed a wider range of request strategies to those used by the NS participants.

More recently, Economidou-Kogetsidis and Halenko's (2022) longitudinal study examined the frequency of request strategies and modification devices in order to track the pragmatic development of spoken requests by ten Japanese adult learners of English during an academic year in the UK. Findings from the study revealed that the learners hardly expanded their pragmalinguistic repertoire as there were only some pragmatic gains in their performance (e.g. a slight drop in the use of want statements). Overall, no dramatic changes were observed in the learners' performance, and the improvements identified at the directness and modification level of request strategies were seen as marginal. More specifically, the learners relied on (and overused) a limited set of request sequences and had clear preferences for particular ways to express (in)directness. At each time period, there was an overwhelming preference for want statements (*'I'd like to'*, *'I want to'*) and an overdependence on preparatory questions (mainly of *'could you'* type) and permissions (*'can you'*). Their lexical downgraders were also found to be limited in scope across time, and tended to follow a predictable pattern across time periods, although, in line with Schauer (2009), there was an increase in the employment of hedges, amplifiers and 'please' towards the end of their sojourn abroad, suggesting a small sign of progress. The authors argue that it is likely that the learners, whose proficiency was rather low, could not retrieve the expressions needed to orally formulate internally modified requests on the spot when completing the oral, computer-animated production task (CAPT) of the study. Overall, the study confirmed that pragmatic gains might often be small, and development may follow a non-linear trajectory, even when living and studying in an EFL environment.

Longitudinal studies inevitably involve a small number of participants. Thus, as Kasper and Rose (2002) maintain, it is important to examine what cross-cultural studies can contribute to the discussion of pragmatic development. Section 3.2.3 therefore reviews the findings of cross-sectional studies in relation to the development of request strategies and internal modification.

3.2.3   *Cross-Sectional Developmental Studies and Pragmatic Development in Requests*

There are a number of cross-sectional studies that have proven fruitful in illuminating certain aspects of interlanguage pragmatic development (Rose, 2000: 33). Scarcella's (1979) early cross-sectional study used role plays to compare requests produced by beginner and advanced Arabic learners of English with those of American NSs. The learners in Scarcella's study employed more direct strategies than the NSs, while the more advanced group displayed more pragmatic characteristics which approximated native-like use. These results were similar to those received in Woodfield's (2008) investigation which also showed that the learner group employed more direct strategies than the NS group. Scarcella's study (1979) also revealed that some request modification devices such as 'please' and alerters ('excuse me') emerged early in the L2 acquisition process, while others such as the joint perspective ('we') became evident in the later stage.

Trosborg's (1995) study, which examined requests, complaints, and apologies by Danish learners across three proficiency levels, found that the learners' usage of request modification increased in parallel with their proficiency level.

However, compared to the NS control group, the learners were found to under-use their request modifiers. At the same time, the study revealed that the learners of all proficiency levels, and the NSs, favoured conventionally indirect strategies, a finding in line with Schauer's (2009) finding above. Importantly, according to Trosborg's study, some internal modification features did not develop in a linear fashion. Although the number of downgraders employed by group II was larger than that of group I[1] (indicating that learners moved closer to NS scores), the most advanced group, group III used fewer downgraders than group II.

Rose (2000) investigated the pragmatic development of request head acts in EFL primary school children in Hong Kong across three levels. His study also showed that conventional indirectness was the most frequent strategy overall, almost exclusively performed with query preparatory with either *can* or *may*. Directness was found to be most frequent among the lower proficient group, a finding which added support to evidence of the reliance on direct requests in the early stages of pragmatic development. Rose's study (2000), however, additionally found that the lower proficient group also used the highest percentage of hints (albeit in the same scenario), a finding which the author himself considers surprising, given the tendency for hints to appear late in both L1 and L2.

In his follow-up study of interlanguage requests, Rose (2009) examined the development of teenage learners' requests. Results indicated ample evidence of pragmalinguistic development, particularly in what appeared to be the onset of pragmatic expansion in the higher proficiency group. Learners in all his three groups made frequent use of the conventionally indirect request strategy, moving away from the earlier pre-basic and formulaic stages found in his 2000 study. While the younger, lower proficiency group in the 2009 study showed a higher frequency of direct requests, the higher proficiency group not only relied on conventional indirectness, but they syntactically modified their requests more by using a wider range of modals and modal expressions such as 'would you mind'.

Félix-Brasdefer's (2007) study with Spanish as a foreign language learners provided further evidence regarding the pragmatic development of requests from the beginning of foreign language instruction to advanced levels of proficiency. Using open role plays to collect data from NSs and learners of three proficiency levels, his study indicated that beginner learners showed a preference for direct strategies and hence little ability to vary their requests

---

[1] Group I in Trosborg's (1995) study comprised pupils from Grade 9 of secondary school who had received approximately five to six years of English language instruction. Her group II comprised high school pupils who had received approximately seven to eight years of instruction in English, while group III involved university students with ten years of instruction in English.

across social situations. In contrast, a strong preference for conventionally indirect requests was observed among intermediate and advanced learners in formal and informal situations, and lower degrees of directness were noted. The realisation of requests by most intermediate and advanced learners did not approximate the request behaviour of NSs. The study also showed that 'early conventionally indirect requests in the beginners group were characterised by interference from the L1, in particular by the learners' inability to use the necessary pragmalinguistic means … to express a polite request with a hearer-oriented perspective' (Félix-Brasdefer, 2007: 270). In fact, Félix-Brasdefer's (2007) study is one of the very few studies which also examined the development of request perspective, something relevant to the focus of the present investigation. The study observed that as learners' proficiency increased so did the number of hearer-perspective requests employed, approximating therefore Spanish NSs' performance. The study further revealed infrequent uses of impersonal requests while inclusive requests were completely absent among the three groups.

Importantly, Félix-Brasdefer's (2007) study identifies four developmental stages of requests, consistent with Achiba's (2003) and Ellis's (1992) investigations discussed above. The first two stages which were identified were the 'pre-basic stage' (consisting of minimal lexical and non-lexical realisations used to express pragmatic intent), and the 'basic stage', characteristic of the emergence of formulas. In the last two proficiency levels, Félix-Brasdefer's (2007: 276) study identified the 'unpacking of formulaic use' stage (characterised by the unpacking of direct requests and a preference for conventional indirectness), and the 'pragmatic expansion' stage as the last stage. In this last stage, requests were modified by a wider range of internal and external markers and more complex grammatical structures prevailed.

Otçu and Zeyrek's (2008) study with role plays focussed on lower-intermediate and upper-intermediate Turkish EFL learners. The study showed that the learners' lexical/phrasal downgraders, syntactic downgraders and subjectivisers exhibited a developmental pattern. With specific reference to syntactic mitigation, the study revealed that the only structure the learners employed was conditional clauses, while tense and aspect were lacking in their request head acts. Neither learner group made use of the same range of syntactic downgraders as the NSs. Regarding lexical/phrasal downgraders and head acts, the study revealed that the upper-intermediate group opted for directness and made a greater use of cajolers unlike the lower-intermediate group which used them quite infrequently.

Goy et al.'s (2012) cross-sectional study similarly investigated the development of internal request modification of Turkish learners of English from two different proficiency levels. The study found that the learners used significantly less syntactic mitigation than the NS group, although a developmental pattern was observed from the beginner to the upper-intermediate group as there was an increase in the learners' use of conditional and conditional clause types. The higher proficiency learners significantly increased their repertoire of lexical/phrasal downgraders compared to beginner learners, although both groups used significantly fewer devices than the NSs.

Savić's cross-sectional study (2015) examined the development of requests in young Norwegian EFL learners. Her results 'revealed clear patterns of pragmalinguistic development with regard to the complexity of head acts and the use of alerters, supportive moves, and downgraders' (2015: 443). In line with previous studies (e.g., Rose, 2000), Savić's (2015) study also showed that conventional indirectness was preferred across all levels, although this preference increased with proficiency level. Lower proficiency learners of level 1 and 2 appeared to display characteristics of the pre-basic stage (stage 1) and the formulaic stage (stage 2) discussed above. Regarding syntactic modification, the use of modal 'can' decreased steadily with level/age and was replaced by 'could', 'would' in level 2, and by a wider variety of structures (e.g., if clauses, *do you have*+ relative clause) in the higher proficiency group (level 3). The higher proficiency group was also found to use a greater variety of lexical/phrasal downgraders although the marker 'please' was employed most extensively by level 2 learners.

More recently, Savić et al.'s (2021) cross-sectional study used a video-based oral discourse-completion task to examine the pragmalinguistic development in the request production of eighty-eight Greek Cypriot and seventy-nine Norwegian young learners, focussing on their request head acts and modification across three proficiency/age groups. This recent study, which is particularly relevant to the study at hand since it also focussed on Greek Cypriot learners (GCLs), found that the 9-, 11-, and 13-year-old GCLs displayed some pragmalinguistic development in their distribution of direct and conventionally indirect strategies. More specifically, their direct strategies decreased significantly with age, while their use of conventional indirectness increased. Certain direct substrategies such as want statements, elliptical statements and imperatives also revealed pragmatic development as they steadily decreased with age. Results from this study also revealed no significant development in the GCLs' use of request modification, with the exception of 'please' which significantly dropped.

3.3 Methods

3.3.1 Participants

Forty learners of English as a foreign language (EFL) and sixteen American NSs provided the data for the present study. More specifically, the learner data came from three groups of three different proficiency levels: fourteen lower-intermediate learners (B1 level in the CEFR – with IELTS score 4.0–5.0), thirteen upper intermediate learners (B2 level in CEFR – with IELTS score 6.0) and thirteen advanced learners (C1–C2 level in CEFR – with IELTS score 7.0 and above)[2]. According to the Cambridge English scale[3] (2015), the IELTS equivalent score of B1 level is 4.0–5.0, the IELTS equivalent of B2 level is 5.5–6.5, while the IELTS equivalent grade of C1–C2 level is 7 and above. This scale was followed in order to group the learners into the three proficiency levels as all of them had taken the IELTS English language exam within two months from the time of the study. All the EFL learners were native speakers of Greek and were living in Cyprus at the time of the study. Some were full-time, undergraduate students at a private university in Cyprus, while others were 12th grade, high school students who were taking English language private lessons for university entry in the UK. Each proficiency group had a mix of university and high school students. In terms of gender, there were fifteen males and twenty-five females, and the gender distribution was similar for each learner group. Their ages ranged from 17–25 and the mean average was 19 years old. None of the learners had lived in an English-speaking country and they had all learnt English as a foreign language through school or private language institutes.

The American NS group which provided the baseline data comprised of sixteen undergraduate students from the USA. At the time of the study, the American students had just arrived in Cyprus in order to spend one semester at a private university in Cyprus as global semester students. They were all female and their ages ranged from 19–22 (the mean age was 21 years old). None of these students was a native speaker of an additional language other than English.

---

[2] The CEFR (Common European Framework of Reference for Languages) is a framework intro-duced by the Council of Europe that was 'designed to provide a transparent, coherent and com-prehensive basis for the elaboration of language syllabuses and curriculum guidelines, the design of teaching and learning materials, and the assessment of foreign language proficiency' (Council of Europe, 2018) www.coe.int/en/web/common-european-framework-reference-languages. It is now extensively used as an international standard for describing language ability in Europe but also in other continents. The CEFR divides language learners into six levels, starting from A1 (breakthrough or beginner) to C2 (proficient user who can understand with ease virtually everything heard or read). www.eui.eu/Documents/ServicesAdmin/LanguageCentre/CEF.pdf. According to CEFR, B1–B2 learners (characterised as 'independent users') 'can deal with most situations likely to arise … and can produce simple connected text on topics which are familiar or of personal interest' (Council of Europe, 2018). B level (B1–B2) is therefore assigned to those language learners who have a lower/upper intermediate proficiency of the foreign language. C level (C1–C2) refers to 'proficient users' of the language and therefore concerns learners who have an advanced/native-like competence of the foreign language.

[3] The Cambridge English scale: www.cambridgeenglish.org/exams-and-tests/cambridge-english-scale/

3.3.2 Instrumentation and Procedures

The data were collected using open-ended, interactive role plays, which can yield spoken data that approximates natural discourse, when administered with care (Félix-Brasdefer, 2007; Kasper, 2000). At the same time, role plays enable the researcher to keep the social and situational variables stable and therefore collect comparable data.

The participants were presented with a cue card which described each situation in detail. After being given time to complete a general background questionnaire and read the cue on the card, the participants role-played the dialogues individually with a female NS of English who was a full-time faculty member at the university. The role-play dialogue was initiated by the faculty member and the students were instructed to respond as they would in a natural conversation. All role plays enabled multiple turns and the average length of each recording was approximately one minute. The dialogues were audio recorded, then transcribed and analysed.

Five role-play situations/scenarios were employed in the study. These were scenarios which the participants were familiar with or were likely to encounter in their lives as students. All the situations required the production of a request but did not predetermine the course and outcome of the interaction (e.g., whether the professor would agree to lend the book or not – see Scenario 1). Following Billmyer and Varghese's (2000) notion of content-enriched situations, the situational prompt deliberately included a lot of detailed contextual information with respect to the setting, time, place, interlocutors' age, and their kind of relationship. The chosen situations also accounted for situational variability as they captured different possible role constellations on the dimensions of social power, distance, and imposition (Brown & Levinson, 1987).

Due to space constraints, the five request role-play situations utilised in this study are briefly described below:

- Scenario 1: *Book Loan*: A student asks a professor he/she hardly knows to lend him/her a book for an assignment. (+Power, +Distance)
- Scenario 2: *Lift Home*: A student asks a professor he/she knows very well and who lives in his/her neighbourhood to give him/her a lift home on a rainy evening. (+Power, -Distance)
- Scenario 3: *Notes*: A student asks his best friend at university to lend him/her lecture notes for an upcoming test. (-Power, -Distance)
- Scenario 4: *Menu*: A student is at an informal restaurant and asks for the menu from the young waiter who seems to have forgotten about them. (-Power, +Distance)
- Scenario 5: *Restaurant Order*: A student is at an informal restaurant and gives his/her order to a young waiter. (-Power, +Distance)

3.3.3   Data Analysis

Requests were analysed first for head act, and were coded according to three levels of directness: (1) direct (e.g., 'Give me your notes'), (2) conventionally indirect (CI) (e.g., 'Can I borrow your notes?'), or (3) non-conventionally indirect/hints (NCI) (e.g., 'Did you go to class yesterday? I couldn't go') (Blum-Kulka et al., 1989). Conventionally indirect requests were further analysed for request perspective which examined whether the request was realised from the viewpoint of the hearer (hearer perspective – HP) ('Can you give me the book?'), the speaker (speaker perspective – SP) ('Can I have the book?'), both participants (joint perspective) (i.e., using the inclusive 'we'), or by avoiding the issue using an impersonal construction (impersonal perspective) (e.g., 'Is it possible to …') (Blum-Kulka et al., 1989).

In addition to strategies employed in the head acts, each of the elicited requests was further analysed and coded with regard to internal mitigation which examined both for lexical/phrasal downgraders and syntactic downgraders. Several taxonomies have been developed in order to account for the different modification devices in requests, but the taxonomy adopted in the present study follows the taxonomy used by Woodfield and Economidou-Kogetsidis (2010). Syntactic downgraders therefore included the conditional structure (e.g., *'Could I* borrow it again?'), conditional clauses ('I was wondering *if I could* borrow one of your books'), tense[4] (past tense forms used with present reference) ('Is it all right if I *asked* for an extension?'), aspect[5] ('I *was wondering* if it's possible to have an extension'), and negation of preparatory condition *('I don't suppose* there's any chance of an extension?'). The analysis for lexical/phrasal mitigation, on the other hand, included seven mitigators: the marker 'please', consultative devices (e.g., 'would you mind', 'do you think'), downtoners (e.g., 'possibly', 'perhaps'), understaters/hedges (e.g., 'a bit', 'a little'), subjectivisers (e.g., 'I wonder', I'm afraid'), cajolers (e.g., 'You know', 'actually') and appealers (e.g., 'OK/right?').

All the requests were coded in the Statistical Package for the Social Sciences (SPSS) for their head act directness level, their mitigating strategies, and their request perspective. Chi-square test of independence were employed to examine the existence of statistical significance. The threshold for statistical significance was set at $p \leq 0.05$.

---

[4] According to Blum-Kulka et al. (1989: 283), past tense forms are coded as downgraders only if they are used with present time reference and can therefore be substituted by present tense forms without changing the semantic meaning of the utterance.
[5] Blum-Kulka et al. (1989: 282) explains that the durative aspect marker counts as a mitigator only if it can be substituted by a simple form (e.g., 'I'm wondering' vs. 'I wonder').

3.4   Results

3.4.1   Head Acts: Levels of Directness and Perspective

This section presents and discusses the results of the study. Table 3.1 displays the overall results for the types of request head acts (direct, conventionally indirect (CI), hints (non-conventionally indirect – NCI), and 'opting out' (don't do the face-threatening act (FTA)) (Brown & Levinson, 1987) for each learner group in all five situations. Figure 3.1 offers a graphic representation of the same results. As shown in Table 3.1 and Figure 3.1, CI was overall the preferred strategy by the NS group (62.9 per cent) while directness was the most frequent strategy not only among the lower proficiency group, but among the most proficient groups as well (B1=52.7 per cent, B2=52.6 per cent, C1=43.5 per cent). We therefore see evidence of reliance not only on direct requests in the early stages of pragmatic development only but also throughout all proficiency stages. It could further be observed from the results that the amount of directness slightly decreased across proficiency levels especially as learners progressed from the B2 to C1 level. Yet, even at the highest proficiency level (C1), their performance did not approximate NS use. Chi-square tests of Independence which were used to establish statistical differences showed that compared to NSs, C1 learners used significantly more direct strategies than the NSs (x^2=11.54 df=1 p<0.01).

A non-linear development was observed in relation to conventionally indirect (CI)strategies. Conventional indirectness was used in 35.7 per cent of B1 learners' requests, then dropped to 27.4 per cent in B2 learners' requests, and increased again to 40.2 per cent in C1 learners' performance. Yet despite this increase, Chi-square tests again showed that C1 learners used significantly fewer CI strategies than the NSs (x^2=10.07 df=1 p<0.01), therefore confirming that the advanced learners' behaviour did not converge with NSs' usage. Some pragmatic development, albeit non-linear, was observed in the use of hints. Hints were employed in 10.1 per cent of lowest proficiency learners' requests and their use increased to 19 per cent in the next proficiency level (B2). However, it slightly decreased to 16.3 per cent in the high proficiency level (C1), a percentage which was again found to differ significantly from NSs' performance (NSs=32.4 per cent, x^2=6 df=1 p<0.01).

The total number of requests is not the same as the number of students as some students produced more than one request in the role play.

3.4.2   Request Perspective

Differences among the groups of participants were observed with respect to the perspective of conventionally indirect requests among the learners. As it

Table 3.1 *Distribution of request head acts by proficiency group across all situations*

HEAD ACTS	B1	B2	C1	NSs
DIRECT	52.7% (68)	52.6% (50)	43.5% (40)	21% (22)
CI	35.7% (46)	27.4% (26)	40.2% (37)	62.9% (66)
HINTS	10.1% (13)	19% (18)	16.3% (15)	32.4% (34)
DON'T DO THE FTA	1.6% (2)	1.1% (1)	0	1.9% (2)
Total	(129)	(95)	(92)	(105)

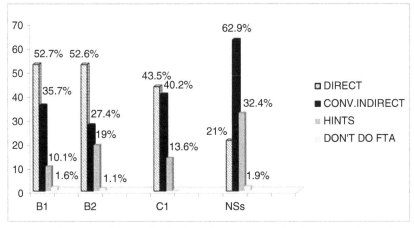

Figure 3.1 Overall distribution of request strategies by type and by proficiency group across all situations

can be seen from Table 3.2, learners preferred hearer-perspective HP requests across all proficiency levels (B1=60.8 per cent, B2=58.8 per cent, C1=76.4 per cent), unlike the NSs who employed mostly SP requests (72.1 per cent). Hence, a reversed developmental trend was observed in the learners' use of request perceptive. SP requests decreased with proficiency level while the opposite trend is evident with HP requests. Impersonal perspective requests were not used at all by low-proficiency learners (B1) but some (8.8 per cent) emerged in the performance of B2 learners which almost approximated NSs' use. Yet, C1 learners made no use of the impersonal perspective at all, deviating again from NSs' performance. Chi-square tests confirmed that the differences between the NSs and C1 learners along the dimensions of SP, HP and impersonal perspective were statistically significant (difference significant at a p=0.00, p<0.01 and p<0.05 respectively).

Table 3.2 *Request perspective of query preparatory structures for all learners across all situations*

	B1 Learners	B2 Learners	C1 Learners	NSs
HEARER	60.8% (31)	58.8% (20)	76.4% (33)	16.2% (11)
SPEAKER	39.2% (20)	32.4% (11)	23.3% (10)	72.1% (49)
IMPERSONAL	0	8.8% (3)	0	11.7% (8)
JOINT	0	0	0	0
Total	(51)	(34)	(43)	(68)

Table 3.3 *Distribution of lexical/phrasal modifiers by proficiency group and type across all situations*

Lexical/Phrasal Downgraders	B1	B2	C1	NSs
'please'*	13.9% (16)	12.5% (10)	16.9% (13)	18.9% (17)
Cons. Devices*	2.6% (3)	16.2% (13)	14.3% (11)	37.8% (34)
Downtoners*	0	0	3.9% (3)	22.2% (20)
Understaters*	0	0	1.3% (1)	10% (9)
Subjectivisers*	0	0	7.8% (6)	43.3% (39)
Cajolers	0	4.3% (5)	0	0
Appealers	0	0	0	0
Total no. of requests	115	80	77	90

* Hints are excluded as they cannot be modified internally with these mitigators] [elliptical requests are included]

Notes:
1. The total number of requests is not the same as the number of students as some students produced more than one request in the role play.
2. The total number of internal modifiers does not amount to the number of requests as more than one modifier was employed in a number of cases within a single request.

3.4.3   Internal Modification

3.4.3.1   Lexical/Phrasal Downgraders   Differences were also observed between the NSs and the learners in the use of lexical/phrasal downgraders. The frequencies for each type of downgrader in each group are shown in Table 3.3. As can be seen from Table 3.3, the NS group employed more lexical/ phrasal mitigation in almost all the markers examined. Chi-square tests of Independence showed that compared to C1 learners, NSs used significantly more consultative devices (X^2=11.634, df=1, p=0.01), more downtoners (x^2=11.735, df=1, p=0.01), more understaters (x^2=5.581 df=1, p<0.05), and more subjectivisers (x^2=26.628 df=1, p<0.01). A noteworthy qualitative finding that could be observed from a closer look at the NS data was the frequency with which NSs combined more than one mitigator within the same request. A typical combination was the use of the subjectiviser (*I was wondering*) with a consultative device (*if possibl*e). In certain cases, as in Examples 1 and 2, an understater/hedge was also added as a third marker. This combination of markers was especially noticeable in the 'book' and 'lift' power-asymmetrical situations (see Examples 1 and 2). This strategy was not observed in the learners' data. Even advanced learners were found to use no more than one marker at a time.

Example 1 [NS data – Scenario 1]
LECTURER: Hello, come on in.
STUDENT: Hi Dr Leigh. How are you?
L: I'm good and how are you?
S: I'm pretty good. Actually, I have a question. I'm in your Geography class and we have that paper that we have to write …
L: Yeah …
S: …. Yeah … erm … and I've been to the library but I found that all the students have checked out all the books that I was looking for and I saw your globalisation book on your desk the other day … *I was wondering* [subjectiv.] *if it would be possible* if [cons.device] I could borrow it *for a few* [under/hedge] days?

Example 2 [NS data – Scenario 2]
STUDENT: Hey Dr Smith …
LECTURER: Oh hi … how are you?
S: Well … I'm very well you know …
L: Good. Good … What are you doing out in the rain?
S: Well … Obviously you know it's raining and need to get back home … and *I was wondering if* [subjectiviser] *it's possible* [cons.device] erh. to get a ride … erh … *maybe* [downtoner] to give me a ride back to … erm …
L: well … I'd absolutely love to take you I just have a few stops to make … and unfortunately I'm a bit busy right now …
S: OK …

Looking at the development of lexical/phrasal mitigators in the learners' performance, it can be observed from Table 3.3 that the learners gradually increased their repertoire of lexical/phrasal markers. While B1 learners relied primarily on the marker 'please' (13.9 per cent), and made only occasional use of the consultative device (2.6 per cent), B2 learners significantly increased the use of the consultative device (16.2 per cent) (x^2=11.656 df=1 p=0.01) and the use of their cajolers (4.3 per cent, (x^2=4.989 df=1 p=<0.05). The C1 learners, on the other hand, expanded their repertoire of markers even further by starting to employ downtowners (3.9 per cent), understaters (1.3 per cent), and subjectivisers (7.8 per cent), which were completely absent from the repertoire of the B1 and B2 groups. The difference between the B2 group and the C1 group in the use of downtowners and subjectivisers was found to be statistically significant (downtoners: x^2=4.55 df=1 p<0.05, subjectivisers: x^2=7.591 df=1 p=0.01). A linear development could therefore be observed in the learners' use of the lexical/phrasal markers, although the more advanced group still lagged behind the NSs.

3.4.3.2 Syntactic Downgraders   The frequencies for each type of syntactic downgrader in each group are shown in Table 3.4. The results are also depicted visually in Figure 3.2. The results indicate that the NS group overall employed a wider repertoire of syntactic modification devices, making extensive use of conditional clauses (e.g., 'If I could ... .') (45.5 per cent), tense (e.g., 'Do you mind if I *borrowed* (vs. borrow) your notes?') (35.2 per cent)), the durative aspect marker (e.g., '*I was wondering* (vs. I wonder)), and conditional structures (25 per cent). It is evident that even the most advanced learners' group (C1) showed no convergence with NS use.

Looking specifically at the learners' performance, some evidence of syntactic pragmatic development can be observed. As can be seen from Table 3.4 and Figure 3.2, B1 learners hardly modified their requests syntactically. A noteworthy increase, however, is observed in the employment of conditional structures and conditional clauses. Conditional structures increased from 5.2 per cent (B1 level) to 30 per cent (B2 level) and then even more to 50.6 per cent (C1 level). Conditional clauses also increased from 7.8 per cent (B1) to 26.2 per cent (B2) and 26 per cent (C1). At the same time new syntactic markers (i.e., tense and aspect) started to appear. These are completely absent from the repertoire of the B1 learners, but some use of tense appears in the requests of B2 learners (tense: 6.2 per cent), while C1 learners make use of both tense and aspect albeit infrequently (tense: 5.2 per cent, aspect:

Table 3.4 *Distribution of syntactic downgraders by proficiency group and type across all five situations*

	B1	B2	C1	NSs
Conditional structures	5.2% (6)	30% (24)	50.6% (39)	25% (22)
Conditional clause	7.8% (9)	26.2% (21)	26% (20)	45.5% (40)
Tense	0	6.2% (5)	5.2% (4)	35.2% (31)
Aspect	0	0	5.2% (4)	30% (26)
Interrogative	0	0	0	1.1% (1)
Negation of prep. condition	0	0	0	0
Total	115	80	77	88

Note: Hints are excluded as they cannot be modified internally with these mitigators] [elliptical requests are included]

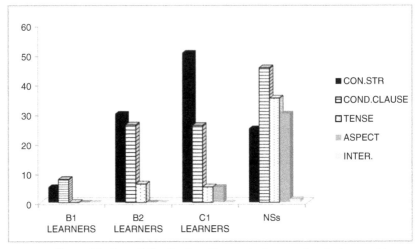

Figure 3.2 Overall distribution of syntactic downgraders by type and by group for all learners in each group over all five situations

5.2 per cent). The low frequency of these two markers by C1 learners stands out as particularly non-target like, given the high frequency of these markers by NSs (tense: 35.2 per cent, aspect: 30 per cent).

The examples below allow one to observe the pragmatic development of syntactic mitigators in the learners' performance. As the grammatical level of the learners increases so does the complexity and length of their requestive structures.

[Scenario 1: Book loan]
1. I want … erh … the book for the … erh … for the geography lesson [no syntactic mitigation] (B1 learners)
2. I *wanted* [tense] to ask you first *if you* [cond. clause] *could* [cond. structure] give me some books. (B2 learners)
3. I *have been meaning* [tense] to ask you *if I* [cond. clause] *could* [cond. struct] borrow your book on the globalization in Europe for assignment? (C1 learners)
4. erm … I *was wondering* [aspect] *if you* [cond. clause] *could* [cond. struct] … if you *had* [tense] a geography book I wanted for an assignment. (C1 learners)

[Scenario 2: Lift]
5. Dr Leigh, can *could you* take me at home? [conditional clause] *If you want* [conditional structure] to go … erh … to take me to my home because you live in the same road. (B1 learners)

6. Yes and I *would like* [cond. structure] to know *if it* [cond. clause] *would be* [cond. structure] okay if I *could* [cond. structure] ... . *if you* [cond. clause] *could take me* [cond. structure] to my home? (B2 learners)
7. I *was wondering* [aspect] *if you* [cond. clause] *could give* [cond. structure] me a ride home *if you are going* [cond. clause] that way ... (C1 learners)

[Scenario 3: Notes]
8. Can I have your notes please? [no syntactic mitigation] (B1 learners)
9. So I *would like* [cond. structure] to ask you *if you* [cond. clause] *could give* [cond. structure] me your notes? (B2 learners)
10. Anyway ... I *would really like it* [cond. structure] *if you* [cond. clause*] could give* [cond. struct] me your notes. (C1 learners)

[Scenario 5: Restaurant]
11. I want a ... a ... Mykonos salad [no syntactic mitigation] (B1 learners)
12. Yes. I *would like* [cond. structure] pork chops. (B2 learners)
13. We *would like* [cond. structure] one nachos with cheese and one Jack Daniels burger. (C1 learners)

3.5   Discussion

The results of the present study clearly suggest that, although there is some development with increasing proficiency, even the advanced learners' performance lags far behind native speakers in the pragmatic areas examined. This finding is not surprising as it corroborates the findings of previous developmental studies in the field (e.g., Bella, 2014; Otçu & Zeyrek, 2008; Schauer, 2004, 2009; Woodfield, 2012). It also lends support to Kasper and Rose's (2002: 190) claim that pragmatics precedes grammar in the early stages of pragmatic development while the reverse seems to be true for advanced learners. Furthermore, this significant divergence in the advanced learners' performance from NS use confirms the claim that 'high levels of grammatical competence do not guarantee concomitant high levels of pragmatic competence' (Bardovi-Harlig, 1999: 686).

The present study also found that requestive directness predominated across proficiency levels but decreased in the higher-proficiency level. This was in line with the finding of previous studies which confirmed that directness decreases with proficiency (e.g. Bella, 2012; 2014; Félix-Brasdefer, 2007; Hassall, 2003; Hill, 1997; Savić et al., 2021; Takahashi & Beebe, 1987). However, the present finding did not agree with Cole and Anderson's (2001) study which showed that participants moved from a direct style to conventionally indirect at the end of their stay in the TL community, nor with Schauer's (2009) and Savić (2015) and Savić et al.'s (2021) studies, which revealed that conventionally indirect requests were employed by the highest number of learners and was preferred across all levels. As directness in the present study persisted across all proficiency levels, it appears that different reasons might be at play behind this preference by the lower and by the higher-proficiency learners. It seems that the lower-proficiency learners of the present study resorted to formulaic direct strategies in order to achieve their interactional goal 'since they do not possess adequate pragmalinguistic means to do it in an appropriate native-like fashion' (Bella, 2014: 55), similarly to Bella's (2014) and Rose's (2000) beginner learners who showed the same preference for directness. The higher proficiency learners, on the other hand, who possess adequate pragmalinguistic means to allow them to opt for more indirectness, might have employed such directness as a *strategic choice* in order to achieve their interactional goal with clarity. Previous studies (e.g., Faerch & Kasper, 1989) found L2 learners to adhere to Grice's (1975) principle of clarity and to prefer explicit and unam-biguous means of expressions. Also, Economidou-Kogetsidis' (2005) study which examined Greek NSs' service encounter requests found Greek speak-ers to prefer explicitness in the form of directness for the sake of clarity and goal-orientedness.

It therefore seems that the present finding is in line with previous interlan-guage and cross-cultural pragmatics studies which focussed on adult Greek speakers (Economidou-Kogetsidis, 2005, 2008, 2011, 2018; Pavlidou, 1994, 1997, 1998; Sifianou, 1989, 1992). These studies have consistently shown that Greek speakers (L2 learners and NSs) favour requestive direct-ness, a finding which has been ascribed to the positive politeness of the Greek society (Bella & Ogiermann, 2019; Sifianou, 1992,) and to the Greek ethos of spontaneity and directness (Triandis & Vassiliou, 1972; Vassiliou et al., 1972). This result therefore points towards the great influence that the L1 language and cultural norms have on the L2 learner's pragmatic perfor-mance, even at an advanced level. It is also in line with Otçu and Zeyrek's (2008) study which found that their upper intermediate learners preferred direct acts. The authors explain that in Turkish, similarly to Greek, 'direct acts may be conventionalised and thus may be preferred by native speak-ers' (2008: 18). At the same time, this finding is in line with Takahashi and Beebe (1987) claim that more advanced learners are more likely to transfer pragmatic functions from their native language because they have more lin-guistic resources.

Of particular importance is also the fact that the participants of the present study were EFL rather than ESL learners and were thus learning English in the FL context. They therefore had no or little exposure to the target language culture. In contrast, the majority of the developmental studies reviewed above have focussed on SA or ESL learners whose pragmalinguistic development might have been affected by factors such as the intensity of interaction with

NSs (Bardovi-Harlig & Bastos, 2011) or length of residence in the TL community (Félix-Brasdefer, 2004; Roever et al., 2014). As Ellis (1992: 20) also argues 'it may be that even with more time the classroom environment is insufficient to guarantee the development of full target language norms, possibly because the kind of "communicative need" that the learners experienced was insufficient to ensure development of the full range of request types and strategies.' Further future research on the pragmatic development of EFL learners is therefore needed in order to shed more light on the relationship between FL context and pragmatic development.

A further possible explanation regarding this finding might relate to the methodology and the proficiency scale that was followed in order to group the participants of the study. It might be that the proficiency difference between the groups was too small to allow for any significant quantitative differences to appear, especially in those cases where a 1.0 IELTS score was the difference that decided the learners' proficiency group.

In addition, the present study revealed a reversed developmental trend in relation to the learners' use of request perspective. The total absence of joint perspective requests in the learners' repertoire is in line with the results of Félix-Brasdefer's (2007) study. However, the learners' preference for HP across all proficiency levels was contrary to Trosborg's (1995) findings which noted a shift to speaker-based strategies with increase in educational level. Even though request perspective among Greek NSs has not been empirically examined (to the best of my knowledge), it can be said that SP requests in Greek (e.g., Μπορώ να έχω τις σημειώσεις σου – Can I have your notes?) tend to be more formal, less natural in spoken Greek and less widely used as compared to HP (e.g., Μου δίνεις τις σημειώσεις σου – Can you give me your notes?). Therefore, the preference on the part of the learners of the present study for HP requests can be seen the result of pragmalinguistic transfer from L1, a phenomenon which seems to persist even with advanced proficiency.

Looking at the participants' oral performance more closely, some salient qualitative patterns emerge which are corroborated by the study's findings regarding internal mitigation. These patterns and the internal mitigation findings suggest a development in the learners' pragmatic competence and are consistent with previous research (Achiba, 2003; Ellis, 1992, Félix-Brasdefer, 2007; Rose, 2000; Savić, 2015) that identified specific stages in the development of requests. More specifically, even though all learners indicated a preference for direct strategies, the specific substrategies that they utilised seemed to change with proficiency and show evidence of pragmatic development. B1 learners relied heavily on unmodified need and want statements for their requests in the book and restaurants situations (e.g., 'I want to have your book to copy some pages', 'For starter, I want potatoes and mushrooms'), and on conventional indirectness of the unmodified 'can you' type in the lift and notes situation (e.g., 'Can you get me to my home?'). The B1 learners therefore appeared to display requestive-behaviour characteristic of stage two (the formulaic stage) and stage 3 (unpacking stage) as described in Kasper and Rose (2002) stages of requestive development. The learners relied heavily on the unmodified formulaic expressions of 'I want'/'I need' type while also using heavily unmodified conventional indirectness. It can therefore be argued that this group was between two stages but moving in the direction of stage 3. Similar to Achiba's study (2003), these B1 learners also made use of the full range of strategies – direct, CI, and even hints. Even though a statistical analysis for each individual situation was not carried out as part of the present study, preliminary findings show little situational varia-tion in the learners' performance. They relied, for example, on the same 'can you' strategy both in the lift situation and in the notes situation, failing to adjust their requests according to the involved imposition, social power and social distance.

B2 learners, on the other hand, used primarily hedged performative direct requests (e.g., 'I would like to ask you if it's possible to'), and want state-ments which were internally modified with a conditional structure (e.g., 'I would like Fanta please'). A shift in modality (from 'can' to 'could') is there-fore evident. These learners were gradually exiting from simple CI forms and moving toward more complex bi-clausal structures (e.g., 'I would like to know if it would be okay if you could take me to my home?'), despite the fact that they still relied on unmodified need/want statements and explicit performatives. It therefore seems that these B2 learners used realisations that could place them in between stages 3 (the unpacking stage) and 4 (the prag-matic expansion stage) which is characterised by increased mitigation and more complex syntactic structures.

Finally, C1 learners employed direct and CI strategies that fell in the prag-matic expansion stage 4 and the fine-tuning stage 5. Their direct requests were characterised by greater syntactic complexity and greater syntactic mitigation. The learners of this level stopped using unmodified need or want statements, and all their direct strategies were longer, biclausal per-formatives of the 'if + clause' type (e.g., 'I would really like to ask you if you could lend me the book for a couple of days so I can use it for my assignment.'). New forms of lexical/phrasal downgraders (i.e., downtoners, understaters, subjectivisers) also started to appear, as well as requests syn-tactically modified for aspect (i.e., durative aspect marker – for example, I was wondering if you had a geography book I wanted for an assignment.'). The study therefore showed that the development of language proficiency gave rise to the use of more numerous and more complex pragmalinguistic means.

3.6   Summary and Conclusions

This study aimed to reveal developmental patterns in request strategies, perspective and internal mitigation (lexical/phrasal and syntactic) in relation to the requests produced by Greek EFL learners across three different proficiency levels. It further aimed to investigate the extent to which the learners' pragmatic development approximates the request behaviour of NS of English.

The results of the present study suggest that, although there is some development with increasing proficiency, even the advanced learners' performance lags far behind NSs in the pragmatic areas examined, a finding which is in line with previous developmental studies (see Chapter 2, this volume, for similar results). It was further revealed that requestive directness predominated across proficiency levels although it decreased in the higher-proficiency level. Some evidence of pragmatic development in relation to learners' request strategies was therefore evident, especially when focussing on the learners' substrategies employed across proficiency levels.

However, the predominance of direct strategies across all levels pointed towards the influence of the L1 and of the norms of the native culture on the L2 learners' pragmatic performance, particularly in the foreign language context. Pragmalinguistic transfer from the L1 was also used to explain learners' preference for hearer-perspective requests across all proficiency levels – a reversed developmental trend and one that resulted in greater divergence from NS use. These findings emphasise the need for more systematic investigations on the role of the L1 and of the native culture in the acquisition of L2 pragmatics by FL learners who receive classroom instruction in a FL context and are not exposed to pragmatic instruction or to the target language culture.

The present study further revealed a linear pragmalinguistic development in the learners' use of internal request modification. Both the repertoires of lexical/phrasal and syntactic markers increased with proficiency therefore confirming the claim that pragmatic development is often 'built on a platform of grammatical competence' (Bardovi-Harlig, 1999: 686). Importantly, both the qualitative and the quantitative results of the study identified specific stages in the development of requests that were in line with the stages described in Kasper and Rose (2002) and in previous studies (Achiba, 2003; Ellis, 1992; Félix-Brasdefer, 2007).

While the present study indicated some requestive developmental trends in the learners' performance, the findings should be treated with caution for a number of reasons. Firstly, the size of the sample population was relatively limited and therefore further investigations with more extensive numbers are needed. Secondly, the present study examined learners from three proficiency levels possibly too close to each other which might have resulted in the existence of less salient proficiency differences from one level to the next. Further investigation could focus on true beginners (A1), true intermediate learners (B2), and more advanced learners of native-like proficiency (C2 level). Finally, the present study did not examine the development of learners' external modification or the situational variation of their performance. Future research on this would be needed in order to shed more light on L2 pragmatic development.

Finally, the finding that even advanced-level EFL learners' performance (in terms of range and frequency) did not converge with NS use has implications for pragmatics teaching in FL contexts. As Taguchi (2012: 54) explains 'although living in the target language environment is no panacea for pragmatic development, the target community has potential to offer unique sociocultural experiences that foster the acquisition of pragmalinguistic forms'. Such opportunities, unless created in the classroom, do not exist for FL learners, and as a result their pragmalinguistic repertoire often expands at an even slower pace. Therefore, pedagogical instruction is warranted and must be included in the curriculum of the FL classroom in order to teach the pragmalinguistic forms and functions of the target language and raise the learners' pragmatic awareness.

References

Achiba, M. (2003). *Learning to Request in a Second Language: Child Interlanguage Pragmatics.* Clevedon: Multilingual Matters.

Bardovi-Harlig, K. (1999). Exploring the interlanguage of interlanguage pragmatics: a research agenda for acquisitional pragmatics. *Language Learning*, 49(4), 677–713.

Bardovi-Harlig, K. (2006). On the role of formulas in the acquisition of L2 pragmatics. In K. Bardovi-Harlig, C. Félix-Brasdefer, & O. Alwiya (eds.), *Pragmatics and Language Learning*, vol. 11. National Foreign Language Resource Center, Honolulu: University of Hawaii Press, pp. 1–28.

Bardovi-Harlig, K. (2013). Developing L2 pragmatics. *Language Learning*, 63(1), 68–86.

Bardovi-Harlig, K., & Bastos, M. (2011). Proficiency, length of stay, and intensity of interaction, and the acquisition of conventional expressions in L2 pragmatics. *Intercultural Pragmatics*, 8(3), 347–384.

Barron, A. (2003). *Acquisition in Interlanguage Pragmatics: Learning How to Do Things with Words in a Study Abroad Context.* Amsterdam and Philadelphia: John Benjamins.

Bella, S. (2012). Pragmatic development in a foreign language: A study of Greek FL requests. *Journal of Pragmatics*, 44(13), 1917–1947.

Bella, S. (2014). Developing the ability to refuse: A cross-sectional study of Greek FL refusals. *Journal of Pragmatics*, 61, 35–62.

Bella, S., & Ogiermann, E. (2019). An intergenerational perspective on im/politeness in Greece. *Journal of Politeness Research*, 15(2), 163–193.

Billmyer, K., & Varghese, M. (2000). Investigating instrument-based pragmatic variability: Effects of enhancing discourse completion tests. *Applied Linguistics*, 21(4), 517–552.

Blum-Kulka, S., House, J., & Kasper, G. (1989). *Cross-Cultural Pragmatics: Requests and Apologies*. Norwood, NJ: Ablex Publishing.

Brown, P., & Levinson, L. (1987). *Politeness: Some Universals in Language Usage*. Cambridge: Cambridge University Press.

Canale, M., & Swain, M. (1980). Theoretical bases of communicative approaches to second language teaching and testing. *Applied Linguistics*, 1(1), 1–47.

Cole, S., & Anderson, A. (2001). Requests by young Japanese: A longitudinal study. *The Language Teacher Online*, 25(8). www.jaltpublications.org/tlt/articles/2001/08/anderson.

Cohen, L., & Morrison, K. (2000). *Research Methods in Education*. London: Routledge.

Council of Europe (2018). Common European Framework of Reference for Languages (CEFR). www.coe.int/en/web/common-european-framework-reference-languages.

Economidou-Kogetsidis, M. (2005). 'Yes, tell me please, what time is the midday flight from Athens arriving?': Telephone service encounters and politeness. *Journal of Intercultural Pragmatics*, 2(3), 253–273.

Economidou-Kogetsidis, M. (2008). Internal and external mitigation in interlanguage request production: The case of Greek learners of English. *Journal of Politeness Research*, 4(1), 111–138.

Economidou-Kogetsidis, M. (2011). 'Please answer me as soon as possible': Pragmatic failure in non-native speakers' e-mail requests to faculty. *Journal of Pragmatics*, 43(13), 3193–3215.

Economidou-Kogetsidis, M. (2018) 'Mr Paul, please inform me accordingly': Address forms, directness and degree of imposition in L2 emails. *Pragmatics*, 28(4), 489–515.

Economidou-Kogetsidis, M., & Halenko, N. ((2022). Developing spoken requests during UK study abroad: A longitudinal look at Japanese learners of English. *Study Abroad Research in Second Language Acquisition and International Education*, 7(1), 24–54.

Ellis, R. (1992). Learning to communicate in the classroom: a study of two learners requests. *Studies in Second Language Acquisition*, 14(1), 1–23.

Faerch, C., & Kasper, G. (1989). Internal and external modification in interlanguage request realization. In S. Blum-Kulka, J. House, & G. Kasper (eds.), *Cross-cultural Pragmatics: Requests and Apologies,* Norwood, NJ: Ablex, 221–247. Félix-Brasdefer, C. (2004). Interlanguage refusals: Linguistic politeness and length of residence in the target community. *Language Learning*, 54(4), 587–653.

Félix-Brasdefer, C. (2007). Pragmatic development in the Spanish as a FL classroom: A cross-sectional study of learner requests, *Intercultural Pragmatics*, 4(2), 253–286.

Goy, E., Zeyrek, D., & Otçu, B. (2012). Developmental patterns in internal modification of requests. In M. Economidou-Kogetsidis and H. Woodfield (eds.), *Interlanguage Request Modification*. Amsterdam: John Benjamins, pp. 51–86.

Grice, P. (1975). Logic and Conversation. In P. Cole & J. Morgan (eds.), *Syntax and Semantics, Volume 3. Speech Acts*. New York: Academic Press, pp. 41–58.

Hassall, T. (1997). Requests by Australian Learners of Indonesia. Unpublished doctoral thesis. Australian National University, Canberra.

Hassall, T. (2003). Requests by Australian learners of Indonesian. *Journal of Pragmatics*, 35(12), 1903–1928.

Hill, T. (1997). The Development of Pragmatic Competence in an EFL Context. Doctoral dissertation. Temple University, Philadelphia.

Kasper, G. (2000). Data collection in pragmatics research. In H. Spencer-Oatey (ed.), *Culturally Speaking: Managing Rapport through Talk across Cultures.* London: Continuum, pp. 316–369.

Kasper, G., & Rose, K. (2002). *Pragmatic Development in a Second Language.* Madison: University of Michigan and Blackwell.

Otçu, B., & Zeyrek, D. (2008). Development of requests: A study on Turkish Learners of English. In M. Puetz & J. N. Aertslaer (eds.), *Developing Contrastive Pragmatics: Interlanguage and Cross-Cultural Perspectives.* Berlin: Mouton De Gruyter, pp. 265–299.

Pavlidou, T. (1994). Contrasting German-Greek politeness and the consequences. *Journal of Pragmatics*, 21(5), 487–511.

Pavlidou, T. (1997). The last five turns: Preliminary remarks on closings in Greek and German telephone calls. *International Journal of the Sociology of Language,* 126, 145–162.

Pavlidou, T. (1998). Greek and German telephone closings: Patterns of confirmation and agreement. *Pragmatics*, 8(1), 79–94.

Roever, C., Stanley Wang, S., & Brophy, S. (2014). Learner background factors and learning of second language pragmatics. *IRAL – International Review of Applied Linguistics in Language Teaching*, 52(4), 377–40.

Rose, K. (2000). An exploratory cross-sectional study of interlanguage pragmatic development. *Studies in Second Language Acquisition*, 22(1), 27–67.

Rose, K. (2009). Interlanguage pragmatic development in Hong Kong, phase 2. *Journal of Pragmatics*, 41(11), 2345–2364.

Savić, M. (2015). 'Can I very please borrow it?': Request development in young Norwegian EFL learners. *Intercultural Pragmatics*, 12(4), 443–480.

Savić, M., Economidou-Kogetsidis, M., & Myrset, A. (2021). Young Greek Cypriot and Norwegian EFL learners: Pragmalinguistic development in request production. *Journal of Pragmatics*, 180, 15–34.

Scarcella, R. (1979). On speaking politely in a second language. In C. Yorio, K. Perkins, & J. Schachter (eds.), *On TESOL'79: The Learner in Focus.*, Washington, DC: TESOL, pp. 275–287.

Schauer, G. (2004). 'May you speak louder maybe'? Interlanguage pragmatic development in requests. In H. S. Foster-Cohen, M. Sharwood Smith, A. Sorace, & O. Mitsuhiko (eds.), *EUROSLA Yearbook.* Amsterdam: John Benjamins, pp. 253–273.

Schauer, G. (2006). The development of ESL learners' pragmatic competence: A longitudinal investigation of awareness and production. In K. Bardovi-Harlig, C. Félix-Brasdefer, & O. S. Alwiya (eds.), *Pragmatics and Language Learning*, Manoa, HI: Second Language Teaching and Curriculum Center, University of Hawaii, pp. 135–163.

Schauer, G. (2009). *Interlanguage Pragmatic Development: The Study Abroad Context.* London: Continuum.

Schmidt, R. (1983). Interaction, acculturation, and the acquisition of communicative competence: A case study of an adult. In N. Wolfson & E. Judd (eds.), *Sociolinguistics and Language Acquisition.* Rowley, MA: Newbury House, pp. 137–174.

Sifianou, M. (1989). On the telephone again! Differences in telephone behavior. *Language in Society*, 18(4), 524–544.

Sifianou, M. (1992). *Politeness Phenomena in England and Greece. A Cross-Cultural Perspective.* Oxford: Clarendon Press.

Taguchi, N. (2012). *Context, Individual Differences and Pragmatic Competence.* Clevedon: Multilingual Matters.

Takahashi, T., & Beebe, L. (1987). The development of pragmatic competence by Japanese learners of English. *JALT Journal*, 8(2), 131–155.

Triandis, C. H., & Vassiliou V. (1972) A comparative analysis of subjective culture. In H. C. Triandis (ed.), *The Analysis of Subjective Culture, Comparative Studies in Behavioral Science.* New York: Wiley, pp. 299–335.

Trosborg, A. (1995). *Interlanguage Pragmatics: Requests, Complaints and Apologies.* Berlin: Mouton de Gruyter.

Vassiliou, V., Triandis, H., Vassiliou, G., & McGuire, H. (1972). Interpersonal contact and stereotyping. In H. C. Triandis (ed.), *The Analysis of Subjective Culture, Comparative Studies in Behavioral Science.* New York: Wiley, pp. 89–115.

Woodfield, H. (2008). Interlanguage requests: a contrastive study. In M. Puetz & J. Neff-van Aertselaer (eds.), *Developing Contrastive Pragmatics: Interlanguage and Cross-Cultural Pragmatics.* Berlin: Mouton de Gruyter, pp. 231–264.

Woodfield, H. (2012). 'I think maybe I want to lend the notes from you': Development of request modification in graduate learners. In M. Economidou-Kogetsidis & H. Woodfield (eds.), *Interlanguage Request Modification.* Amsterdam: John Benjamins, pp. 9–49.

Woodfield, H., & Economidou-Kogetsidis, M. (2010). 'I just need more time': A study of native and non-native students' requests to faculty for late submission. *Multilingua*, 29(1), 77–118.

4   Placing Oneself in the Reader's Shoes
Developing Pragmatic Awareness of Perlocutionary Acts

Sara Gesuato

4.1   Introduction

In real-life interactions, if messages are formulated in atypical ways, misunder-standings and/or social friction – surprise, embarrassment, or irritation – may ensue. For instance, if an utterance is formally accurate, semantically plausible, and situationally relevant, but misleading in content and/or interpersonally inappropriate, the interlocutor will take it for what it conventionally means, interpreting it as a deliberate choice, and developing relevant emotional, cogni-tive, and behavioural reactions accordingly (Thomas, 1983). This is a problem for L2 users interacting with L1 users (e.g., Grundy 2008: 73), because the latter might not make allowances for the former's not-so-easily-detectable communi-cative incompetence.

Things are different in the L2 classroom. Here, if an utterance is grammati-cally accurate but socially inappropriate and/or misleading content-wise, the teacher, as an expert educator with a mentoring agenda, is expected to identify and account for mistakes in the L2 user's discourse, providing supportive, cor-rective feedback in view of better future performance. The language teacher's leniency towards the L2 learner's interactional mistakes originates from two circumstances. One, the teacher knows that learning involves making mistakes, and that learners are practising interaction rather than interacting for real. Two, the teacher is not considered responsible for informing/reminding students of norms of social conduct and shaping their behaviour – unlike what happens in the L1 socialisation process (e.g., Gleason & Perlmann, 1985: 102; Jeon & Kaya, 2006: 167) – nor is he/she expected to be knowledgeable about culturally variable social norms to be presented as more or less contextually appropriate.[1]

As a result of the teacher's tolerance in the sheltered environment of the language classroom, students may experience the negative academic effects of their less-than-perfect discourse (e.g., poor marks); however, they are unlikely to be alerted to the social consequences this may bring about – personal

---

[1] Also, as a reviewer points out, the sensitive nature of certain types of discourse does not easily lend itself to feedback.

(Economidou-Kogetsidis, 2016; Laughlin, Wain & Schmidgall, 2015: 1) or professional (Sirikhan & Prapphal, 2011) – or to develop preventive or repair interactional strategies. However, students *should* know that what their language teachers recognise as improperly worded communication is socially bothersome and objectionable to others. This awareness should inform teaching-learning practices (Wolfe, Shanmugaraj, & Sipe, 2016: 400, 412; see Chapters 7 and 8, in this volume), lest learners are left ill-prepared to deal with pragmatic challenges (Laughlin et al., 2015: 1). Thus, learners should be sensitised to the consequences of their choices (Cohen, 2008: 220) and tested on their ability of seeing such consequences (Yamashita, 2008: 207), for example, in virtual or technology-mediated environments (see Chapters 1 and 8), while remaining free to decide how exactly to behave (Cohen, 2008: 220; Sykes, 2010: 258; cf. the notion of 'pragmatic resistance' (i.e. dissociation from L2 norms) in Chapter 2, this volume).

Such an awareness-raising agenda requires research on pragmatic perception, which, until recently, has been scant (DeWaard Dykstra, 2011: 97), especially regarding 'the effect on the interlocutor' (Roever, 2011: 467). This can be explored through post-event comments that 'identify people's face sensitivities and evaluative reactions', revealing 'the cognitive underpinnings of their reactions' (Spencer-Oatey, 2007: 653–4). This chapter aims to contribute to the research on the assessment of learners' ability to produce extended discourse (Roever, 2011: 463), by exploring how English as a Native Language (ENL) university lecturers perceive English as a Foreign Language (EFL) learners' written thanks in terms of their 'adequacy', here intended as successful achievement of interactional goals in a way that is efficient and acceptable to the addressee and the situation (Pallotti, 2009: 596, 599). I first set the context for my research questions by outlining the literature on pragmatic perception of L2 discourse. Then I present my research method and illustrate the findings. Finally, I comment on the findings, drawing conclusions in relation to the research questions.

4.2   Studies on Pragmatic Perception

How discursive/interactional behaviour is perceived has become an object of analysis in pragmatics research.[2] The focus has been on speech acts, especially requests (Alcón-Soler, 2015; Alemi & Khanlarzadeh, 2017; Economidou-Kogetsidis, 2016; Hendriks, 2010; Savić, 2018; Sydorenko, Maynard, & Guntly, 2014; Wolfe et al., 2016), but also apologies (Tajeddin & Alemi, 2014), refusals (Alemi & Tajeddin, 2013), compliments (Alemi & Rezanejad,

---

[2] I do not provide an extensive literature review, only mentioning recent publications.

2014), compliment responses (Alemi, Eslami, & Rezanejad, 2014), sugges-tions (Koike & Pearson, 2005), or combinations (Bektas-Cetinkaya, 2012; Chen & Liu, 2016; Sirikhan & Prapphal, 2011; Taguchi 2011a, 2011b). These studies examine how teachers rate foreign/second language learners' commu-nicative practices, elicited under experimental conditions (Alcón-Soler, 2015; Alemi & Khanlarzadeh, 2017; Alemi & Tajeddin, 2013; Alemi et al., 2014; Economidou-Kogetsidis, 2016; Savić, 2018; Tajeddin & Alemi, 2014).

The assessment criteria considered by raters in these studies are mainly politeness (Chen & Liu, 2016; Cohen, 2014; Economidou-Kogetsidis, 2011, 2015, 2016; Hudson, Detmer, & Brown, 1995; Ishihara, 2010; Savić, 2018) and appropriateness (Alcón-Soler, 2015; Alemi & Khanlarzadeh, 2017; Alemi & Tajeddin, 2013; Bektas-Cetinkaya, 2012; Savić, 2018; Sirikhan & Prapphal, 2011; Sydorenko et al., 2014; Taguchi, 2011b).[3] Others include illocution-specific features – for example, acknowledgement of the imposition (Economidou-Kogetsidis, 2016) and reasonableness of the request (Hendriks, 2010; Taguchi, 2011b) – and/or language users' traits such as competence, power, and agreeableness (Hendriks, 2010; Economidou-Kogetsidis, 2016; Savić, 2018), reliability and conscientiousness (Wolfe et al., 2016), and envis-aged reactions (Savić, 2018). Instead, assessment data typically consist in rat-ings of properties on Likert scales (Alcón-Soler, 2015; Alemi & Khanlarzadeh, 2017; Chen & Liu, 2016; Cohen, 2014; Economidou-Kogetsidis, 2016; Ishihara, 2010; Koike & Pearson, 2005; Savić, 2018; Sydorenko et al., 2014; Taguchi, 2011b; Tajeddin & Alemi, 2014; Wolfe et al., 2016) and occasion-ally in open comments (Alcón-Soler, 2015; Alemi & Rezanejad, 2014; Chen & Liu, 2016; Economidou-Kogetsidis, 2015; Savić, 2018; Sydorenko et al., 2014; Taguchi, 2011b; Tajeddin & Alemi, 2014; Wolfe et al., 2016).

Although insightful, most of the abovementioned studies have two limita-tions. First, their assessment criteria are loosely or not defined, and a priori selected by the researchers, disregarding the extent to which they are clear to raters. Second, these criteria are grounded in theories relevant to trained researchers, but oblivious of what potential interlocutors may consider appropriate in interaction, which is crucial to develop pragmatic compe-tence (Sydorenko et al., 2014: 21, 23). Only a few studies have examined how raters motivate their assessment of speech act discourse (e.g., Alemi & Khanlarzadeh, 2017; Alemi & Tajeddin, 2013) or the emotional impact that discourse may have on the addressee (Change, 2011; Culpeper et al., 2010; Wolfe et al., 2016; Economidou-Kogetsidis, 2011, 2015, 2016).

---

[3] More specific criteria comprise clarity (Taguchi, 2011b), amount of information (Sirikhan & Prapphal, 2011), sequencing of components (Sydorenko et al., 2014), relevance (Chen & Liu, 2016), grammaticality (Ishihara, 2010; Taguchi, 2011a), and phrasing (Cohen, 2014).

This study investigates how raters assess discourse without being primed for specific assessment categories and explores their reactions to discourse also as ordinary interlocutors. The research questions (RQs) are: (RQ1) what evaluative dimensions do raters identify as relevant to speech act discourse? (RQ2) How do these tie in with their ratings of the texts? (RQ3) How important are these dimensions considered to be? (RQ4) Are these dimensions also relevant in judging the accuracy/appropriateness of L2 speech act discourse?

4.3   Method

The research consisted of three phases. In Phase 1, I compiled a corpus of learner discourse (i.e., sixty-nine written thanks produced by sixty-nine EFL Italian graduate students; Section 4.3.1) and collected fifteen ENL teachers' comments on and ratings of the student texts (Sections 4.3.1.1, 4.3.1.2, 4.3.2.1, 4.3.2.2). In Phase 2, I elicited from eleven ENL teachers ratings of the importance of features relevant to email writing in general and to written thanks in particular (Sections 3.1.3, 3.2.3). In Phase 3, two bilingual assessors identified possible problematic linguistic-textual aspects in a subset of the texts, observing whether these could be related to the writers' Italian L1 background (Sections 4.3.1.4, 4.3.2.4).

4.3.1   Participants and Instruments (Phase 1-a)

To examine how written thanks produced by EFL students are perceived by ENL teachers – in their general discursive properties and possible interference phenomena from the students' L1 background – I first collected student texts and lecturers' assessment of them.

The dataset consists of sixty-nine thank-you messages (about 8,000 words), written by as many Italian EFL graduate students enrolled at Padua University in the Foreign Languages and Literatures degree course or in the International Communication and Cooperation degree course. Although not collected for research purposes, the texts were elicited under monitored conditions, in test settings, and cannot be considered spontaneously produced data. They thus formed a convenience sample. Forty-four texts were produced in four end-of-course exam sessions in 2015 by second-year graduate students, who had attended a class focussed on speech acts. Twenty-five were produced in 2016 by first-year students as part of their entry tests. The former group had to answer open-ended pragmatics-oriented questions about a speech act, and to write one speech act on the basis of a scenario. The latter had to take a reading and listening comprehension test, and to write an argumentative text on a topic of general interest described in a prompt as well as a speech act on the basis of a scenario.

Given that all the thanking speech acts were elicited by means of scenarios, they qualify as written-for-written discourse completion tasks (WDCTs)

(Bardovi-Harlig & Shin, 2014). For the second-year students, the relevant scenarios were 'Computer virus' (three texts), 'Office hours' (thirty-three texts), 'Holiday' (one text) and 'Teaching assistant' (seven texts).[4] For the first-year students, the prompt was only 'Computer virus' (twenty-five texts). The scenarios indicated the addressee's status relative to the writer's (i.e., peer or superior), the degree of social distance between the writer and the addressee (i.e., intimate) and the magnitude of the benefit (i.e., high). As an example, the 'Computer virus' prompt is presented below, followed by two sample student texts:[5]

Last week your computer was not working very well due to a virus. A friend of yours offered to help you out by introducing you to a friend of his/hers, a computer expert. Much to your relief, in a couple of days your friend's friend fixed the problem, and you expressed all your gratitude to him/her promptly and profusely. But now you feel grateful to YOUR friend too. You email him/her. What do you write?

Text A
> *Dear Jane,*
> *Thank a lot for introducing me your friend Mark. He made a wonderful job with my computer and he took just a couple of day! Now I can continue my research for my thesis project. I'm so happy. I thought I had lost all my documents and lot of time. Luckily Mark arranged everything! As he was so nice and quick, I was wondering to give a present to him. Do you have any suggestion?*
> *Thanks,*
> *[name]*

Text B
> *Dear Carol,*
> *thank you very much for your help with my computer.*
> *I would like to express all my gratitude and hope to see you soon*

In the examination settings in which the texts were collected, the main goal was to gauge students' ability to write moderately elaborate texts as relevant to high-value benefits. For the second-year students, an additional goal was to determine their ability to formulate texts appropriate to the addressee's relative status.

4.3.1.1 Open-Ended Questions (Phase 1-b-i) Assessors' views of and reactions to the texts elicited through the WDCTs were explored through a written questionnaire. The assessors included fifteen ENL university lecturers of various nationalities (Australian: one; Canadian: one; US: one; British:

---

[4] The different number of texts in each set is due to the varying number of test takers present at any given exam session.
[5] The others are available from the author on request.

twelve), with teaching experience at university ranging from eight to thirty-six years. Most were lecturers I knew personally, while two were referred to me by a colleague. I contacted all via email, and they agreed to participate out of personal interest in the topic. I chose lecturers rather than 'naïve' native speakers because I wanted assessors able to provide two types of feedback: indications of their reactions to the texts as ordinary interlocutors – something they could do due to their practice in social interaction (Taguchi, 2011c: 618) – and evaluations of the 'technical' characteristics of the texts – something they could do as experts in English (language teaching).[6] On average, every assessor examined six texts.

The questions the assessors addressed formed the first part of a two-part questionnaire (for the second part, see Section 4.3.1.2), and were meant to explore the lecturers' impressions of, and the envisaged emotional, cognitive, and behavioural reactions to, the students' texts. I chose these questions after reading works on addressees' reactions to and attitude towards addressers (e.g., Hacking, 2008; Koike, 1996; Schauer, 2006; Scher & Darley, 1997), and after examining data collected in a pilot study, in which three assessors often referred to these conceptual domains: what they liked vs. disliked about the texts, what they considered realistic vs. unrealistic in their content, and what their intimate (i.e. cognitive, emotional) and external (i.e. visible) reactions to the texts and/or their authors might be. I phrased the questions in general terms so as not to excessively influence the assessors' responses. For the same reason, the assessors were not trained to complete their task. My goal was to tap into what the ENL readers would 'freely' consider relevant when judging the quality of the texts. Any form of coaching might have revealed my expectations of them and thus affected their answers (cf. Chen & Liu, 2016: 237).

Table 4.1 reports the open-ended questions, and the responses given by two assessors on the two student texts reproduced above:

Questions A) and B) explored the readers' likes and dislikes through reference to positive and negative types of emotional responses (i.e., 'gut reactions') to the texts, respectively. Questions C) and D) investigated the readers' rational impressions of the texts (i.e., 'logic and making sense'). (In these four questions, near-synonyms served to clarify to the respondents what evaluative dimensions I was considering.) Questions E) and F) addressed the participants' likely reactions to the texts, including those experienced but left unexpressed, those manifested verbally or non-verbally, and those projected in the long-term.

---

[6] In my email invitation, they were asked to put themselves in the addressee's shoes in the first part of the questionnaire and to put on their teacher hat in the second one.

Table 4.1 *Open-ended questions and sample responses relevant to two student texts*

Questions	Descriptions	Responses for Text A	Responses for Text B
A)	What, if anything, do you find annoying/irritating/unacceptable? That is, what makes you feel uncomfortable and why?	*Nothing*	*The brevity of the email makes it feel as though it were not heartfelt*
B)	What, if anything, do you find pleasant/enjoyable/satisfactory? That is, what makes you feel relaxed, at ease and why?	*She hasn't gone over the top in thanking*	*Nothing in particular*
C)	What, if anything, do you find unnatural and implausible (or nonsensical)? That is, what makes you feel incredulous and surprised and why?	*Nothing*	*That there seems to be so little to say*
D)	What, if anything, do you find natural and plausible (or sensible)? That is, what makes you feel things are 'normal', as expected, reasonable, decent/fair?	*Asking my advice on a gift for my friend*	*To receive thanks, I suppose, although it does feel a little forced*
E)	All in all, how might you react to this text and its author, whether intimately (i.e. in your mind/heart) or with your external behaviour (i.e. through what actions, if any, and/or with what attitude)?	*I'd be happy to reply*	*Fairly neutrally though maybe I might feel a little 'cold' towards this person*
F)	More generally, do you think that the reception of the above text would/ might sustain/enhance, jeopardise/ compromise or have no effects whatsoever on your long-term relationship with the interlocutor? Why?	*It would enhance our relationship because I approve of her intention to give my friend something*	*It wouldn't jeopardise our relationship but I might feel a little hesitant before proffering my help again (though wouldn't deny it if it were asked for)*
G)	Any other general comments? [Optional]		

4.3.1.2 Ratings of the Texts (Phase 1-b-ii)
In the second part of the questionnaire, the same ENL lecturers also evaluated the same student texts on a 1–10 scale along linguistic-textual and interactional-communicative parameters. Table 4.2 lists these rating criteria and the ratings given to the two student texts above.

Table 4.2 *Rating criteria and sample responses relevant to two student texts*

Criteria	Descriptions	Text A	Text B
1)	The communicative purpose is easy to recognise.	10	10
2)	The content is relevant to the communicative purpose.	10	6
3)	The text contains the right amount of information.	10	4
4)	The text is well organised (e.g., it has an opening, a closing, conceptual paragraphs, logical transitions between and sequencing of topics/paragraphs).	10	4
5)	The text appears to make sense (e.g., the information provided is truthful, consistent, motivated).	10	5
6)	The writer is aware/considerate of my circumstances.	10	0
7)	The register is appropriate to the context (e.g., formal vs informal; technical vs intimate; enthusiastic vs aloof).	10	4
8)	The text is easy to process (e.g., it shows accurate grammar, correct spelling, natural/typical lexis and collocations, enough cohesive devices).	9	9
9)	Overall the text is effective (e.g., useful, valid, plausible, clear).	10	4
10)	Overall the text is interpersonally appropriate (e.g., enjoyable, agreeable, non-confrontational).	10	3
11)	Overall the text is aesthetically pleasing (e.g., attractive, not sloppy).	10	5
12)	Other (please specify) [Optional]		

I had the assessors first 'spontaneously' comment on the texts and then rate them to avoid priming them for specifically labelled notions. The terms expressing the evaluation criteria were not 'explained' (i.e., glossed or illustrated in sample texts), and it is possible they meant different things to the assessors. However, I assumed that, given their expertise, the assessors would be familiar with the denotation of these terms, which represented a condensed version of the comments collected in the pilot test. (That is why they were expressed as statements, as in the original comments, like *The communicative purpose is easy to recognise*, rather than abstract nominalised formulae like *Recognisability of communicative purpose*.) The choice of a 1–10 rating scale was motivated on two grounds: first, having a high number of points would enable assessors to make fine distinctions across degrees of given properties; second, an even number of points would lead assessors to unambiguously rate each text as either positive (ratings from 6 to 10) or negative (ratings from 1 to 5) along the criteria. (The demarcation between the positive and negative side of the continuum was not made visually prominent in the questionnaire lest the assessors should think they were 'merely' passing/failing the texts rather than describing their characteristics.)

Table 4.3 *Strategies/components to be rated in terms of importance in written production in general*

Question	Strategy/component
1	Context-appropriate openings, closings
2	Enough contextualising background information
3	Consideration for the addressee's circumstances
4	Brevity and to-the-pointness
5	Logic
6	Textual organisation
7	Personalised approach
8	Context-appropriate register
9	Aesthetically pleasing and easy-to-process text

4.3.1.3 Positive and Negative Strategic and Textual Features (Phase 2)   In Phase 2 of the study, about six months after the abovementioned questionnaire was administered,[7] I contacted the same ENL university lecturers again and asked them to complete another questionnaire, similarly distributed via email (see Section 4.3.1.1), which explored their opinions on positive and negative features of written email communication in general and written thanks in particular. I derived these features from comments obtained in the pilot study. After analysing their content, through repeated readings, I identified their common traits, and reformulated them in a simplified, succinct fashion (see Tables 4.3, 4.4, 4.5, and 4.6). The different number of items in each set of features is due to the varied range of comments gathered in the pilot study. The goals were to ascertain which features the assessors agreed upon as relevant evaluative descriptors of written email texts/thanks – to be later used for classroom-based assessment activities – and to indirectly check whether these features made sense to the assessors.

Only eleven of the original lecturers (ten British and one Canadian) agreed to participate. They were instructed to rate on a 1–10 scale the extent to which they considered important the positive features relevant to written production in general (see Table 4.3) and those relevant to the written speech act of thanking in particular (see Table 4.5) as well as to rate the seriousness-inadequacy of the complementary negative features relevant to general written production (see

---

[7] The time lapse was supposed to be three months, that is, enough for the assessors not to have fresh memories of the first questionnaire and enough for me to analyse the data collected through it. Personal circumstances forced a delay.

Table 4.4 *Strategies/components to be rated in terms of inadequacy in written production in general*

Question	Strategy/component
1	Context-inappropriate openings, closings
2	Not enough contextualising background information
3	Unawareness/disregard of addressee's circumstances
4	Rambling on with irrelevant, obvious, repetitive information
5	Poor logic
6	Poor textual organisation
7	Lack of a personalised approach
8	Context-inappropriate register
9	Inaccurate and sloppy text

Table 4.5 *Strategies/components to be rated in terms of importance in written acts of thanks*

Question	Strategy/component
1	Showing enthusiasm for the benefit received
2	Explaining what is good about the benefit
3	Acknowledging the effort the addressee went to
4	Not taking the benefit received for granted
5	Offering to reciprocate the benefit

Table 4.6 *Strategies/components to be rated in terms of inadequacy in written acts of thanks*[8]

Question	Strategy/component
1	Using an inappropriate tone (e.g., too informal; over-dramatic/gushing)
2	Appearing to be taking advantage of the addressee's generosity
3	Comparing the addressee to other people, albeit favourably
4	Misleading the addressee with an unclear communicative purpose
5	Causing embarrassment to the addressee, albeit in good faith
6	Imposing on the addressee with one's reciprocal gesture
7	Leaving the onus of the next steps to the addressee

Table 4.4) and those relevant to the written speech act of thanking (see Table 4.6). The assessment criteria selected were considered important/serious with ratings from 6 to 10, and unimportant/non-serious with ratings from 1 to 5.

---

[8] Questions 2, 3, and 4 in Table 4.6 summarise comments about writers appearing to go 'too far', such as: expressing the desire to receive future benefits (Question 2), describing their generous behaviour as unusual when compared to that of other people (Question 3), giving the impression they were writing not only to thank but also to pay compliments or make a request (Question 4), and expressing excessive gratitude and the intention to reciprocate tangibly (Question 6).

4.3.1.4 Linguistic-Textual Problem Areas (Phase 3)   About five months later,[9] two of the L1 English university lecturers who had participated in the two previous questionnaires were involved in Phase 3 of the research. They were a female lecturer of Canadian nationality and a male lecturer of British nationality, who had both grown up as English and Italian bilinguals. I emailed them an Excel file with the written thanks relevant to the 'Computer virus' scenario (i.e., thirty-three, about 2,800 words) and for each, I asked them to answer these questions:

1) What specific formal problem areas, if any, can you spot in the text (e.g., punctuation, spelling, lexis, word order, inflectional morphemes, derivational morphemes, sequencing of information units)?
2) Which ones are likely to be due to interference from Italian, in your opinion?

The first question tapped into the assessors' expertise, focussing on the 'technical' aspects of the texts (see the features listed in parentheses). The goal was to detect whether the texts shared certain deficiencies or drawbacks. The second question tapped into the assessors' intuitive native-speaker knowledge, and the goal was to reveal peculiarities sounding atypical of English, but which reminded them of Italian phraseologies and/or communicative practices. The assessors returned the files with their comments via email, and were given a small monetary reward for their time.

4.3.2   Data Coding

At the end of each phase of the research, I coded the data collected, as specified below.

4.3.2.1 Responses to Open-Ended Questions (Phase 1-b-i)   The assessors' comments (see RQ1) varied in their formulation and content. First, they were encoded in words, phrases, sentences or combinations thereof (e.g., *Nothing; Neutral reaction, but I would feel cold towards this person*). Second, they were expressed from variable perspectives: the assessor's, the writer's or an impersonal one (e.g., *I would be hesitant to proffer my help again; She hasn't gone over the top in thanking*). Third, they mentioned properties of the texts, the writer's behaviour, the reader's experiences and/or attitude (e.g., *Saying so little; I'd be happy to reply; Brevity suggests that thanks are not heartfelt*).

To make the comments comparable across the texts, I coded their content under inductively identified conceptual categories (see Table 4.7 for

---

[9] The time lapse was supposed to be two months, to give the assessors time to 'forget' about their previous tasks, but the assessors' personal circumstances caused a delay.

Table 4.7 *Sample codings of the assessors' comments*

Questions	Original comments on Text A	Codings	Original comments on Text B	Codings
A)	*Nothing*	Nothing	*The brevity of the email makes it feel as though it were not heartfelt*	Limited length; Insincerity
B)	*She hasn't gone over the top in thanking*	Appropriate amount/ intensity of content	*Nothing in particular*	Nothing
C)	*Nothing*	Nothing	*That there seems to be so little to say*	Limited content
D)	*Asking my advice on a gift for my friend*	Inquiring about reciprocation	*To receive thanks, I suppose, although it does feel a little forced*	Verbal reciprocation
E)	*I'd be happy to reply*	Verbal reply; Positive attitude	*Fairly neutrally though maybe I might feel a little 'cold' towards this person*	No effect; Negative attitude
F)	*It would enhance our relationship because I approve of her intention to give my friend something*	Enhancing relationship; Positive attitude	*It wouldn't jeopardise our relationship but I might feel a little hesitant before proffering my help again (though wouldn't deny it if it were asked for)*	Compromising relationship; Negative attitude

examples). I established the categories iteratively, through a back-and-forth process of data examination, data coding, data re-examination and category revision.[10] To aim at intra-rater reliability, I coded the corpus on two occasions, which were about a year apart. When I noticed discrepancies in category assignment between my first and my second coding, I re-examined the relevant parts of the corpus, and made a final decision.[11]

Table 4.7 exemplifies the process of category assignment. I coded some comments twice, if these appeared to convey two main notions (e.g., the answer to Question A) for Text B). Also, I sometimes reassigned comments

---

[10] Similar circular processes of category identification and labelling are reported in move analyses of genres or speech acts, most also providing for inter-rater reliability checks (e.g., Cortes, 2013: 37; Hartung & Wilson, 2016: 259; Henry & Ho, 2010: 844; Henry & Roseberry, 2001: 156–157; Hyland & Hyland, 2001: 190; Jucker et al., 2008: 277; Kumar & Stracke, 2007: 463), exceptions being Ädel (2014: 72) and Tseng (2011). Cf. also Chapter 5, this volume, for a similar process of qualitative data analysis.

[11] Since I was involved in this project on my own, I could not aim at inter-rater reliability by comparing my codings with those of another researcher.

that were not directly relevant to the question they were answers to (e.g., the answer to Question D) for Text B, 'it feels forced' was coded as 'Insincerity' and reported as relevant to Question A)). Then I determined the dispersion of the comment categories, that is, how many texts they applied to. I considered this a more accurate measure of relative textual prominence than raw or normalised frequency counts of comment categories for two reasons. One is that certain assessors provided a given comment repeatedly about the same text, or differently formulated comments about the same text, but which I categorised under the same heading.[12] The other is that not all the texts were commented on by the same number of assessors (see Section 4.3.1.1).

4.3.2.2 Ratings of Texts along Parameters (Phase 1-b-ii)   The assessors' ratings of the texts along given assessment parameters (see RQ2) were averaged out for each text – even when, as in the case of Text B, 0 (zero) was chosen as a rating option, which was technically outside the relevant scale. The averaging of the ratings produced the overall numerical evaluation of the texts (e.g., 9.90 vs. 4.45 for Texts A and B, respectively). I later compared the global average rating of each text to its coded comment categories, checking whether they converged toward a positive or negative assessment. I considered a numerical rating positive if it ranged between 6.00 and 10.00, and negative if it ranged between 1.00 and 5.59. I considered the comment categories relevant to each text positive, negative or neutral on the basis of the lexis they were encoded in.

4.3.2.3 Ratings of Features (Phase 2)   In Phase 2 of the research, I averaged out the ratings of the positive vs negative features of written production and of written thanks across the respondents (see RQ3). I considered an average rating positive if its value ranged between 6.00 and 10.00, and negative if it ranged between 1.00 and 5.59. I then compared each average rating to the dispersion value of comparable comment categories collected in the first questionnaire (Phase 1), if applicable, to check if overlaps in content and similarity in positive or negative orientation could be determined.

4.3.2.4 Specific Linguistic-Textual Problems (Phase 3)   In Phase 3 of the research, I analysed the data from the third questionnaire (see RQ4). I coded the responses to the first question, about possible problem areas, and the second question, about possible L1 interference phenomena, for these categories: formal encoding, namely spelling and punctuation; grammar, specifically

---

[12] For example, one assessor answered Question E) with 'I'd be pleased and happy to continue our friendship' and Question F) with 'Enhance, as mentioned above, I'd be happy to continue our friendship and appreciate being invited to do something specific (rather than a vague "let's meet up sometime")'.

Table 4.8a *Codings of problem areas in Text A*

Questions	Female Italian-Canadian assessor on Text A	Codings	Male Italian-British assessor on Text A	Codings
1) Problem areas	Plurals (thank, day, lot and suggestion should all have -s); prepositions ('for introducing me TO your friend Mark'; I was wondering to give --> I was wondering about giving / I was thinking of giving); wrong words (arranged --> took care of)	b) grammar c) lexis	spelling (e.g., Thank a lot, instead of Thanks a lot), lexis (e.g., arranged, made a wonrdeful [sic] job), grammar, prepositions ('introducing me your friend Mark' instead of 'introducing me to your friend Mark' or '… and lot of time' instead of 'and a lot of time'), wrong use of 'I was wondering'	a) formal encoding b) grammar c) lexis
2) Problem areas due to L1 interference	probably all in the above column	b) grammar c) lexis	He made a wonderful job: ha fatot [sic] un ottimo lavoro he took just a couple of day: ha impiegato solo un paio di giorni	c) lexis

morphology, tenses, prepositions, word order, compounding, articles, extra or missing words; lexis, namely word choice, phrases, literal translations, register; and structure, which included paragraphing, sequencing of content, amount of content, logic/coherence, transitions, and anaphora. I assigned the responses to these categories by considering their lexical formulation. Responses mentioning two or more problems received multiple codings; those specifying multiple problems relevant to the same domain were coded once for the relevant category. To illustrate the procedure, Tables 4.8a and 4.8b reproduce the responses given about Texts A and B, and how I categorised them:

The number of problematic aspects identified in the texts did not necessarily correlate with the overall positive or negative impression the texts made. Text A, which received positive comments and ratings, was associated with a higher number of problematic features than Text B, which received negative comments and ratings. This suggests that alternative ways of measuring texts' inadequacies serve complementary purposes, highlighting the severity or scope of these deficiencies vs recording their frequency of occurrence.

To determine the prominence of the categories, I counted how often they were instantiated for each question prompt with regard to each assessor. Since for each prompt a given problem area was marked once at most, the counting reflects both the frequency of occurrence of that category and its dispersion.

Table 4.8b *Codings of problem areas in Text B*

Question prompt	Female Italian-Canadian assessor on text B	Codings	Male Italian-British assessor on Text B	Codings
1) Problem areas	We don't start emails with a lowercase letter ('thank you very much ...') and there is no closing name	a) formal encoding d) structure	Missing information. The student misunderstood the prompt	d) structure
2) Problem areas due to L1 interference	We don't start emails with a lowercase letter	a) formal encoding	I would like to express all my gratitude (vorrei esprimerti tutta la mia gratitudine)	c) lexis

Additionally, I qualitatively compared the responses to the two question prompts about problem areas with those given by the same assessors about eleven months earlier in answer to the first open-ended question in the first questionnaire (see Section 4.3.1), namely 'What, if anything, do you find annoying/irritating/unacceptable? That is, what makes you feel uncomfortable and why?' My goal was to check to what extent they were relevant to the same features, namely formal encoding, lexis, grammar and structure. Specifically, I qualified the 'annoying aspects' responses relevant to each text as coinciding with, overlapping with, or diverging from, the 'problem areas' responses given about the same text depending on whether, respectively, they mentioned exactly the same specific problems, some of the same problems, or none of the same problems. I assumed that the assessors could not remember their earlier responses, and thus that their 'problem areas' responses could not have been influenced by their earlier 'annoying aspects' responses. The following comments exemplify reference made to overlapping problems: 'We don't start emails with a lowercase letter ("thank you very much ...") and there is no closing name' vs 'It's way too short and lacks a closing name'. The following comments, instead, illustrate mention of different problems: '"a university research" --> "research" is uncountable so it should be "a university research project/a study"' vs 'That the beginning letter of the first line isn't capitalised and that there are a few too many exclamation points'.

4.4   Findings

4.4.1   Open-Ended Comments on the Texts (Phase 1-b-i)

The comments to the open-ended questions in the first questionnaire are relevant to RQ1, about the evaluative dimensions the raters identified as relevant to speech act discourse. Their codings were numerous (i.e., 29, 26, 21, 19, 36, and

Table 4.9 *Frequency of thematic categories of responses to questions A), B), C), and D) in the first questionnaire*

	Codings for A)		Codings for B)		Codings for C)		Codings for D)	
Themes	Types	Tokens	Types	Tokens	Types	Tokens	Types	Tokens
1) General communication/ interaction	5	30	3	10	4	25	1	3
2) Illocution-specific communication/ interaction	13	38	15	82	9	25	10	55
3) Formulation	8	34	7	28	9	22	3	17
4) Other	3	31	1	19	2	33	4	18

14 for questions A), B), C), D), E), and F), respectively), each applying to a few texts (e.g., *Excessive formality* for A): three tokens; *Brevity* for B): four tokens; *Acknowledging cost of benefit* for D): three tokens; *Mixed feelings* for F): four tokens). Only a few were relatively frequent (e.g., *Excessive intensity/emotionality/involvement* for A): fourteen tokens; *Impression: sincerity* for B): eight tokens; *Choice of content* for C): nine tokens; *Replying: pleasantries* for E): twenty-three tokens; *Negative attitude: wariness* for F): fourteen tokens). I grouped the coded comments under three themes: (1) general (written) content-related and strategic communicative competence, (2) context-specific strategic communicative competence, and (3) accuracy and style of formulation, while classifying the generic ones such as *Little/nothing* or *Everything* as *Other*.

The comments grouped under Theme (1) mentioned characteristics of the texts, actions of their writers and/or effects of either, which could be relevant to various topics and/or motivated by various purposes (e.g., Comment 'Polite, but not too friendly'; Comment coding 'Adequate intensity/emotionality/involvement'). Instead, the comments relevant to Theme 2) referred to characteristics of the texts, actions of their writers and/or effects of either, which focussed on the thanking illocution motivating the texts like the appreciative acknowledgement of a benefit, and the cancellation of the social debt incurred thanks to a reciprocation gesture (e.g., Comment: 'Reasonable is the recognition of time spent and possible bother'; Comment coding: 'Acknowledging cost of benefit'). The comments contributing to Theme (3) signalled textual properties or writers' choices affecting the organisation and accuracy of the text, that is, matters of grammar and style (e.g., Comment: 'It is written poorly'; Comment coding: 'Formulation').

Table 4.9 shows the frequency of occurrence of the themes. Since the figures lump together various codings, and since each text was associated with multiple categories, the totals do not correspond to the number of texts.

Here I report on the codings applicable to ten or more texts, showing their relevance to the questionnaire items. The assessors found these features unsatisfactory/unpleasant in the texts (Question A)): telling the addressee something they already know; not sounding heartfelt; and providing too much information or not sequencing it properly (Theme 1). A frequent coding category in this group was *Excessive intensity/emotionality/involvement* (fourteen texts; e.g., *She's a bit over the top*). They also mentioned the following as inadequate illocution-relevant strategies (Question A)): thanking too much; volunteering to reciprocate in an exaggerated way; or making a reluctant-sounding reciprocation gesture (Theme 2). A frequent coding category in this group was *Inappropriate topic/content* (ten texts; e.g., 'The mention of my colleagues not being very helpful is out of place.'). Finally, the assessors mentioned 'unsavoury' formulations like: using the wrong register; writing 'shouty' capital letters; formulating sentence-long paragraphs; using idioms incorrectly; and making grammar mistakes (Theme 3). On the positive side, in the thanking texts, they appreciated the following (Question B)): providing the right amount of content (Theme 1); reciprocating through thanking; mentioning the positive effects of the benefit received; explaining why the favour was important; making a non-imposing counter-offer and not thanking too much (Theme 2); and using an enthusiastic or friendly tone (Theme 3). The only frequent coding category in this set was *Gratitude (for benefit)*, relevant to Theme 2 (thirteen texts; e.g., *That the student took the time to write with thanks and expressed a desire to acknowledge the help received.*).

Features classified as unnatural/surprising in thanks (Question C)) included: informing the addressee of something they already know (Theme 1); offering disproportionate compensation; making an offer that is difficult to contextualise-understand (Theme 2); using register-inappropriate lexis, and being inconsistent in referring to the same person (Theme 3). The only frequent coding category in this group was *Excessive intensity/emotionality/involvement*, relevant to Theme 1 (fourteen texts; e.g., *'passionate' [...] 'honour' [...] this is really over-dramatizing things*). Instead, the following features ware considered natural and sensible (Question D)): being informed of the circumstances of the event under discussion (Theme 1); taking action so as to reciprocate; giving options as to whether to accept the reciprocal gesture; explaining why the benefit was important (Theme 2); and using a friendly tone (Theme 3). Here the only frequent coding category was *Expressing gratitude* (twenty-four texts; e.g., *'really wanted to tell you how grateful' is too much gratitude for an office hour visit.'*).

The range of reactions envisaged by the assessors (Question E)) was limited. The emotional-cognitive reactions included: feeling pleased and appreciative; feeling neutral or generically well-disposed; and feeling annoyed, surprised or embarrassed due to the writer's actions or attitude. A frequent coding here was *Positive emotional impact: happy/pleased* (twenty-three texts; e.g., *I would be pleased to receive this*). The 'tangible' reactions included: not taking anything from the writer, replying to them, and accepting their reciprocation gesture. A frequent thematic coding identified a verbal reaction, that is, *Replying: pleasantries* (twenty-three texts; e.g., *I'd probably write back and say 'glad I could help.'*).

The participants foresaw the following long-term effects of the thanks (Question F)): sustaining the relationship (e.g., through a continued or balanced friendship), compromising or ending the relationship, and not affecting it. The two frequent coding categories in this group were *Enhancing/sustaining relationship* (twenty-seven texts; e.g., *Definitely it would contribute to a good working relationship*) and *Negative attitude: wariness* (fourteen texts; e.g., *I might try to avoid any further particular contact in order to avoid any embarrassment that might arise from reference to gifts or such*).

4.4.2   Rating of the Texts (Phase 1-b-ii)

The assessors' ratings of the student texts provided an answer to RQ2, about possible connections between the characteristics of the texts and their quantitative assessment. The global numerical ratings ranged between 2.2 and 10, the average being 6.3. Most texts (i.e., 73.1 per cent) were evaluated positively, twenty-eight being rated between 6.0 and 7.9, and 21 between 8 and 10. The average values for the assessment criteria were positive, the highest being 9.1 for recognisability of communicative purpose and the lowest 7.0 for register appropriateness.

The average ratings of the texts generally matched the codings of the comments provided in answer to Questions A), B), C), and D) in the first questionnaire in their positivity or negativity (see Section 4.4.1). That is, the texts that received mostly or only positive comments also received ratings of or above 6.0, and those that received mostly or only negative ratings also received ratings of or below 5.9. However, there were a few mismatches regarding the seventeen texts whose global numerical ratings ranged between 6 and 8. More specifically, ten texts that received negative comments were later positively rated in numerical terms; five more texts received both positive and negative comments and yet were later given positive numerical ratings; and finally, two texts received mixed comments, but negative ratings.

4.4.3   Ratings of Features (Phase 2)

The ratings of assessment criteria provided answers to RQ3 about the importance attributed to the evaluative dimensions of the texts. As shown in Table 4.10, the positive features of general written production received high ratings in terms of importance, with values over 7.0, the average being 7.9. The highest value (i.e., 8.6) was attributed to *Brevity and to-the-pointness*, and the lowest (i.e., 7.5) to *Textual organisation*. In parallel, the negative features received high ratings in

Table 4.10 *Degree of importance attributed to positive features and degree of inadequacy attributed to negative features of general written communication*

Features	Descriptions	Perceived importance: 1–10	Descriptions	Perceived inadequacy: 1–10
1	Context-appropriate openings, closings	8.2	Context-inappropriate openings, closings	7.4
2	Enough contextualising background information	8.2	Not enough contextualising background information	8.1
3	Consideration for the addressee's circumstances	7.1	Unawareness/disregard of the addressee's circumstances	8.0
4	Brevity and to-the-pointness	8.6	Rambling on with irrelevant, obvious, repetitive information	8.4
5	Logic	8.2	Poor logic	8.3
6	Textual organisation	7.5	Poor textual organisation	7.0
7	Personalised approach	7.6	Lack of a personalised approach	6.6
8	Context-appropriate register	8.2	Context-inappropriate register	7.3
9	Aesthetically pleasing and easy-to-process text	7.6	Inaccurate and sloppy text	8.0
Global		7.9		7.6

terms of perceived inadequacy, their values ranging from 6.6 for *Lack of a personalised approach* to 8.4 for *Rambling on with irrelevant, obvious, repetitive information*, the average value being 7.6. Interestingly, not all pairs of complementary positive vs negative features were associated with very similar values. For example, the positivity of an appropriate register was more keenly felt than the negativity of an inappropriate one; similarly, the negativity of the disregard of the addressee's circumstances was rated higher than the positivity of its counterpart. More generally, a stronger sensitivity was registered to matters of content (ratings of features 2, 3, 4, and 5) than form (ratings of features 1, 6, 7, 8, and 9).

The features considered important vs inadequate in written thanks in particular also received high ratings (see Table 4.11). However, the positive and negative features did not form matching pairs, nor were they equivalent in number. The positive features received ratings above 6.0, the average being 7.9; in particular, *Showing enthusiasm for the benefit received* obtained the highest (9.1) and *Offering to reciprocate the benefit* the lowest (6.2). Also, six of the seven negative features received high ratings, with *Appearing to be taking advantage of the addressee's generosity* obtaining the highest (8.0),

Table 4.11 *Degree of importance attributed to positive features and degree of inadequacy attributed to negative features of written thanks*

Features	Descriptions	Perceived importance: 1–10	Descriptions	Perceived inadequacy: 1–10
1	Showing enthusiasm for the benefit received	9.1	Using an inappropriate tone (e.g., too informal; over-dramatic/gushing)	7.6
2	Explaining what is good about the benefit	8.5	Appearing to be taking advantage of the addressee's generosity	8.0
3	Acknowledging the effort the addressee went to	7.8	Comparing the addressee to other people, albeit favourably	6.5
4	Not taking the benefit received for granted	8.0	Misleading the addressee with an unclear communicative purpose	7.7
5	Offering to reciprocate the benefit	6.2	Causing embarrassment to the addressee, albeit in good faith	7.3
6			Imposing on the addressee with one's reciprocal gesture	7.1
7			Leaving the onus of the next steps to the addressee	5.7
Global		7.9	Global	7.1

and *Comparing the addressee to other people, albeit favourably* the lowest (6.5). Instead, *Leaving the onus of the next steps to the addressee* was rated negatively (5.7), maybe because it was not considered particularly relevant to thanks, which usually do not require long negotiations.

4.4.4   Formal Problem Areas (Phase 3)

Phase 3 of the project aimed to reveal whether the assessors' evaluative dimensions were comparable in content to the judgements on the accuracy/appropriateness of L2 speech act discourse (RQ4). The two bilingual assessors who identified inadequate characteristics of the texts provided their comments in slightly different ways. In detecting problem areas, the male British assessor listed general aspects/components of the texts (e.g., word order, grammar, punctuation, spelling). Instead, in detecting problem areas relatable to the writers' L1 background, he provided quotes from the texts, accompanied by the source language expressions they were presumably translated from. Here are some of his responses:

(1) *I have no more virus and it is fast.: non ho più virus ed è veloce*
(2) *whenever I'll need any help I'll phone him (quando avrò bisogno di aiuto lo chiamerò); [...] at the sea (al mare); [...] Thank you very for everything (grazie molte di tutto)*
(3) *I can pay you a coffee (ti posso pagare un caffè). How I could have done ... (come avrei potuto fare – a poor expression also in Italian)*
(4) *Finally I can email you: finalmente ti posso scrivere un email*
(5) *I can't explain you how grateful I am: non riesco a spiegarti quanto ti sia grata.*
(6) *next Monday is the last call to hand my thesis: lunedì prossimo è la scadenza per consegnare la tesi*
(7) *So, I would be really happy to invite you two out for a pizza to express all my gratitude: quindi sarei felice (poor choice of words even in Italian) to invitarvi fuori per una pizza per esprimervi tutta la mia gratitudine.*
(8) *I really thought I couldn't make it with the thesis: pensavo non ce l'avrei fatta con la tesi.*

Instead, when answering the first question, the female Canadian assessor mentioned general areas for improvement (e.g., *mistakes in lexis*) and specific problematic characteristics (e.g., *the greeting and sentence structure albeit simple are too formal*); she also quoted excerpts, accompanying them with suggested reformulations or corrections (e.g., *preposition: 'dinner in my place' 'at my place'*); alternatively, she referred to rules of grammar/textuality (e.g., *We don't start emails with a lowercase letter ('thank you very much ...') and there is no closing name*). Here are some examples:

(9) *'I thought it would have been impossible' 'would be impossible' (reporting future thoughts in the past)*
(10) *'you have never been in Padua' 'to Padua' (preposition).*
(11) *Thanks God' with no -s ...*
(12) *'Mark has been very kind and efficient to fix' 'in fixing' (wrong construction)*
(13) *'in debt' 'I owe you'*
(14) *and 'take a coffee' 'get/have a coffee' (vocab mistakes)*
(15) *'I have a research' should be 'I have some research / I have a research project / I have a study' (research is uncountable).*
(16) *'[...] I feel like the sentence "Eliot with his experience saved me" is unnatural in English; it should be "with his experience, Eliot saved me'*
(17) *'for introducing me TO such an incredible guy' (missing preposition).*

In answering the second question, the Canadian assessor virtually always identified the L1-related problem areas by referring to her answers provided to the previous question about general problem areas (e.g., through formulae like *all of the above* or *the first two mentioned above*).

Table 4.12 *Problematic aspects in a subset of the texts*

Problematic aspects	Respondents	Comment codings			
General problem areas		Formal encoding	Grammar	Lexis	Structure
	British assessor	15	21	24	4
	Canadian assessor	4	22	13	2
L1 interference	British assessor	0	7	25	0
problem areas	Canadian assessor	3	19	12	0

Table 4.13 *Categories of problem areas identified in a subset of the texts in the answers to question A) of the first questionnaire, and degree of similarities with the problem areas mentioned in relation to L1 interference*

Problematic aspects	Area/Degree of similarity	British assessor	Canadian assessor
Annoying aspects (Question	Formal encoding	5	5
A) in the first	Grammar	11	11
questionnaire)	Lexis	16	12
	Structure	8	6
Comparison with L1	Same	0	0
interference problems	Similar	3	11
	Different	22	14

The problems most frequently mentioned were lexico-grammatical, and those identified as relatable to the writers' L1 background more often lexical than grammatical (Table 4.12). A similar focus on lexico-grammar is found in the bilingual assessors' responses to Question A) in the first questionnaire; e.g.,

(18) *Some expressions are too colloquial (pampered), while others are arti-ficial [...]. I also found the concluding expression (Much love and all our best) rather weird.*

(19) *I felt I needed to write you. One does not write a person, one writes to a person*

However, despite the *broad* thematic similarities between the issues attrib-uted to L1 interference and those perceived as annoying, the specific topics mentioned by the same assessors on the two occasions often differed (see Table 4.13). This may partly be due to the different formulation of the questions.

4.5   Discussion

RQ1 explored how written thanks are perceived. The participants commented on the positive and negative impressions of the texts (e.g., naturalness/unnaturalness;

agreeability/irritability), expressing their likely cognitive-emotional and aesthetic-moral responses to them. They also envisaged their intimate, verbal and non-verbal reactions to the writers, and the long-term effects of the texts on their relationship with the addressees. The assessors were sensitive to: communicative effectiveness (i.e., adherence to the Cooperative Principle), the respect of transaction-specific sociopragmatic norms (i.e., the options/constraints relevant to the interlocutors' complementary speech act roles, the display of reader-friendliness and consideration of the addressee's circumstances, and also the formulation, register, and genre-specific conventions of speech act discourse (cf. Alcón-Soler, 2015; Alemi & Khanlarzadeh, 2017; Alemi & Tajeddin, 2013; Economidou-Kogetsidis, 2011, 2015; Savić, 2018). Similar answers were sometimes given to the questions about the annoying and implausible aspects of the texts (i.e., Questions A) and C) in the first questionnaire) and also to those about the satisfactory and logical features of the texts (i.e., Questions B) and D) in the first questionnaire). Therefore, these questions were not perceived to be addressing the distinct emotional vs cognitive reactions to the texts. Further piloting of the data collection instrument or standardisation training through an instruction sheet might have prevented this. Also, follow-up one-on-one interviews with the raters might have clarified the reasons for these overlaps.

RQ2 examined the degree of convergence of different assessment methods. The numerical ratings of the texts generally matched the codings of the open-ended comments on those texts. That is, positive vs negative impressions of and/or foreseen reactions to the written thanks were usually associated with, respectively, positive vs negative ratings of 'technical' aspects of the texts. This suggests that textual properties may have an impact on the addressees, partly revealing the writer's communicative competence. However, differences also emerged: not all the texts were consistently rated as (in)adequate in all their dimensions. Also, there were occasional mismatches in the positivity or negativity of the comments on vs the ratings of the texts, the former revealing areas for improvement that might have gone unnoticed. Reasons for this inconsistency may be: that the two assessment methods were relevant to partly different aspects of the texts; that the methods led the assessors to orient to the texts as finished products in the case of ratings, but as a writing process in the case of comments (Alemi & Tajeddin, 2013); and that the raters were not trained beforehand, differently from other studies (e.g., Chen & Liu, 2016).

RQ3 considered the importance attributed by ENL lecturers to textual-strategic features of general written communication and written thanks. The participants appreciated effectiveness (i.e., clarity, understandability) and social-transactional acceptability (i.e., context-appropriateness, regard for interlocutors' face wants). They saw them as interrelated dimensions, observing that rationality and coherence strengthen perceived interpersonal acceptability because they reduce the addressee's processing effort. Finally, they attributed communicative adequacy to features like structure (framing moves and sequencing of content), informativity (amount of content), relevance (context awareness) and form (visual 'first impression').

RQ4 investigated the specific linguistic-textual features assessors identified as problematic and relatable to the writers' L1 background. The literature on this topic suggests that L1 interference phenomena may affect pragmalinguistic and sociopragmatic aspects of L2 discourse such as the use of politeness strategies (Alcón-Soler, 2013; Chivarate, 2011), the formulation and content of speech act strategies (Eslami-Rasekh, 2004; Hendriks, 2010) and the frequency of use of register/-genre-specific interactional strategies (e.g., framing moves; Economidou-Kogetsidis, 2011). Studies also show that different types of errors are perceived as bothersome to different degrees (Wolfe et al., 2016) depending on their nature and context (e.g., Beason, 2001). For the two bilingual assessors consulted, grammar and lexis were more prominent problem areas than form and structure, and lexico-grammatical mistakes were often attributed to interference from the writers' L1. However, since I counted whether the assessors' comments applied to a given text rather than how often they were made, the importance attributed to word choice and phraseologies does not adequately stand out. Many more observations were made about 'faulty' lexis than faulty grammar. Similarly, lexical problems were identified as the most common source of 'irritation' in the assessors' answers to Question A) in the first questionnaire. Apparently, according to these assessors, when a text failed, it mostly failed in the selection and combination of terms, perceived as all-important for reader-friendliness and addressee-appropriateness. On the other hand, in answering Question A) in the first questionnaire, the two assessors frequently mentioned specific features different from those indicated when identifying L1-interference phenomena. They may thus have reacted differently to the differently formulated sets of questions – as 'ordinary interlocutors' in the former case, but as teachers in the latter one. Of course, other assessors might have provided different comments.[13]

Overall, the lecturers provided holistic assessment of the L2 discourse – identifying its technical strengths and weaknesses, and presenting their views, as potential addressees, on its effectiveness, appropriateness and envisaged consequences. They were sensitive to, and held the writers responsible for, communicative effectiveness and the respect of transaction-specific sociopragmatic norms. In analysing written (speech act) discourse, they attributed equal

---

[13] Raters vary in their perception of discourse appropriateness, application of criteria, sensitivity to illocution-specific pragmalinguistic and sociopragmatic norms, and impressions of general communicative effectiveness in terms of content and form (e.g., Alcón-Soler, 2015; Alemi & Khanlarzadeh, 2017; Alemi & Rezancjad, 2014; Taguchi, 2011b; Tajeddin & Alemi, 2014).

importance to the writers' display of reader-friendliness and consideration of the addressee's circumstances. Finally, the two assessors who explored the specific problems in a subset of the texts indicated that grammatical and, especially, lexical choices had a bearing on the impressions the texts made on the reader.

4.6   Conclusion

This study has addressed two issues relevant to the long-term goals of language teaching and learning. One is that it is important to examine pragmatic competence 'beyond the sentence-level to understand whether learners can produce speech acts with an acceptable degree of efficiency, including considerations such as discourse management, grammaticality of expressions, and strategic skills' (Taguchi, 2006: 515). The other is that, if L2 students receive feedback on the lexico-grammatical (de)merits of their discourse, without being alerted to its foreseeable outcome, such as the interlocutors' reactions, this leaves a gap in their communicative competence, namely, their ability to predict and address the consequences of their interactional choices.

A small-scale investigation was presented on the perceived adequacy of (goal-oriented) written discourse. On the one hand, it considered assessors' open-ended comments on pragmatic features applicable to *entire* texts, speech acts in general and thanks in particular, highlighting the importance of supportive moves and compliance with expectations (cf. Alemi & Tajeddin, 2013). On the other, it reported on: how language teachers judged the likely impact of foreign language learners' written thanks on their addressee, the value they attributed to the learners' written texts, and the problem areas, especially due to L1 interference, they deemed responsible for less-than-ideal accuracy and appropriateness. The participants motivated their reactive impressions of the texts and their authors' projected 'attitude', as if they were the addressees (i.e., as ordinary interlocutors), indicating that the (perceived) respect, violation, or misunderstanding of social-textual norms is likely to determine multi-faceted intimate and observable reactions. They also identified the aspects of the texts that they deemed relevant to their assessment, in their role as teachers (i.e., as external observers).

The study showed that, when discourse was considered from the receiving end, communicative adequacy depended on several properties, like the choice of content, its formulation, its fitness of purpose, and its contextual relevance, which had interpersonal-social effects. This was evident in comments linking textual features to readers' impressions, and those describing the texts in terms of their writers' projected attitude. This is along the lines of other studies, which showed the relevance of 'appropriateness of linguistic expressions, grammaticality of the expressions, and comprehensibility of the expressions' to the quality of speech acts (Taguchi, 2006: 529), or which reported how grammatical errors may indicate 'a lack of respect', which may lead the reader to stop reading, and that lack of clarity of purpose may be confusing or bothersome (Wolfe et al., 2016: 409–410; (cf. also Beason, 2001).

The literature indicates that L2 learners need to know that people outside the educational context are not likely to react kindly to pragmatic errors (Wolfe et al., 2016). It is thus crucial 'to direct L2 writers' attention to the embedded social norms and cultural assumptions of particular linguistic features. [...] Only when L2 learners develop this awareness of the interconnectedness between form, use, and meaning of a second language can they enlarge the intercultural pragmatic competence and successfully socialise themselves into the new discourse community' (Chen, 2010: 45). The study therefore suggests the following pedagogical implications. It is important to promote learners' communicative and face-work skills through guided reflection on the potential impact of their discourse. This may involve checking whether function-specific and general communicative requirements are met (cf. Ishihara, 2010; Sydorenko et al., 2014); exploring the connections between discursive and especially lexical choices and their interactional effects, despite the difficulties involved (Lumley, 2002); and engaging in peer feedback tasks favouring the adoption of an addressee-centred perspective on their discourse. Teachers could prepare students for real-life interactional exchanges by presenting addressees' likely views on the effectiveness, appropriateness, and envisaged consequences of their communicative choices. A focus on the perception of discourse can be used as a diagnostic tool for measuring language learners' interactional competence, as an intervention tool highlighting areas for focussed instruction, and as an assessment tool, providing feedback on the social implications of interaction.

The study presents limitations which future research could address. First, the data considered is relevant to one source linguistic background (Italian), one target linguistic background (English), and one speech act (thanking). More speech acts from varied linguistic and cultural backgrounds should be explored. Also, the speech acts considered were assessed by experts. Although teachers can be consulted as ordinary interlocutors due to their practice in social interaction (Taguchi, 2011c: 618), other assessors in the role of envisaged addressees (e.g., linguistically untrained native speakers, peers) might have offered complementary types of assessment (cf. Economidou-Kodgetsidis, 2016), being motivated by different interpretations of it (cf. Alcón-Soler, 2013). Third, in Phases 1 and 2 of the project, the participants' expertise as assessors was taken for granted given their professional background; in the future, it may be useful to train raters (e.g., through examples, instructions, or explanations) to verify whether they understand the questionnaire items in the way intended by the researcher. Fourth, although similarities were found between the assessors' comments on and their ratings of the texts, reliable correlations were not established; thus, associations between discursive choices, evaluation parameters and envisaged reactions are to be investigated. Fifth, my categorisation of the assessors' responses aimed at intra-rater reliability, but was nevertheless subjective, and may have painted a fragmented or simplified picture of the data. Having at least two researchers develop the codings of assessors' responses, preferably through a lexis-driven approach, may reduce classification bias. Sixth, my analysis of the quantitative data was limited to outlining dispersion values; if these were combined with frequency counts, a more balanced interpretation of the assessment of texts would emerge. Finally, data was repeatedly collected only through written questionnaires; a better understanding of what makes discourse appropriate could be achieved by validating data collection instruments, for instance through follow-up interviews with study participants, in view of developing reliable assessment tools.

References

Ädel, A. (2014). Selecting quantitative data for qualitative analysis: A case study connecting a lexicogrammatical pattern to rhetorical moves. *Journal of English for Academic Purposes*, 16, 68–80.

Alcón-Soler, E. (2013). Pragmatic variation in British and International English language users' e-mail communication: A focus on requests. *Revista Espanola de Linguistica Aplicada*, 26, 25–44.

Alcón-Soler, E. (2015). Teachers' perceptions of email requests: insights for teaching pragmatics in study abroad contexts. In S. Gesuato, F. Bianchi, & W. Cheng (eds.), *Teaching, Learning and Investigating Pragmatics: Principles, Methods and Practices*. Newcastle upon Tyne: Cambridge Scholars Publishing, pp. 13–31.

Alemi, M., Eslami, Z. R., & Rezanejad, A. (2014). Rating EFL learners' interlanguage pragmatic competence by non-native English speaking teachers. *Procedia – Social and Behavioral Sciences*, 98, 171–174.

Alemi, M., & Khanlarzadeh, N. (2017). Native and non-native teachers' pragmatic criteria for rating request speech act: The case of American and Iranian EFL teachers. *Applied Research on English Language*, 6(1), 67–84.

Alemi, M., & Rezanejad, A. (2014). Native and non-native English teachers' rating criteria and variation in the assessment of L2 pragmatic production: the speech act of compliment. *Issues in Language Teaching (ILT)*, 3(1), 65–88.

Alemi, M., & Tajeddin, Z. (2013). Pragmatic rating of L2 refusal: Criteria of native and nonnative English teachers. *TESL Canada Journal/Revue TESL du Canada*, 30(7), 63–81.

Bardovi-Harlig, K., & Shin, S.-Y. (2014). Expanding traditional testing measures with tasks from L2 pragmatics research. *Iranian Journal of Language Testing*, 4(1), 26–49.

Beason, L. (2001). Ethos and error: How business people react to errors. *College, Composition and Communication*, 53(1), 33–64.

Bektas-Cetinkaya, Y. (2012). Pre-service EFL teachers' pragmatic competence. The Turkish case. *International Journal of Language Studies*, 6(2), 107–122.

Change, L. (2011). Interlanguage pragmatic development: The relation between pragmalinguistic competence and sociopragmatic competence. *Language Sciences*, 33(5), 786–798.

Chen, H.-I. (2010). Contrastive learner corpus analysis of epistemic modality and interlanguage pragmatic competence in L2 writing. *Arizona Working Papers in SLA & Teaching*, 17, 27–51.

Chen, Y.-S., & Liu, J. (2016). Constructing a scale to assess L2 written speech act performance: WDCT and e-mail tasks. *Language Assessment Quarterly*, 13(3), 231–250.

Chivarate, B. (2011). Perception of politeness in English requests by Thai EFL learners. *3L: The Southeast Asian Journal of English Language Studies*, 17(2), 59–71.

Cohen, A. D. (2008). Teaching and assessing L2 pragmatics: What can we expect from learners? *Language Teaching*, 41(2), 213–235.

Cohen, A. D. (2014). Towards increased classroom assessment of pragmatic ability. *Iranian Journal of Language Testing*, 4(1), 5–25.

Cortes, V. (2013). 'The purpose of this study is to': Connecting lexical bundles and moves in research article introductions. *Journal of English for Academic Purposes*, 12(1), 33–43.

Culpeper, J., Marti, L., Mei, M., Nevala, M., & Schauer, G. (2010). Cross-cultural variation in the perception of impoliteness: A study of impoliteness events reported by students in England, China, Finland, Germany and Turkey. *Intercultural Pragmatics*, 7(4), 597–624.

DeWaard Dykstra, L. (2011). Reconceptualizing the goals for foreign language learning: the role of pragmatics instruction. In V. M. Scott (ed.), *AAUSC Volume 8: Principles and Practices of the 'Standards' in College Foreign Language Education*. Boston, MA: Heinle Cengage, pp. 86–105.

Economidou-Kogetsidis, M. (2011). 'Please answer me as soon as possible': Pragmatic failure in non-native speakers' e-mail requests to faculty. *Journal of Pragmatics*, 43(13), 3193–3215.

Economidou-Kogetsidis, M. (2015). Teaching email politeness in the EFL/ESL classroom. *ELT Journal*, 69(4), 415–424.

Economidou-Kogetsidis, M. (2016). Variation in evaluations of the (im)politeness of emails from L2 learners and perceptions of the personality of their senders. *Journal of Pragmatics*, 106, 1–19.

Eslami-Rasekh, Z. (2004). Face-keeping strategies in reaction to complaints. *Journal of Asian Pacific Communication*, 14(1), 181–197.

Gleason, J. B., & Perlmann, R. Y. (1985). Acquiring social variation in speech. In H. Giles & R. N. St. Clair (eds.), *Recent Advances in Language, Communication and Social Psychology*. London: Lawrence Erlbaum, pp. 86–111.

Grundy, P. (2008). *Doing Pragmatics*. London and New York: Routledge.

Hacking, J. F. (2008). Socio-pragmatic competence in Russian: How input is not enough. In S. L. Katz & J. Watzinger-Tharp (eds.), *Conceptions of L2 Grammar: Theoretical Approaches and their Application in the L2 Classroom*. Boston, MA: Heinle Cengage, pp. 110–125.

Hartung, K. J., & Wilson, D. G. (2016). Conversational moves that matter: Bridging learning outcomes and patterns of speech in informal cross-organizational conversations among top-level learners. *Adult Education Quarterly*, 66(3), 254–272.

Hendriks, B. (2010). An experimental study of native speaker perceptions of non-native request modification in e-mails in English. *Intercultural Pragmatics*, 7(2), 221–255.

Henry, A., & Ho, D. G. E. (2010). The act of complaining in Brunei – then and now. *Journal of Pragmatics*, 42(3), 840–855.

Henry, A., & Roseberry, R. L. (2001). A narrow-angled corpus analysis of moves and strategies of the genre: 'Letter of Application'. *English for Specific Purposes*, 20(2), 153–167.

Hudson, T., Detmer, E., & Brown, J. D. (1995). *Developing Prototypic Measures of Cross-Cultural Pragmatics, Technical Report # 7*. Manoa, HI: University of Hawai'i at Manoa: Second Language Teaching and Curriculum Center.

Hyland, F., & Hyland, K. (2001). Sugaring the pill: Praise and criticism in written feedback. *Journal of Second Language Writing*, 10(3), 185–212.

Ishihara, N. (2010). Assessing learners' pragmatic ability in the classroom. In D. Tatsuki & N. Houck (eds.), *Pragmatics: Teaching Speech Acts*. TESOL Classroom Practice Series, Alexandra, VA: TESOL, pp. 209–227.

Jeon, E. H., & Kaya, T. (2006). Effects of L2 instruction on interlanguage pragmatic development. A meta-analysis. In J. M. Norris & L. Ortega (eds.), *Synthesizing Research on Language Teaching and Learning*. Amsterdam and Philadelphia: John Benjamins, pp. 165–211.

Jucker, A. H., Schneider, G., Taavitsainen, I., & Breustedt, B. (2008). Fishing for compliments: Precision and recall in corpus-linguistic compliment research. In A. H. Jucker & I. Taavitsainen, eds., *Speech Acts in the History of English*. Amsterdam and Philadelphia: John Benjamins, pp. 273–294.

Koike, D. A. (1996). Transfer of pragmatic competence and suggestions in Spanish foreign language learning. In S. M. Gass & J. Neu (eds.), *Speech Acts Across Cultures, Vol. 11*. Berlin: Mouton de Gruyter, pp. 257–281.

Koike, D. A., & Pearson, L. (2005). The effect of instruction and feedback in the development of pragmatic competence. *System*, 33(3), 481–501.

Kumar, V., & Stracke, E. (2007). An analysis of written feedback on a PhD thesis. *Teaching in Higher Education*, 12(4), 461–470.

Laughlin, V. T., Wain, J., & Schmidgall, J. (2015). *Defining and Operationalizing the Construct of Pragmatic Competence: Review and Recommendations*, Research Report ETS-RR-15-06.

Lumley, T. (2002). Assessment criteria in a large-scale writing test: What do they really mean to the raters? *Language Testing*, 19(3), 246–276.

Pallotti, G. (2009). CAF: Defining, refining and differentiating constructs. *Applied Linguistics*, 30(4), 590–601.

Roever, C. (2011). Testing of second language pragmatics: Past and future. *Language Testing*, 28(4), 463–481.

Savić, M. (2018). Lecturer perceptions of im/politeness and in/appropriateness in student e-mail requests: A Norwegian perspective. *Journal of Pragmatics*, 124, 52–72.

Schauer, G. A. (2006). Pragmatic awareness in ESL and EFL contexts: Contrast and development. *Language Learning*, 56(2), 269–318.

Scher, S. J., & Darley, J. M. (1997). How effective are the things people say to apologise? Effects of the realization of the apology speech act. *Journal of Psycholinguistic Research*, 16(1), 127–140.

Sirikhan, S., & Prapphal, K. (2011). Assessing pragmatic ability of Thai hotel management and tourism students in the context of hotel front office department. *Asian EFL Journal Professional Teaching Articles* 53, 72–94.

Spencer-Oatey, H. (2007). Theories of identity and the analysis of face. *Journal of Pragmatics*, 39(4), 639–656.

Sydorenko, T., Maynard, C., & Guntly, E. (2014). Rater behaviour when judging language learners' pragmatic appropriateness in extended discourse. *TESL Canada Journal/Revue TESL du Canada 19*, 32(1), 19–41.

Sykes, J. M. (2010). (In)commensurable discourse: researchers and practitioners bring pragmatics to language learning. *Studies in Hispanic and Lusophone Linguistics*, 3(1), 253–263.

Taguchi, N. (2006). Analysis of appropriateness in a speech act of request. *Pragmatics*, 16(4), 513–533.

Taguchi, N. (2011a). Do proficiency and study-abroad experience affect speech act production? Analysis of appropriateness, accuracy, and fluency. *International Review of Applied Linguistics in Language Teaching (IRAL)*, 49(4), 265–293.

Taguchi, N. (2011b). Rater variation in the assessment of speech acts. *Pragmatics*, 21(3), 453–471.

Taguchi, N. (2011c). Pragmatic development as a dynamic, complex process: General patterns and case histories. *The Modern Language Journal*, 95(4), 605–627.

Tajeddin, Z., & Alemi, M. (2014). Criteria and bias in native English teachers' assessment of L2 pragmatic appropriacy: content and FACETS analyses. *Asia-Pacific Education Research*, 23(3), 425–434.

Thomas, J. (1983). Cross-cultural pragmatic failure. *Applied Linguistics*, 4(2), 91–112.

Tseng, F.-P. (2011). Analyses of move structure and verb tense of research article abstracts in applied linguistics journals. *International Journal of English Linguistics*, 1(2), 27–39.

Wolfe, J., Shanmugaraj, N., & Sipe, J. (2016). Grammatical versus pragmatic error: Employer perceptions of nonnative and native English speakers. *Business and Professional Communication Quarterly*, 79(4), 397–415.

Yamashita, S. (2008). Investigating interlanguage pragmatic ability: What are we testing? In E. Alcón-Soler & A. Martínez-Flor (eds.), *Investigating Pragmatics in Foreign Language Learning, Teaching and Testing*, Bristol: Multilingual Matters, pp. 201–223.

5 'Hey, You, Can I Loan Your Yellow Pencil?'
Young Norwegian EFL Learners' Metapragmatic Appraisal of Requests

Milica Savić and Anders Myrset

5.1 Introduction

This chapter presents a cross-sectional study exploring young Norwegian EFL learners' appraisal of requestive behaviour in English and their metapragmatic awareness of the linguistic and contextual features influencing request production and interpretation. The pool of interlanguage pragmatics (ILP) studies with young language learners, especially those investigating requests, seems to be growing steadily. However, compared to the research with adult learners, this is still a significantly under-researched area (Portolés, 2015; see also Chapter 6, this volume), with comprehension (Lee, 2010), metapragmatic awareness (Myrset & Savić, 2021) and developmental studies (Chiba, 2017) being particularly sparse. In an attempt to address these research gaps, the present study is perception-oriented and investigates metapragmatic development in young English as a foreign language (EFL) learners, attending third, fifth, and seventh grade of primary school, aged approximately 9, 11, and 13 years old. The results presented in this chapter are part of a broader study and the scope has thus been limited to the following research question: What indicates metapragmatic awareness among primary school EFL learners with regard to the speech act of requesting? Specifically, to what extent is the appraisal of requests in EFL developmental?

5.2 Theoretical Background

5.2.1 Conceptualising Metapragmatic Awareness

Within ILP, the term metapragmatic awareness has been defined in a number of ways (for an overview, see McConachy, 2018). McConachy (2018) argues that a limitation of many definitions of pragmatic and metapragmatic awareness (as the two terms have often been used 'inconsistently and interchangeably' within the field of second language (L2) learning (2018: 23)) is a disregard of how first language (L1) experiences shape meaning in the L2. Consequently, these definitions fail to acknowledge the multiple languages learners draw on in their pragmatic behaviours. He therefore suggests that L2 pragmatic awareness development involves recognising L1-L2 pragmatic differences, which enables the learner to avoid 'unintended pragmatic transfer'. Drawing a distinction between pragmatic and metapragmatic awareness, he continues: 'When the scope of "pragmatic" awareness goes beyond knowledge of specific pragmatic norms and develops into a broader capacity for reflection on pragmatic decision making and interactional effects, the nature of the awareness can be viewed as developing towards the "meta-pragmatic"' (McConachy, 2018: 28).

The complexity of reflection inherent in this conceptualisation of metapragmatic awareness may not be easily attainable by primary school L2 learners. Namely, '[a]s they are still in the process of acquiring logical reasoning and abstract concepts, their access to metalanguage remains limited, especially under the age of 8' (Ishihara & Chiba, 2014: 86). Additionally, children's understandings of L1 pragmatics and ability to verbalise them are still not fully developed (Bernicot, 1991; Bernicot, Laval, & Chaminaud, 2007; Collins, Lockton, & Adams, 2014; Laval, 2003). Yet, this should not be interpreted as children being incapable of reflecting on and discussing language use. They can indeed demonstrate metapragmatic knowledge of linguistic form, social situation or their interplay in L1 at the age of 5 (Bernicot, 1991), with a 'developmental shift' in 'the ability to talk about the rules of verbal interactions by relating what has been said to the context in which it has been said' (Collins et al., 2014: 32) happening approximately at the age of 7 (Bernicot, 1991; Collins et al., 2014).

Due to the sparse research in L2 contexts with young learners (Myrset & Savić, 2021), we have taken conceptualisations of metapragmatic awareness used in research with young L1 speakers as a point of departure (Bernicot, 1991; Wilkinson & Milosky, 1987). However, it is important to acknowledge the differences between the process of developing metapragmatic awareness in L1 and L2, the latter necessarily involving multiple frames of reference originating from different languages (Kecskes, 2014; McConachy, 2018). Therefore, for the purposes of the present study, we will view metapragmatic awareness about requestive behaviour as the learners' ability to verbalise reflections on the linguistic form of requests, the contextual features influencing requestive behaviour, or their interplay, with or without employing L1 as a frame of reference.

5.2.2 Metapragmatic Development in Young EFL Learners: Previous Research

Few studies have explored L2 metapragmatic development in requestive behaviour with young EFL learners. Those that have involved participants of different age and L1 backgrounds: 176 Cantonese children aged 7, 9, and 12 (Lee, 2010), 13 English-Swedish bilinguals aged 5–8 (Cromdal, 1996), 402 Spanish-Catalan trilinguals aged 4–5 and 8–9 (Portolés, 2015), and 127 Spanish trilinguals aged 8–9 (Portolés & Safont, 2018). In addition, they used different elicitation techniques: a multiple-choice comprehension test (Lee, 2010), a politeness differentiation task and observations (Cromdal, 1996), and a computer-based judgement task (Portolés, 2015; Portolés & Safont, 2018). These studies tended to focus on learners' comprehension and/or evaluation of requests of different directness levels: direct, conventionally indirect (CI), and/or hints, differing with regard to 'the degree to which the speaker's illocutionary intent is apparent from the locution' (Blum-Kulka, House, & Kasper, 1989: 278).

Previous research suggests that even young learners are able to comprehend L2 direct and indirect requests (Lee, 2010), showing an ability to judge the appropriateness of requests (Cromdal, 1996; Portolés, 2015; Portolés & Safont, 2018). One study found that 'the pragmatic development of these groups of young learners of English is close to that of L1 children' (Lee, 2010: 361), while another revealed that the participants' pragmatic awareness originated from a 'multilingual proficiency', rather than their L1 or L2, with learners showing 'a high degree of pragmatic awareness, even though their pragmatic systems were not fully developed, especially in English' (Portolés, 2015: 170). Moreover, Lee (2010) suggests that younger learners tend to rely on literal meanings, which facilitates comprehension of direct speech acts in particular, while older learners rely on a host of other features to arrive at the interpretation, such as contextual information, general world knowledge, speaker intention, and sequential utterance development. These studies investigated learners with different L1 backgrounds compared to the participants in the present study. As a vast body of research has shown that L1 pragmatic norms may influence L2 pragmatic choices in complex ways (Chapter 3, this volume; Yates, 2010), some information about Norwegian requests may shed light on our participants' understandings of EFL requestive behaviour.

5.2.3   Requestive Behaviour in Norwegian

This section introduces some general Norwegian tendencies regarding request formulations and address terms which may serve as a background for interpreting the results of the present study. However, there is considerable variation in pragmatic behaviours within national cultures (e.g., Eelen, 2001) and thus, learners sharing a national background 'are not necessarily culturally situated in the same way' (McConachy, 2018: 33).

Fretheim (2005: 145) states that 'verbal politeness in Norwegian is not of the conspicuous sort'. Specifically focussing on Norwegian requests, he explores the ways in which concerns for the hearer's negative face (Brown & Levinson, 1987) can be expressed. He enumerates the following linguistic devices employed in conventionally indirect requests: modal questions with *Kan jeg* (*Can I*) or *Kunne jeg* (*Could I*); the modal verb *få* followed by the infinitive (e.g., *Kan jeg få undersøke = Can I examine*) or the past participle (*Kunne jeg få undersøkt = Could I have [...] examined*); the use of the verb of belief *tro* (= *think, believe*; *Tror du jeg kunne = Do you think I could*); the past tense (*Jeg lurte på = I wondered if*); the interrogative past form of the verb *gå an* (= *be possible, be feasible; Gikk det an å bestille = Could I order*). The use of the past tense, together with a reference to the hearer's ability or attitude, is 'the safest politeness strategy' in Norwegian requests (Fretheim, 2005: 157). The Norwegian counterpart of the marker *please* is not an appropriate mitigating device in requests with a high level of imposition or in highly face-threatening requests (Fretheim, 2005) and can be interpreted as an attempt to communicate impatience or annoyance.

As for address terms, titles and names are seldom used as either attention getters or relationship reinforcers (Røkaas, 2000) and use of endearment terms is not conventionalised (Fretheim, 2005). In spoken discourse, the most commonly used attention getter is the second person singular pronoun *du* (Fretheim, 2005; Røkaas, 2000). In their study of address terms in English and Norwegian, Dittrich, Johansen, and Kulinskaya (2011: 3809) hypothesise that 'the strategy of omitting formal titles during interactions in order to reduce the distance and power between parties negotiating everyday requests is less likely to be found in the UK and USA as compared with Nordic countries'. Their results demonstrate that in conversations with non-intimates of equal social status the UK participants pay more attention to title usage and regard proper forms of address as more important than the Norwegian participants.

Research into Norwegian EFL users' requestive behaviour has only investigated production (e.g., Krulatz, 2016; Savić, 2015) and, to the best of our knowledge, prior to the current project (Savić, 2021; Savić, Economidou-Kogetsidis, & Myrset, 2021; Savić & Myrset, 2021), only one study investigated primary school learners (Savić, 2015), which is in keeping with the principal focus on (young) adults in ILP research. Thus, the present study aims to add to the sparse research on young EFL learners' metapragmatic development and to contribute to the field by expanding the range of the data collection techniques employed to elicit metapragmatic data from young language learners (Myrset & Savić, 2021).

5.3 Present Study

5.3.1 Instrument

As young learners' L2 metapragmatic development is an under-researched area, without a well-established and validated methodology (Myrset & Savić, 2021), devising age-appropriate data collection techniques was a significant part of this project.[1] This section presents the data collection techniques employed, piloted with two fourth-grade groups to determine whether the tasks were appropriate for the learners' age and level of English, adequate for eliciting relevant metapragmatic data, sufficiently engaging and whether the small-group set-up was suitable for the chosen tasks (Punch, 2002).

The instrument comprised a pre-task followed by two tasks. The pre-task was a video-prompted oral discourse completion tasks (VODCT) prompted by four videos aimed at eliciting requests (similar to Flores-Salgado and Halenko's computer-animated production task in Chapter 7, this volume), but also serving as a rapport-building and warm-up activity before the cognitively more demanding tasks (Punch, 2002). The first task (Emoticon task) was an individual metapragmatic appraisal task based on a selection of requests produced in the VODCT, followed by a group discussion of the learners' appraisals. The second task was a group ranking task, but it is not reported on in this chapter and will not be elaborated on further (for a detailed description of the tasks, see Myrset & Savić, 2021). Group discussions and task-based activities, conducted in 'friendship groups' (Pinter & Zandian, 2014: 72), were chosen to reduce the pressure young participants might feel and to facilitate sharing and actively co-constructing meaning with their peers.

The VODCTs were based on four English language learning videos,[2] containing a total of thirteen different scenarios for request production in various settings: a fast food restaurant, a classroom, a store, and dinner at a friend's place. The children in the videos produced requests addressing a range of interlocutors: a server, a classmate, a teacher, parents, a friend, and a friend's mother. Additionally, visual support was provided: for example, if the child in the video wanted to order two hamburgers, a picture of a child and a thought bubble with two hamburgers was shown to the group (Figure 5.1).

As a request elicitation technique, the VODCT is subject to some of the criticism directed at the traditional written DCT (e.g., Ogiermann & Bella, 2020); however, in the present study, its main purpose was to generate requests for metapragmatic appraisals and discussions. Learner- rather than researcher-generated requests were used for two reasons: firstly, having produced them and seen the specific context, the learners could relate to them more easily; secondly, this ensured that they were familiar with the language in each request (Bernicot, 1991). Three to four requests produced in the VODCT were selected for group discussions in the Emoticon task according to the following criteria: a) all three directness levels were represented, that is, if the group produced at least one direct, CI request and hint, they were selected; b) to ensure

---

[1] This is the first of a series of studies within this research project. The other studies include Myrset and Savić (2021), Savić (2021), Savić, Economidou-Kogetsidis and Myrset (2021), and Savić and Myrset (2021).

[2] https://youtu.be/49QFHWIky-k

Figure 5.1 A visual prompt for the video-prompted oral discourse completion task (VODCT) (a snapshot from https://youtu.be/49QFHWIky- k?t=27s)

Figure 5.2 Request appraisal sheet

variety, requests with varied internal and external modification and alerters were included; c) requests clearly demonstrating L1 influence were selected.

The Emoticon task consisted of a metapragmatic appraisal task and a group discussion. Each request was accompanied by an appraisal sheet containing a happy (☺), neutral (☺), and frowny (☹) emoticon and Post-It notes (Figure 5.2). These were used for individual appraisals: Post-It notes were placed on the facial expression that best represented whether a request was appraised as 'nice', 'so-so', or 'not so nice'.[3] The appraisals were followed by a discussion and suggestions for possible improvements of the requests appraised as ☺ or ☹. Inspired by O'Kane's (2008) Pots and Beans activity[4],

---

[3] This was the wording employed by the researcher when giving instructions in Norwegian. 'Nice' is our translation of the Norwegian adjective 'fin'.

[4] To support the children's meaning-making, in O'Kane's (2008) study the child was provided with six pots with labels indicating different aspects of their participation in the project, together with three beans for each pot. The child put one to three beans in each pot, depending on their

this task included both verbal and non-verbal participation and created a visual representation of the learners' appraisals used as support in the ensuing group discussions.

5.3.2   Participants

The sample consisted of seventy-nine primary school learners, attending third (n=24), fifth (n=28), and seventh grade (n=27), aged roughly 9, 11, and 13, learning English as a compulsory school subject from the age of 6. Their expected English proficiency levels on the Common European Framework of Reference for Languages were as follows: approaching A1 for third graders, A1-A2 for fifth graders and A2-B1 for seventh graders (Hasselgreen, 2005).

The third- and fifth-grade learners were from the same school, while the seventh graders were from two schools with comparable socio-economic backgrounds (Stavanger municipality, 2017). This was a convenience sample in that the teachers from the researchers' networks were invited to partici-pate. The learners whose parents were native speakers of English and/or who had lived in an English-speaking country were not included in the sample. Information about the project was sent to the parents and written consent was obtained prior to the data collection.

5.3.3   Procedures

The data was collected at the two schools in February 2018. The teach-ers formed groups consisting of four learners that would complete the tasks together, the only criterion being that the group members were comfortable working together. Altogether, there were twenty groups (nineteen groups of four and one group of three). Two researchers were present at all times: one leading the activities and facilitating group discussions, the other taking notes and providing materials for the tasks.

Before the tasks, the learners were informed about what they were going to do, what the scope of the study was, and that there were no right or wrong answers, to feel more comfortable contributing (Punch, 2002). In the VODCT, the videos were paused before each request and the learners were told what the child needed and who the request should be addressed to. The group was then asked what they thought the child would say: for example, 'The girl is hungry. This is what she orders. What do you think she says?' The groups produced a total of eighteen to thirty-one (average: 24.5) requests. All of these

---

perception of how actively they participated in or prepared for the different activities. One bean meant 'not very good'/'not much', while three beans meant 'really good'. The number of beans in each pot served as a prompt for the ensuing discussion.

Table 5.1 *Number of requests appraised by grade and directness level*

Directness level	3rd	5th	7th	Total
Direct	6	6	6	**18**
CI	11	18	19	**48**
Hints	4	4	3	**11**
Total	**21**	**28**	**28**	**77**

were written down by one of the researchers and, according to predetermined criteria, three to four were selected for appraisal.

The learners were provided with requests, an appraisal sheet for each and Post-It notes. For each request, they individually placed a post-It note on the emoticon that best represented their appraisal. After appraising all the requests, they were invited to share their reasoning behind the placement of Post-It notes and provide suggestions for possible improvements of the requests appraised as ☺ or ☹.

Due to limited time, three third-grade groups appraised only three requests, whereas all the other groups appraised four. The number of requests appraised by each grade, together with their distribution across the three directness levels, is presented in Table 5.1.

The VODCT was conducted in English, whereas the Emoticon task was conducted in Norwegian since the learners' use of English might have affected their ability to express their opinions as well as their confidence and willingness to participate in the discussion. However, some seventh-grade groups chose to perform all the tasks in English.

The three tasks lasted approximately 30 minutes per group. The recordings ranged from 28.13 to 37.20 minutes (average: 32.34 minutes). The research as a whole is therefore based on 10.8 hours of audio recorded data, supported by the researchers' notes. The recordings were transcribed by two research assistants.

5.3.4 Data Analysis

The transcriptions were analysed using the NVivo Pro 11 qualitative data analysis software (QSR International), employing the constant comparison method (Savin-Baden & Major, 2013). Due to the study's exploratory nature, the coding categories were developed exclusively from the data, that is, all the codes were inductive (Savin-Baden & Major, 2013). The sometimes unconventional language use by the young study participants (Punch, 2002) posed a challenge in the process of identifying the codes. After multiple readings of the transcriptions and agreeing on the preliminary codes, the two researchers

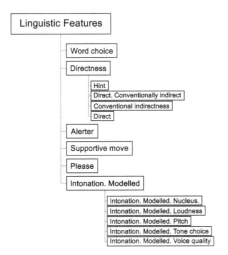

Figure 5.3 Codes for linguistic features

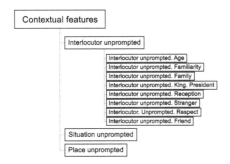

Figure 5.4 Codes for contextual features

independently coded three recordings and compared the coding to ensure satisfactory inter-coder reliability. While the researchers were in complete agreement about coding most of the material, some codes needed to be discussed and further refined. After calibrating, the researchers proceeded with the coding, each focussing on the data from one task for the sake of consistency. To ensure reliability, during the final stage, the coding of the whole dataset was examined by both researchers and full agreement was reached. The multiple rounds of coding and constant comparison between the passages to identify in/consistencies ensured that the researchers did not impose a priori codes and their own perceptions on the data, which is a concern when doing research with children (Punch, 2002). Once established, the codes were labelled using standard terminology for pragmatics, for ease of reporting, and some codes were grouped into broader themes. For example, the utterance *'she said "hi"'*[5] (III.6[6]) was initially coded as 'Hi' and relabelled to 'Alerter' before reporting. Similarly, the utterances a) 'Maybe a friend at your age, but not, like, someone older' (VII.6), b) *'But if I said it to my dad'* (V.1) and c) *'because you don't exactly know that person'* (VII.4) were initially coded as a) 'friend' and 'age', b) 'family', and c) 'someone you don't know' respectively, before being relabelled to 'Interlocutor. Friend', 'Interlocutor. Age', 'Interlocutor. Family', and 'Interlocutor. Familiarity' and grouped under a broader category 'Interlocutor'. The codes reported on in this chapter are provided in Figures 5.3 and 5.4. Reflections on linguistic features, or linguistic considerations, included the language form or content of any semantic component of requests, such as alerters, head acts, internal modifiers, and supportive moves (Blum-Kulka et al., 1989). Contextual features comprised extralinguistic considerations, such as interlocutor characteristics, place or type of communicative situation. Quotations are provided throughout to illustrate the participants' ways of articulating ideas.

5.4   Results

This section presents the findings, focussing on the participants' metapragmatic appraisal and awareness of relevant considerations for requestive behaviour in English. The appraisal of requests of different directness levels across the grades has been adopted as the organising principle. The data for each directness level – direct, CI, and hints – is presented separately. The frequencies of positive (☺), neutral (☺), and negative (☹) ratings of different request types are presented first, followed by the metapragmatic comments that accompanied them. The linguistic and contextual features identified in the comments are subsequently summarised before their frequency of occurrence across the grades is presented.

5.4.1   Direct Requests

Direct requests were produced and appraised by eighteen out of the twenty groups, the exception being one fifth- and one seventh-grade group (Table 5.2).

Direct requests were appraised quite negatively by the third graders, not a single one being considered appropriate. Half of these were heavily influenced by Norwegian request formulations. In Table 5.3, Example (1) illustrates the direct translation of the Norwegian phrase 'Jeg vil ha' (I will have), sometimes

---

[5] Since the group discussions were mostly conducted in Norwegian, the translations into English (done by the authors) are given in italics. The words or phrases produced in English by the participants are not italicised.
[6] III.6 (third grade, group 6)

Table 5.2 *Appraisal of direct requests*

	☺	☺		☹	Total
3rd		9		15	24
5th	5	10		9	24
7th	5	12	1	5	23

Note: Occasionally, learners asked to place their Post-It between two emoticons.

Table 5.3 *Examples of direct requests*

Grade	Example	
3rd	1	I will have a kite.
	2	Two drinks (please).
5th	3	I want a fork.
	4	I want to order two hamburgers.
	5	I'm still hungry. I want more soup.
7th	6	I'd like to order two hamburgers.
	7	I would also like some soda.
	8	I want that one.

used to make requests in the participants' L1. Such requests were also identified in Norwegian second-grade EFL learners' request production in Savić (2015). Interestingly, while the third graders produced 'I will have' requests in the VODCT, their consistently negative appraisals clearly indicated a developing awareness that such requests were inappropriate in English. In the discussions, these were often contrasted with the conventionally indirect 'Can I/you' ones, regarded as more polite:

Excerpt A

LEARNER: *Ehh, because she[7] says 'can' and not 'I will have' [...] She is polite.* (III.1)

Example (2) in Table 5.3 represents an elliptical request, consisting only of a noun phrase or a noun phrase followed by the marker 'please'. In this case, the appraisal was more favourable, with nine middle-option responses (☺). All the groups were unanimous with regard to how these requests could be improved so as to be considered 'nicer'. They suggested reformulating them as CI requests, beginning with the modal verb 'can' and containing 'please',

[7] The learners often talked about the requests as if they had been produced by the children in the videos and not by themselves.

for example: 'Can I have two Cokes, please?' The third graders' perceptions of polite requestive behaviour in English as equating modal questions with 'can' and including 'please' were expressed very clearly both in the request reformulations and in all the group discussions. Excerpt B is representative of most comments about direct requests:

Excerpt B

LEARNER: *She didn't say* 'please'. *Just* 'Two cokes' [...] *She could have said, for example,* 'Can I have two cokes, please', *because in a way she wasn't so polite to the person standing there.* (III.5)

The fifth graders tended to view direct requests slightly less negatively. The majority of their direct requests were want statements or hedged performatives. Except in two cases, Examples (3) and (4) were appraised as neutral or inappropriate (Table 5.3). When asked why a direct request was appraised as ☺, a learner explained that *'in a way, she just said it'* (V.7), suggesting the request was rather abrupt. Another linguistic feature that four fifth-grade groups associated with the abruptness of direct requests was intonation. The relevance of intonation was grasped only intuitively. The four learners who attempted to manipulate intonation when producing direct requests appeared to associate loudness with directness. When contrasted with CI requests, direct ones were pronounced more loudly and with more prominence placed on the nucleus, as in Excerpt C:

Excerpt C

LEARNER: In a way, what's nice is to say, 'can I please get this nice hat? It was very cool.'
RESEARCHER: Mhm.
LEARNER: *And if it was said in a bad way, you could have said,* 'BUY ME[8] the hat.' (V.3)

Example (4) received only negative appraisals, one of the explanations being that *'the person* [being addressed] *may think that [...] the person* [requesting] *will be quite angry if you don't do it fast enough'* (V.3). This introduces the recipient perspective, indicating a shift from a principal focus on linguistic form in third grade to a growing awareness of the effect on the interlocutor. Example (5), including a grounder, was appraised positively by three out of four learners although the head act was equally direct. The supportive move thus seemed to contribute to positive appraisals.

The most common suggestion for improvement was to employ a CI request. The modal verbs employed included 'may' (May I have a fork, please?) and

---

[8] Capital letters were employed to signal emphasis.

'could' (Could I please get two hamburgers?) as well as 'can' (Can I get two hamburgers, please?), the only modal found in the third graders' improved requests. Additionally, one improved request contained a supportive move (Can I please have two hamburgers? I am very hungry.) because the learner thought *'the person prepares it a bit more quickly because you said you are hungry'* (V.3), suggesting a developing awareness of the linguistic elements outside the head act.

The appraisals of direct requests by the seventh graders were evenly distributed between positive and negative, with the largest number being in the middle. Table 5.3 provides examples of requests rated most positively (6), neutrally (7), and most negatively (8). Similar to the younger participants, four out of six seventh-grade groups suggested using a CI modal question with 'Can I' or 'Do you think I can' instead. However, their discussions displayed greater complexity regarding the interplay between contextual and linguistic features, which may have been a reason for appraising some direct requests more positively. The exchange in Excerpt D was prompted by the request 'I would take two cokes, please'. The group disregarded the grammatically awkward formulation and focussed on the appropriateness of such a request in a fast food restaurant as opposed to a regular restaurant.

Excerpt D
LEARNER: Maybe (-) I think (-) ehmmm, she orders from a FAST food restaurant, not from a, like, also, NORmal restaurant, maybe, like, so yeah (-) it's like, 'Would you have some drinks', and, yeah 'Could I get two cokes?' That's, like, *fine, you know.*
RESEARCHER: Does it make a difference if it's a restaurant or a FAST food restaurant?
LEARNER: I mean, *yes, like, I personally think that in a way if we are, in a way, talking about McDonald's, it's like (-) erm (-)*[9]
[…]
LEARNER: *It's like, really fast there all the time, I mean, it's like, you that goes up and orders, and I feel that it's, like, a bit more (-), like, what's it called (-) a bit more proper in an ordinary restaurant.*
[…]
LEARNER: *I feel that, for example, at McDonald's, that they, like, just ask you what you want to have, and then you say what you want, and that's your order, and then you wait, and they, like, do things pretty fast. But at a restaurant it's a bit like we have to be pleasant and speak properly.* (VII.5)

The group portrays ordering at a fast food restaurant as highly routinised, thus allowing for more directness. They seem to perceive this service encounter as task oriented and therefore more expedient than in ordinary restaurants.

[9] This turn demonstrates the learner's self-initiated switching between English and Norwegian to express themselves more clearly.

Orienting to a specific communicative situation and elaborating on its characteristics to determine the appropriateness of a request was only identified with some seventh graders. Another group voiced their concern about the inappropriateness of the request 'Orange paper, please' with regard to the classroom context:

Excerpt E
LEARNER: *Because [...] it sounds like that particular person you are asking is your servant or something like that. Just like that* {snaps fingers} *'Give it to me'.* (VII.1)

As the learner snapped his fingers to explain, the request might have been perceived as too direct and thus inappropriate for the teacher–learner relationship.

In sum, direct requests were appraised quite negatively by the third graders, while in the seventh grade, considering some contextual features had a positive impact on their appraisal. However, the metapragmatic discussions in all the grades displayed much variation both regarding the issues raised and the learners' ability to articulate their opinions and co-construct explanations.

5.4.2   Conventionally Indirect Requests

CI requests represent the directness level most commonly produced in the VODCTs, and, consequently, most often appraised. Nonetheless, there was substantial variation in the formulation of the head act, alerters, internal modification and supportive moves.

The third graders considered over 85 per cent of CI requests 'nice' (☺). Without any exceptions, the head act was a modal 'Can I/we' question, sometimes accompanied by an alerter and/or a supportive move. However, these strategies external to the head act did not appear to play a role in the third graders' appraisal of requests. Examples (9) and (10) represent requests considered ☺ by all the learners, while (11) was regarded as ☹ (Table 5.5). As in the discussions about direct requests, the importance of the linguistic form, that is, including 'can' and 'please', was acknowledged when discussing CI requests. The following exchange took place when the learners were asked why they considered Example (9) 'a nice way to ask':

Excerpt F
LEARNER: *Because she says* 'can' *and* 'please' *instead of* 'I will'.
RESEARCHER: *Yes, so she says* 'can' *and* 'please'. *Yes?*
LEARNER: *They're very polite.*
              [...]
LEARNER: *She doesn't just say what she wants.* (III.1)

Table 5.4 *Appraisal of CI requests*

	☺		☺		☹	Total
3rd	38		6			44
5th	56		12	1	3	72
7th	33	7	26	5	3	74

Table 5.5 *Examples of CI requests*

Grade		Example
3rd	9	Can I have a kite, please?
	10	The kite is very beautiful. Can we buy it, mum?
	11	Mommy, Daddy, can I have this kite?
5th	12	May I have a few crayons, please?
	13	Hey, you, can I loan your yellow pencil?
	14	Can we come another time? It was very fun here.
7th	15	May I borrow a crayon?
	16	The dinner was really good, so I was wondering if I could come another day.
	17	All my friends have one. Can I have one?

While one group mentioned that a request was 'nice' because '*she said "hi"*' (III.6), none of the other groups regarded alerters as important, and only a single group mentioned supportive moves as relevant for their appraisals. A profound change in this respect appeared in fifth-grade request production and metapragmatic discussions.

The fifth graders also appraised CI requests as the most appropriate, with almost 78 per cent of positive ratings. The CI requests appraised included requests comprising only the head act (Example (12)), the head act preceded by alerters (Example (13)), and including supportive moves (Example (14)) (Table 5.5). Only two CI requests, one with no internal and external modification (Can we come back tomorrow?) and one accompanied by a grounder but with no internal modification (This hat is nice. Can I have it?) received no positive appraisals. An important reason for this was that the head act did not contain the marker 'please', which was considered crucial for polite requests: '"please" *is a polite way to finish or open or include in the middle of a sentence*' (V.7). Requests with 'please' were also regarded as '*a good way to say things to your parents if you want something*' (V.2). Consequently, the suggestions for improving CI requests always included adding 'please'.

The importance of supportive moves was acknowledged both through the appraisal and in metapragmatic discussions. The following exchange was prompted by Example (14) (Table 5.5):

Excerpt G

RESEARCHER: *So, here you have all said that this was a nice way to ask. What makes this (-)*

LEARNER: *Because you are saying that it was nice to be there and that you would like to come back.*

[...]

LEARNER: *I think this was a pretty nice way to ask, instead of just saying 'can I come back?' (V.2)*

This exchange appears to highlight the importance of the supportive move, explaining why they would like to come back and at the same time giving a compliment to the hosts. Indeed, complimenting the host and thanking for the dinner were considered highly significant by many groups. One possible reason could be the 'takk for ...' (thank you for) routinised phrase in Norwegian, typical of social leave-taking situations (Røkaas, 2000), which some learners explicitly referred to during the discussions: '[The request was polite] *because she thanked for the food* (takk for maten)' (V.6).

Finally, alerters, such as 'Mommy, Daddy' and 'teacher', were not viewed as essential, since many CI requests without them received ☺ appraisals, but when employed, they positively contributed to appraisals. An alerter worth addressing from the L1-L2 influence perspective is 'Hey, you', in Example (13). This request was appraised as ☺ by three out of four learners in the group, one learner specifically emphasising the alerter contributed to its politeness. Both the attention getter and the address term seem to be embedded in the L1. Namely, 'hei' is the greeting term employed with a wide variety of interlocutors, and the second person singular pronoun 'du' is often used as an attention getter in spoken discourse in Norwegian (Fretheim, 2005), regardless of the social status and age of the addressee (Røkaas, 2000). On the other hand, this function is customarily performed in English by titles and/or names (Røkaas, 2000). Thus, this issue may be worth addressing in the early stages of EFL instruction so that the learners can make informed choices about their positioning in relation to the interlocutors and become sensitised to the potential consequences of their choices on the interlocutors' evaluations.

The seventh graders' appraisal of CI requests differed markedly from that of the younger participants. Only thirty-three out of seventy-four CI requests (44.6 per cent) were appraised positively. Table 5.5 shows examples of a request that was viewed as ☺ (Example 15), one that was ☹ (16), and the only request that received predominantly negative ratings (17)

While the marker 'please' still played a central role, a broader set of contextual and linguistic features was considered, including the familiarity with the interlocutor, their age, their potential perception of the request, the place where the interaction is taking place, and specific word choices, which were rarely discussed by the younger participants. For example, Excerpt H illustrates an exchange about a linguistic feature – the use of the modal verb 'may' as compared to 'can' – which took place when the participants were asked about their positive appraisal of Example (15):

Excerpt H

LEARNER: Because you ask and not, cause, like, kind of, order […] And it's more, like, friendly.
        […]
LEARNER: Yeah, she asked, like, polite, and (-)
LEARNER: And it's, like, 'may', so if it's not ok, it's, like, it's ok to say no. (VII.6)

The positive appraisal of 'may' is thus discussed in the light of offering freedom of choice to the addressee (Brown & Levinson, 1987). Specific word choices were also considered with regard to their interplay with certain interlocutor characteristics, as demonstrated in the discussion about the request 'It was a pleasure being here. It would be cool to come back' in Excerpt I:

Excerpt I

LEARNER: I feel like it's kind of weird that he says 'cool', like (-)
LEARNER: Me too.
LEARNER: I will say it to my friends, so yeah (-)
RESEARCHER: Yeah.
LEARNER: But it's not, like, kind of, so polite to ask, if she said to her mom. I think it's weird to say like that.
RESEARCHER: Yeah.
LEARNER: THEN it's weird. Yeah. But (-) […]
LEARNER: But if you talk, like, to adult and say like that, like, 'cool' (-) Maybe to, like, a teenager, like, 18, like, yeah, then it's, like (-) Maybe a friend at your age, but not, like, someone older.
        […]
RESEARCHER: But what if it was an adult and we wanted to ask, what would you say then?
LEARNER: It was a pleasure being here. It would be, erm (-)
LEARNER: Nice.
LEARNER: Yeah, nice to come back. (VII.6)

This quotation opens with the group's reflection on the appropriateness of using the word 'cool' in a conversation with a friend's mother as opposed to a friend. From this specific context provided in the video, the learners transition to a more general discussion about the appropriateness of this word choice in a conversation with an older interlocutor, introducing age as a relevant variable. Indeed, the influence of the various interlocutor-related features was the most commonly raised contextual consideration. Later in the discussion, they introduce the friend's house as the place of interaction that would also affect word choice. From a methodological point of view, the last three turns clearly exemplify group members co-constructing meaning through building on their peers' ideas, which is further explored in Savić (2021).

The relevance of supportive moves was also acknowledged. One group focussed on the sequencing of the strategies, while another considered the content of the supportive move prompted by request (16).

EXCERPT J

LEARNER: You, like, say just that the dinner was good, not that it was nice to BE there. And, I, yeah (-) and come just for the dinner, not for, like be with the people there.

RESEARCHER: Mmm. Okay.

LEARNER: *I thought it was better than red [☹] because they asked, they did say that it was very good, so THAT was something positive, but they just said, they just said the FOOD was good, and not that it was, it was, like, fun to be there.* (VII.5)

The much wider range of considerations regarding both the linguistic realisations of CI requests and interlocutor-related factors seems to have contributed to more nuanced appraisals performed by the seventh graders as compared to the third graders, who mainly focussed on specific linguistic features.

5.4.3   Hints

Only three to four hints were appraised by each grade as relatively few hints were produced in the VODCT (Table 5.6).

The hints appraised by the third graders included one addressed to the parents in a toy shop (18) and to a classmate in class (19) (Table 5.7). Nearly all the hints were appraised as ☺, which may be a sign of insecurity regarding their communicative function; hence, the option in the middle might have seemed to be the safest one. All the third-grade discussions about hints, such as the one in Excerpt K, clearly demonstrated that they equated the expression of requestive intent with the marker 'please'. Only a single learner in this group felt that 'please' was not necessary as (19) could be interpreted as a question seeking information rather than a request. Therefore, the group suggested rephrasing this request as 'Do you have a yellow pencil, please?'

Excerpt K

RESEARCHER: 'Do you have a yellow pencil?' *Why is it in the middle?*
          [...]

LEARNER: *They didn't say 'please' either.*

RESEARCHER: *They didn't say 'please'.*

LEARNER: *No, they should have done it.*

RESEARCHER: *Anything else?*

LEARNER: *Yes, in a way, they don't have to say 'please'. She just asked if you have, so (-)*

LEARNER: *But it's nicest to say 'please'.* (III.5)

Table 5.6 *Appraisal of hints*

	☺	☺	☹	Total
3rd	1	1	14		16
5th	7		6	3	16
7th	5		6		11

Table 5.7 *Examples of hints*

Grade	Example	
3rd	18	I like the little kite.
	19	Do you have a yellow pencil?
5th	20	I can't use the chopsticks.
	21	I also like this hat.
	22	Do you have a yellow pencil?
7th	23	Maybe we can play another time, too.
	24	Do you have a yellow pencil?

The appraisal of hints and the discussions prompted by hints in the fifth-grade groups were markedly different. Examples of three hints, one produced at a dinner table at a friend's place (20), one in a shop with parents (21), and one in a classroom conversation with a classmate (22) are given in Table 5.7. Appraisals of Examples (20) and (22) were almost evenly distributed between ☺ and ☺, while Example (21) was appraised much more negatively. However, all the discussions revealed that the groups struggled to determine the communicative intent behind these hints, as demonstrated by a learner's initial reaction when appraising Example (20): *'This was a bit difficult'* (V.1). The exchange in Excerpt L was prompted by the researcher's question about why three learners had appraised hint (21) negatively.

Excerpt L
LEARNER: *Because, like, 'I also like this hat'.*
LEARNER: *And then she just gets it. It becomes a bit like 'I want this hat, please?' Kind of.*
RESEARCHER: *Yes, yes.*
LEARNER: *Yes, but I (-) It was she (-) Or, we don't really know, but it doesn't quite sound like she asked either. If she could get the hat. I just think that (-)*
RESEARCHER: *Mhm.*
LEARNER: *Or did she? Was that, like, the intention?*
        […]
LEARNER: *But if I said it to my dad, it would be kind of wrong, I think.* (V.1)

This discussion demonstrates rather convincingly the learners' insecurity regarding the speaker's intention. The learners oscillated between interpreting Example (21) as an inappropriate direct request and a statement that may actually not be a request at all, concluding that it was difficult to make a decision. This appears to show that these fifth graders are beginning to develop an understanding of hints and their function. As this discussion evolved, a learner introduced the interlocutor as playing a role in determining the appropriateness of the hint.

The appraisals of hints in seventh grade were almost equally distributed between positive and neutral evaluations. Requesting through Example (24) (Table 5.7) received two positive and two neutral ratings. The seventh graders proposed two different explanations of this hint: one that viewed the hint as open to two interpretations, in which case it was appraised as appropriate, and one that considered it less appropriate because the requestive intent had not been stated explicitly, but they kept changing their mind throughout the exchange. Hints have been found difficult to discuss metapragmatically by 10-year-olds in L1 as well (Bernicot et al., 2007), so this finding should not be surprising with L2 learners.

5.4.4   Summary: Linguistic and Contextual Features Identified

As demonstrated in the excerpts, various linguistic and contextual features, revealing developing metapragmatic awareness, came up in the discussions of request appraisals (Table 5.8). The third graders mostly focussed on the use of the marker 'please' and/or on contrasting direct and indirect formulations through examples (Excerpts A, B, C, F, and K). Indeed, these two linguistic features were very prominent in all age groups. 'Directness' in Table 5.8 refers to all the exchanges in which the learners contrasted the use of modal questions and imperatives through examples and/or commented on their potential effect on the interlocutor, as well as comments about the in/appropriateness of requests of different directness levels, including the ones about the communicative intent behind hints (Excerpt L). 'Please' was also a central topic in all the grades. New considerations emerging in the fifth-grade groups included supportive moves (Excerpt G), intonation (Excerpt C), and specific word choices. While no new linguistic considerations appeared in the seventh grade, the discussions about the content of supportive moves (Excerpt J), and word choice (Excerpts H and I) were more diverse and in-depth.

Contextual features were explored much less frequently in the discussions about request appraisals (Table 5.9). They were usually mentioned in relation to the specific linguistic features of the requests that prompted the discussions. Interlocutor characteristics, in particular the interlocutor's age (Excerpt I) and, most often, whether they were the learners' friends (Excerpt I) or family

Table 5.8 *Linguistic features*

	3rd	5th	7th	Total
Alerters	3	5	3	**11**
Directness	15	26	22	**63**
Intonation (modelled)	0	5	4	**9**
Please	15	20	20	**55**
Supportive moves	1	12	11	**24**
Word choice	0	4	2	**6**
Total	**34**	**72**	**62**	**168**

Table 5.9 *Contextual features*

	3rd	5th	7th	Total
Interlocutor	1	4	8	**13**
Place	0	1	3	**4**
Situation	1	2	5	**8**
Total	**2**	**7**	**16**	**25**

members (Excerpts I and L), seemed to be most readily connected to the appraisals. The place where the exchange takes place (Excerpt D) and the communicative situation (Excerpt D) were occasionally brought to bear on interpretation. While these features were overall discussed fairly rarely, there was an increase in their number and frequency from third to seventh grade; namely, the third graders remarked on their relevance only twice, and the seventh graders acknowledged their importance in sixteen discussions without being prompted by the researcher.

5.5   Discussion

This study set out to explore primary school EFL learners' metapragmatic awareness with regard to requests, more specifically, the development in their request appraisals from third to seventh grade. Before discussing the findings, some limitations of the study will be highlighted as they need to be considered when interpreting the findings. Firstly, despite the care taken not to impose our views, as in all qualitative research, especially with children, we still risk misinterpreting or misrepresenting the participants' thoughts. To minimise this risk, we have provided many illustrative direct quotations, particularly due to potential differences in child and adult language use (Punch, 2002). Another limitation concerns the considerable differences in the depth of the discussions in the groups of learners of the same age, as well as the observed variation in individual learners' contributions to the discussions. It is, therefore, not possible to make generalisations regarding specific age groups even within the small sample in this study. However, the individual ratings in the metapragmatic appraisal task provided insight into each learner's appraisal, thus providing a 'quantifiable measure' (O'Kane, 2008: 138) of all children's views. Generalising to a wider population is also rendered impossible due to the small convenience sample in this exploratory study.

Turning to the findings, direct requests were appraised increasingly more positively from the third to seventh grade, while the opposite was the case with CI ones. Although this was rather surprising, similar results were obtained by Wilkinson et al. (1984: 2136), albeit with 6- to 8-year-old English native speakers: 'direct requests were increasingly likely to be judged appropriate with increasing age'. Given the general preference for CI requests in different varieties of English (e.g., Blum-Kulka et al., 1989; Fukushima, 2003), the older learners' less favourable response to conventional indirectness could potentially be indicative of their aligning with their L1 norms, perceived to be more direct (Røkaas, 2000). However, this interpretation is rendered less plausible in the light of the learners' metapragmatic discussions. These suggest that the increase in the number of linguistic and contextual considerations with age has made the appraisal more nuanced. The considerations included, for instance, the content of supportive moves, specific word choices, the effect of the request on the interlocutor, the interlocutor's age and familiarity, and the place and nature of the communicative situation. Whereas the third graders focussed solely on linguistic considerations, with a principal focus on the use of 'please' and conventional indirectness, the learners in the fifth and seventh grades also considered contextual features, suggesting a development of metapragmatic awareness across the three grades. Additionally, some fifth and seventh graders employed intonation to highlight the inappropriateness of direct requests, demonstrating a developing intuition of the impact of intonation on the effect of the request.

The linguistic considerations concerning modal questions and the importance of 'please' were consistent across the grades, and the reformulations tended to reflect this. This may be accounted for both by the fact that the modal verb *kan* is commonly employed in indirect requests in Norwegian (Røkaas, 2000) and the similarity of the sentence structure in the two languages, which may easily lead to overgeneralisations. Overreliance on a single modal verb in young Norwegian learners' request production was also observed by Savić (2015), where 'can' appeared in almost 95 per cent of head acts produced by second graders and over 70 per cent in fourth and sixth graders' requests, and by Savić et al., (2021), examining request production strategies in the current VODCT dataset, where 'can' was employed in nearly 90 per cent of the 9- and

13-year-old learners' requests. However, in all these studies, the older learners utilised a broader range of modal verbs and, in this one, showed an awareness of the impact of modal verb choice on the interlocutor.

The positive appraisal of requests containing the marker 'please' is in line with much previous research, which has found it to be one of the most salient features of polite English requests for young learners, both in L2 (Cromdal, 1996; Portolés, 2015) and L1 contexts (Wilkinson & Milosky, 1987). However, while in the L1 context first graders were more sensitive to the presence of the marker 'please' than the third graders (Wilkinson & Milosky, 1987), in our sample the frequency of 'please' in suggested improvements and metapragmatic discussions did not decrease with age. The vast majority of older learners felt they needed to use 'please' *'almost always'* (V.7) or *'in each sentence'* (VII.6) and few exchanges reflected an awareness of alternatives. While such statements could be viewed as 'articulation[s] of simplistic views of language' (McConachy, 2018: 163), as Kádár and House (2020) argue, 'please' functions as a marker for framing utterances as requests. Indeed, their contrastive investigation revealed that, in English, 'please' is the most frequently used single expression for requesting, appearing across a range of standard situations. When it comes to Norwegian requests, there is no equivalent of 'please' and its closest counterpart has 'limited applicability' (Fretheim, 2005: 158); consequently, the learners' reflections about the use of 'please' in EFL requests indicate a developing awareness of requestive frames in EFL. Although the learners in the current study appeared to overgeneralise the use of 'please', their understandings of its function can be a springboard for creating a more nuanced understanding of linguistic and contextual variability.

When appraising CI requests, the fifth and seventh graders considered modification outside the head act itself, adding supportive moves in their reformulations. These were also present in metapragmatic discussions, which suggests that the learners' age appears to play a role in the perception of the importance of supportive moves. While fifth and seventh graders acknowledged their relevance, specifically focussing on the content of compliments, the younger learners did not discuss them. No previous studies that we are aware of have examined the role of supportive moves in young L2 learners' request appraisal; however, these results indicate a developmental pattern similar to the one identified in young Norwegian learners' production of request strategies, that is, a steady increase in the use of this external modification strategy with age. (Savić, 2015; Savić et al., 2021).

Hints proved to be the most challenging to appraise and discuss, indicating uncertainty about their appropriateness and communicative function. Because of the discrepancy between hints' locutionary and illocutionary force, children may regard hints in the form of declaratives as 'problematic' (Wilkinson et al., 1984). Bernicot et al. (2007) found that the ability to comprehend hints develops earlier than metapragmatic knowledge about them. Their 10-year-old participants were unable to articulate 'the discrepancy between "what is said" and "what is meant"' (Bernicot et al., 2007: 2129) by L1 hints. This supports the findings in our study, where the participants produced hints, but demonstrated uncertainty when appraising their appropriateness. However, in some of the fifth and seventh graders' metapragmatic discussions, the speaker's intentions were brought to bear on the interpretation, revealing a developing awareness about the communicative potential of hints in English. Lee's (2010) study revealed that 7- to 12-year-old L2 learners' ability to comprehend hints was adequate (over 70 per cent) even in the youngest group and it only increased with age. Nevertheless, a comparison between our findings and the aforementioned studies should be exercised with caution due to the differences in the participants' age; L1 and L2 contexts; the definitions of terms, that is, indirect requests comprising both what we refer to as CI requests and as hints (Lee, 2010; Wilkinson et al., 1984); and the operationalisations of metapragmatic awareness across the studies.

Contextual considerations featured less prominently in the exchanges. They included references to interlocutor characteristics, specifically their age and familiarity with the speaker, as well as the situation and place where the request is produced. These considerations appeared more often in the fifth- and seventh-grade exchanges, revealing a developing awareness about the interplay between the linguistic form and contextual factors. These results support the findings of previous research in L2 contexts (Cromdal, 1996; Lee, 2010). In a study of processing strategies in speech act comprehension, Lee's 9- and 12-year-old participants, as opposed to the 7-year-old ones, employed 'a range of strategies such as the sub-processing strategy of sequential development […] or macro strategies of attending to speaker and utterance-answer relationship' (2010: 363). However, the findings in L1 contexts seem to indicate that reliance on the communicative context precedes an awareness of linguistic conventions (Bernicot et al., 2007; Laval, 2003). The difference in the results may be accounted for by the variation between L1 and L2 contexts, the differences in the participants' age and the operationalisations of metapragmatic awareness. In addition, task effects might have played a role. Namely, a potential reason for fewer discussions about the context in our dataset could be that the context was provided in the videos, which might have rendered such discussions unnecessary.

5.6   Conclusion

This chapter has investigated the metapragmatic appraisal of requests by young Norwegian EFL learners, aged 9, 11, and 13. Older learners appraised direct requests more positively, whereas the trend was the opposite with CI requests. Interpreting hints proved difficult due to the discrepancy between the linguistic form and the speaker's intention. However, an awareness of their potential to function as requests was first observed in the fifth grade. Linguistic considerations, such as directness, the use of the marker 'please' or the relevance of supportive moves, featured more prominently than contextual ones in metapragmatic discussions in the dataset examined. However, an increase of contextual considerations with older learners revealed a development in their ability to relate these, specifically the interlocutor, place, and communicative situation, with linguistic realisations of requests, resulting in more nuanced appraisals. Considering that young learners' metapragmatic awareness is still under-researched, this study contributes to our understandings of how learners in these age groups draw on a range of linguistic and contextual features to make sense of EFL requestive behaviour.

The task-based data collection techniques created multiple opportunities for the learners to engage in group negotiation and co-construction of meaning (O'Kane, 2008; Myrset & Savić, 2021). Moreover, the dialogic approach to data collection and the use of visual stimuli provided insights into – as well as support for – learner reflections about language use (Myrset & Savić, 2021; Savić, 2021). Thus, combining dialogic approaches and task-based techniques to explore young EFL learners' metapragmatic awareness in different L1 contexts is a promising avenue for future research. We believe that creating opportunities for young learners to voice their reflections will enrich our understandings of their metapragmatic development and afford novel empirical and pedagogical insights.

Acknowledgements

We would like to express our sincere thanks to those who participated in the study: the teachers for giving us access to learners and facilitating the data collection, the learners for enthusiastically sharing their reflections about language use, and the student assistants for helping us with transcribing the recordings. Furthermore, we want to thank Professor Emeritus Andrew D. Cohen for sharing his insights on an early draft of this chapter; Dr Silje Normand and Dr Rebecca Charboneau Stuvland at the University of Stavanger for engaging discussions during the planning of our project; and the two anonymous reviewers.

References

Bernicot, J. (1991). French children's conception of requesting: The development of metapragmatic knowledge. *International Journal of Behavioural Development*, 14(3), 285–304.

Bernicot, J., Laval, V., & Chaminaud, S. (2007). Nonliteral language forms in children: In what order are they acquired in pragmatics and metapragmatics? *Journal of Pragmatics*, 39(12), 2115–2132.

Blum-Kulka, S., House, J., & Kasper, G., eds. (1989). *Cross-Cultural Pragmatics: Requests and Apologies.* Norwood, NJ: Ablex Publishing Corporation.

Brown, P., & Levinson, S. C. (1987). *Politeness: Some Universals in Language Usage.* Cambridge: Cambridge University Press.

Chiba, A. (2017). Investigating young learners' L2 pragmatic competence in telling uncomfortable truths. In G. Brooks (ed.), *The 2016 PanSIG Journal.* Tokyo: JALT, pp. 46–54.

Collins, A., Lockton, E., & Adams, C. (2014). Metapragmatic explication ability in children with typical language development: Development and validation of a novel clinical assessment. *Journal of Communication Disorders*, 52, 31–43.

Cromdal, J. (1996). Pragmatic skills and awareness in bilinguals: Children's directives in school contexts. *Working Papers on Childhood and the Study of Children*, 10, 1–38.

Dittrich, W., Johansen, T., & Kulinskaya, E. (2011). Norms and situational rules of address in English and Norwegian speakers. *Journal of Pragmatics*, 43(15), 3807–3821.

Eelen, G. (2001). *A Critique of Politeness Theories.* Manchester and Northampton, MA: St. Jerome Publishing.

Fretheim, T. (2005). Politeness in Norway: How can you be polite and sincere? In L. Hickey & M. Stewart (eds.), *Politeness in Europe.* Clevedon: Multilingual Matters Ltd, pp. 145–158.

Fukushima, S. (2003). *Requests and Culture: Politeness in British English and Japanese, 3rd ed.* Bern: Peter Lang.

Hasselgreen, A. (2005). The new læreplan proposal for English – reading between the lines. *Språk og språkundervisning*, 2, 7–10.

Ishihara, N., & Chiba, A. (2014). Teacher-based or interactional?: Exploring assessment for children's pragmatic development. *Iranian Journal of Language Testing*, 4(1), 84–112.

Kádár, D., & House, J. (2020). Ritual frames: A contrastive pragmatic approach. *Pragmatics*, 30(1), 142–168.

Kecskes, I. (2014). *Intercultural Pragmatics.* Oxford: Oxford University Press.

Krulatz, A. (2016). Competent non-native users of English? Requestive behaviour of Norwegian EFL teachers. *Nordic Journal of English Studies*, 15(4), 24–44.

Laval, V. (2003). Idiom comprehension and metapragmatic knowledge in French children. *Journal of Pragmatics*, 35(5), 723–739.

Lee, C. (2010). An exploratory study of the interlanguage pragmatic comprehension of young learners of English. *Pragmatics*, 20(3), 343–373.

McConachy, T. (2018). *Developing Intercultural Perspectives on Language Use: Exploring Pragmatics and Culture in Foreign Language Learning.* Bristol: Multilingual Matters.

Myrset, A., & Savić, M. (2021). 'If an astronaut were on the moon …': Eliciting metapragmatic data from young L2 learners. *Applied Pragmatics*, 3(2), 163–193.

Ogiermann, E., & Bella, S. (2020). An interlanguage study of request perspective: Evidence from German, Greek, Polish and Russian learners of English. *Contrastive Pragmatics*, 1(2), 180–209.

O'Kane, C. (2008). The development of participatory techniques: Facilitating children's views about decisions which affect them. In P. Christensen & A. James (eds.), *Research with Children: Perspectives and Practices*, 2nd ed. New York and London: Routledge, pp. 125–155.

Pinter, A., & Zandian, S. (2014). 'I don't ever want to leave this room': Benefits of researching 'with' children. *ELT Journal*, 68(1), 64–74.

Portolés, L. (2015). *Multilingualism and Very Young Learners: An Analysis of Pragmatic Awareness and Language Attitudes*. Berlin: Walter de Gruyter.

Portolés, L., & Safont, P. (2018). Examining authentic and elicited data from a multilingual perspective. The real picture of child requestive behaviour in the L3 classroom. *System*, 75, 81–92.

Punch, S. (2002). Research with children: The same or different from research with adults? *Childhood*, 9(3), 321–341.

Røkaas, F. (2000). Potential for misunderstandings: Social interaction between Norwegians and Americans. In M. Isaksson & F. A. Røkaas (eds.), *Conflicting Values: An Intercultural Challenge*. Sandvika: Norwegian School of Management BI, pp. 111–129.

Savić, M. (2015). 'Can I very please borrow it?' Request development in young Norwegian EFL learners. *Intercultural Pragmatics*, 12(4), 443–480.

Savić, M. (2021). Co-constructing metapragmatic understandings: How young EFL learners talk about making requests. *The European Journal of Applied Linguistics and TEFL*, 10(2), 153–176.

Savić, M., Economidou-Kogetsidis, M., & Myrset, A. (2021). Young Greek Cypriot and Norwegian EFL learners: Pragmalinguistic development in request production. *Journal of Pragmatics*, 180, 15–34.

Savić, M., & Myrset, A. (2021). 'But in England they're certainly very polite, so you mustn't forget that': Young EFL learners making sense of pragmatic practices. In T. McConachy & A. J. Liddicoat (eds.), *Teaching and Learning Second Language Pragmatics for Intercultural Understanding*. London and New York: Routledge, pp. 40–59.

Savin-Baden, M., & Major, C. (2013). *Qualitative Research: The Essential Guide to Theory and Practice*. London and New York: Routledge.

Stavanger municipality. (2017). *Levekår i Stavanger: Geografisk Fordeling – Rapport nr. 7* [Living conditions in Stavanger: Geographical Distribution – Report no. 7], Stavanger: Stavanger Kommune.

Wilkinson, L. C., & Milosky, L. M. (1987). School-age children's metapragmatic knowledge of requests and responses in the classroom. *Topics in Language Disorders*, 7(2), 61–70.

Wilkinson, L. C., Wilkinson, A. C., Spinelli, F., & Chiang, C. P. (1984). Metalinguistic knowledge of pragmatic rules in school-age children. *Child Development*, 55(6), 2130–2140.

Yates, L. (2010). Pragmatic challenges for second language learners. In A. Trosborg (ed.), *Pragmatics across Languages and Cultures*. Berlin: De Gruyter Mouton, pp. 287–308.

Part II

Instructed Pragmatics

6   Interlanguage Pragmatic Development in a German EFL Secondary School Context

Investigating Input and Output Focussing on the Speech Acts of Agreement and Disagreement

Gila A. Schauer

6.1   Introduction

Although a number of studies have been conducted over the years that examined speech acts in instructional materials (e.g., Uso-Juan, 2007; Ogiermann, 2010; Nguyen, 2011; Limberg, 2015; Glaser, 2020; Schauer, 2020), and a smaller number of studies have been conducted that explored the interlanguage pragmatic development of L2 learners in an instructed context (e.g., Rose, 2000; Warga, 2004; Rose, 2009; Glaser, 2014; Sadeghidizaj, 2014; Halenko, 2021), very few studies have focussed on both – the input provided via instructional materials and the output produced by L2 learners (cf. Schauer, 2019). This is regrettable because it means that potential links between instructional input and learners' output have not received much research attention to date. This study aims to shed some light on interrelationship between input and output by investigating two speech acts, agreements and disagreements, which according to the Standing Conference of the Ministers of Education and Cultural Affairs of the Länder in the Federal Republic of Germany (KMK, 2003), EFL learners in intermediate level secondary schools need to master in order to achieve the standards required for the intermediate school leaving certificate.

Being able to agree and disagree is an essential part of intermediate L2 learners' communicative competence because it enables them to take part in discussions and voice their opinions. While as Pomerantz (1984: 83–84) notes 'agreement is a preferred next action across a large diversity of initial assessments', disagreements also play an important role in everyday-life interactions. As Angouri and Locher (2012: 1551) argue 'expressing opposing views is an everyday phenomenon; […] [and] as in all language usage, the ways in which disagreement is expressed – and not only its occurrence per se – will have an impact on relational issues […].'

Thus, although not as frequent and unavoidable as greetings or requests, agreements and disagreements constitute speech acts that L2 learners need to be able to understand and produce if they want to exchange their views with others. This is why the present study focusses on both of them by investigating (dis)agreement input in instructional materials and (dis)agreement output by young EFL learners of two different proficiency levels. In the following, I will review studies that focus on speech acts in instructional materials followed by studies that examine L2 learners' pragmatic development in instructed contexts.

6.2   Literature Review

6.2.1   Pragmatic Content in Instructional Materials

To date a number of studies have been conducted that examine instructional materials from an interlanguage pragmatic perspective. I will briefly summarise some of the issues that were commented on in speech act studies not focussing on agreements or disagreements, as those will be discussed later in this chapter. Pragmatic investigations of teaching materials have found that there is often an unsystematic introduction and repetition of speech acts (e.g., Schauer & Adolphs, 2006; Ogiermann, 2010; Nguyen, 2011; Schauer, 2019), that only a limited number of speech act strategies are provided in textbook series (e.g., Ogiermann, 2010; Limberg, 2015; Barron, 2016), that specific speech acts are less frequently focussed on in exercises than others (e.g., Diepenbroek & Derwing, 2013), that the number of speech acts presented decrease in a textbook series (e.g., Ogiermann, 2010; Ekin, 2013; Limberg, 2015; Schauer, 2019; Glaser, 2020), that modifiers and contextual information are poorly presented (e.g., Usó-Juan, 2007; Barron, 2016), that some speech acts do not feature at all in individual textbooks (Vellenga, 2004), and that materials frequently do not provide complete and therefore authentic conversations (e.g., Bardovi-Harlig, 2001; Schauer, 2019, 2020).

Nguyen (2011) and Ren and Han (2016) analysed the presentation of (dis) agreements and several other speech acts in Vietnamese and Chinese textbooks. Nguyen examined the inclusion of twenty-seven different speech acts in two material types (student books and work books) of one textbook series for three consecutive years of upper secondary school learners from years 10–12, whereas Ren and Han focussed on thirteen different speech acts in ten recent EFL textbooks in use at Chinese universities. Nguyen found that while agreements and disagreements were included in all three student books, agreements were only included in the workbook for year 10 and disagreements were not included in any of the workbooks. While it certainly would have been helpful for the EFL learners to encounter agreements and disagreements in both student and workbooks, it needs to be noted that compared to some of the other speech acts analysed in the study, agreements and disagreements were at least presented in one material type each year. In contrast, some other speech acts only featured in one or two workbooks, for example, advising in the workbook for year 10 or thanking in the workbooks for years 10 and 12.

In contrast to Nguyen's (2011) study, Ren and Han (2016) analysed dis(agreements) as one category, that is, no separate data on agreements and disagreements are available. They found that (dis)agreements were only included in three of the ten textbooks they had analysed and therefore presented as (in) frequently as complaints, greetings, refusals, but more frequently than apologies or expressions of gratitude which were only featured in two textbooks. The speech act included in the majority of the ten Chinese university-level textbooks was the combined category of advice/suggestion. It is unfortunate that (dis)agreements were analysed as a combined category and not as two separate speech acts in this study, since being able to express agreement and disagreement is important in academic discussions and it would therefore have been interesting to see whether both speech acts were included similarly or whether preference was given to one over the other.

The number of studies providing an in-depth analysis of agreements and disagreements in instructional materials is still rather small. In a study that compared agreements included in five different secondary school English textbooks used in Hong Kong, Seto (2009) found that the textbooks differed considerably regarding the number of agreements included which ranged from three to twenty-six and thus provided very different input opportunities for the ESL learners using them. In addition, the individual agreements presented in the textbooks also differed considerably from one-word agreements, for example, *certainly, absolutely*, that also varied across the books, to complete sentences, for example, *I agree [with you]*. Seto's findings suggest that apart from standard expressions such as *I agree* there is relatively little agreement amongst the textbook writers and/or publishing houses with regard to which expressions should be included for secondary school learners.

Liew (2016) compared three textbooks from the international New Headways series (intermediate, upper intermediate and advanced) to their corresponding Malaysian textbooks for the secondary school. She found that New Headway books contained a considerably higher number of agreements than the Malaysian books, ninety-four and forty-two respectively. She also noted that both books included fewer disagreements than agreements with New Headway featuring thirty-four compared to twenty-three included in the Malaysian series. Regarding the actual agreement expressions, she found that the Malaysian series contained more formal options, such as *I agree [with you]* or *that's true*, while New Headway included a higher number of shorter and/or more informal expressions such as *yeah*. Headway's preferences for informal over formal options also held for disagreements: Headway did not include the more formal *I don't agree* option included in the Malaysian series and instead contained more attack-like statements, such as *In your dreams; Fat chance*. The studies by Seto (2009) and Liew (2016) suggest that there appears to be relatively little agreement among textbook writers and/or publishing houses with regard to which (dis)agreement expressions L2 learners of English should be exposed to.

6.2.2   *L2 Learners' Pragmatic Development in Instructed Contexts*

Concerning L2 learners' development in instructed contexts, a considerable number of studies have focussed on the effect of implicit versus explicit instruction. The majority of studies comparing these two different teaching methods found that explicit instruction results in better learning outcomes than implicit instruction (e.g., House, 1996; Alcón-Soler, 2005; Nguyen, Pham, & Pham, 2012; Fordyce, 2014; Sadeghidizaj, 2014; but see Martínez Flor & Alcón-Soler, 2007, for different findings). In a study comparing output-focussed versus comprehension-focussed pragmatic instruction that was based on video-vignettes and delivered to adult learners at university, Jernigan (2012) found that learners in the output-focussed group achieved significantly better results in the pragmatic awareness task than the comprehension-focussed group but that there was no significant difference in learners' productive pragmatic competence that was tested with a discourse completion task (DCT). Examining the effect of paper-based versus computer-based instruction to no instruction on adult EFL learners, Halenko (2021) found that the group receiving computer-based instruction outperformed the other two groups. Finally, cross-sectional developmental studies that compared the pragmatic performance of L2 learners in different proficiency levels at educational institutions found that with increasing proficiency in the L2, learners tended to use fewer direct strategies and increased their use of conventionally indirect strategies (e.g., Rose, 2000, 2009; Félix-Brasdefer, 2007, but see Warga, 2004 for different results concerning French as a foreign language learners).

With regard to studies focussing on (dis)agreements, Glaser (2014) examined the effect of inductive versus deductive teaching approaches on disagreements and offer refusals in her investigation involving university students enrolled in undergraduate programmes. Her study involved a variety of data elicitation techniques, such as DCTs, role plays, and reflective essays. She found that 'the instruction was generally effective in both conditions as measured by an increased use of target features' (2014, p. 284). Also focussing on adult learners in university language programmes, Bardovi-Harlig, Mossman, and Vellenga (2015) explored ESL learners' use of different pragmatic routines that can be used to agree or disagree, for example, *that's right, that's true, I don't think so* (most of these routines will be categorised as (dis)agreement tokens in the present study). They were interested in examining whether 'instruction ha[s] a positive effect on the use of pragmatic routines as measured by oral production in conversation simulations' (Bardovi-Harlig, Mossman, and Vellenga, 2015: 328) and therefore compared two groups – one receiving instruction on pragmatic routines and one that only completed the pre-test and the post-test without receiving instruction. The test used was a computer-delivered oral production test. Bardovi-Harlig,

Mossman, and Vellenga (2015: 339) found that in the group receiving instruction 'the use of expressions for agreements increased from 13.1% at the pretest to 50% at the posttest (*That's right*), [and] 21.2% to 41.2% for disagreements [...], while the control group did not show a significant change [...].'

6.2.3   Issues Rarely Focussed on Concerning Pragmatic Input and Output in Instructed Settings

As mentioned above, none of the studies reviewed here has investigated both input provided by instructional materials used in compulsory secondary school EFL classes and output produced by EFL learners learning English with these materials in the final years of compulsory education. In addition, intermediate secondary school learners are very rarely focussed on in interlanguage pragmatics studies to date, as those tend to either focus on primary school learners (e.g., Rose, 2000; Schauer, 2019; Chapter 5, this volume), advanced secondary school learners (e.g., Warga, 2004), or university learners (e.g., Félix-Brasdefer, 2007; Glaser, 2014; Bardovi-Harlig, Mossman, & Vellenga, 2015). The research questions this study intends to answer are:

1. How are (dis)agreements represented – if at all – in the EFL Lighthouse textbooks and audio materials for intermediate secondary schools from grade 5 to grade 10?
2. Do EFL learners of different year groups use different agreement and disagreement strategies?
3. Do the agreements and disagreements produced by the learners indicate a link between instructional input and output?
4. Do the data indicate differences in pragmatic competence among the two learner groups? And if so, what are they?

6.3   Method

For the present investigation, input and output data were analysed. In the following, I will first describe the input data, that is, the textbooks and the accompanying audio tracks, and will then introduce the young EFL learner participants and the data elicitation instrument with which the output data were collected.[1] This will be followed by the procedure section in which the agreement and disagreement strategies that were focussed on in the analyses are described.

---

[1] Different definitions exist for the term 'young learners', however, Ellis (2014: 75) states: 'The term "young learner" is often used in the ELT profession to refer to any learner under the age of 18.'

6.3.1   Input: Teaching Materials

The input data investigated for this study consists of six EFL textbooks belonging to the Lighthouse series published by the major German publishing house Cornelsen that were used at the secondary school in which the output data were collected, as well as their accompanying Lighthouse audio CDs. The textbooks are intended for EFL learners from years 5 to 10 at German intermediate secondary schools. The page counts for the individual textbooks from book 1 to book 6 are: 232, 256, 256, 272, 272, and 280. This shows that the page numbers increase over the years and that the final textbook contains about fifty more pages than the first one. All parts of the books, apart from study skills, grammar, vocabulary, and dictionary sections, were analysed. All audio texts included on CDs accompanying the textbooks were also examined, as they featured texts that were integral parts of the textbooks. Both, textbooks and audio CDs, are freely available to language learners, that is, none of them were only available to teachers, and could be purchased from the publishing house, bookshops, or other retailers.

I decided to focus on two components of the material pool offered by the publisher for three reasons: (1) it seemed unlikely that EFL teachers using the textbook series would not use both the textbook and the audio CD when teaching (as certain picture stories presented in the book are only included on the audio cd and it would be difficult for learners to understand the stories otherwise); (2) it was less clear whether teachers would use any of the other materials offered by the publisher or recommend that all learners purchase them (e.g., additional vocabulary booklet, additional grammar booklet, etc.) and my aim was to get an overview of what all EFL learners in the individual years are likely to encounter; and (3) space constraints would not have allowed a detailed analysis of all accompanying materials.

6.3.2   Output: Participants

Two groups of EFL learner participants took part in the cross-sectional developmental study: twenty-eight learners in year 8 and thirty-one learners in year 10 of a Regelschule (an intermediate secondary school) in a small city in the German state of Thuringia. The Regelschule is attended by students from years 5 to 10 in Thuringia, which means that the learners in year 10 were in their final year and left the school soon after data collection had taken place. In Thuringia, two hours of foreign language education are compulsory[2] in years 3 and 4 of primary school, thus learners in year 8 typically have had six years of compulsory

---

[2] Primary schools can also elect to begin their foreign language instruction in year one of primary school but this does not seem to be widely done (cf. Schauer's 2019 survey of EFL teachers in Thuringia in which 84 per cent of the EFL primary school teachers stated that they worked in a primary school in which EFL instruction began in year 3). Although primary schools in Thuringia can choose which foreign language is offered at their institution (the options are: English, French, Italian or Russian), the majority of schools offer English as a foreign language (Schulportal Thüringen, n.d.).

EFL but at least a minimum of four years of EFL instruction in year 8 if they attended a primary school in which another foreign language was taught.

Of the twenty-eight students in year 8, sixteen were female and twelve were male. The average age of the learners in this year group was 14 years. Three of the learners in this group had spent two to three weeks in English-speaking countries (Australia, Canada, and the United States) during their holidays. In year 10, twenty-one of the thirty-one students were female and ten were male. Their average age was 15.10 years. In this group, fourteen learners had spent four days to two weeks in an English-speaking country while on vacation – all of the learners in year 10 who had been to an English-speaking country had been to England and one had also spent one week in Ireland. None of the learners in either group had taken part in a student exchange programme. Apart from one learner in year 8 who stated that he had two native languages (German and Italian), all other learners stated that they were monolingual German native speakers. Due to data protection guidelines, no information on the proficiency level of individual learners could be obtained.

6.3.3 Output: Date Elicitation Instrument

The data were collected with a written illustrated DCT that contained twelve scenarios in addition to a section with personal background questions (e.g., age, gender, sojourns in English-speaking countries). The images had been added to the questionnaire in order to make it more visually appealing and also to provide further contextual information. To ensure that both learner groups could understand and complete the questionnaire, specific words that learners in year 8 may not know were translated into German (see Appendix).

The questionnaire scenarios were designed in cooperation with an MEd student who knew the school where the data collection took place well and could therefore provide information on situations and contexts that would be familiar to the EFL learners' own learning experience. To provide a reason for why all interactions in the scenario were taking place in English, the EFL learners were told that they should imagine that they were taking part in exchange programme with a 15-year-old English female and were staying with her and her family in London for three months taking part in typical family, school, and spare-time activities during that time.

All learners were familiar with student exchange programs, because Lighthouse 3 and Lighthouse 5 contain content on student exchange programmes. In addition, learners were also used to scenarios similar to the ones included in the questionnaire, since exercises similar to DCT scenarios feature regularly in the Lighthouse textbooks. The scenarios included in the questionnaire involved interactions with a variety of different individuals and focussed on the following topics: (1) 'Beautiful day' (breakfast interaction with host mother), (2) 'Barbecue' (interaction with host father), (3) 'Dog' (interaction with host sister), (4) 'German food' (interaction with school friend), (5) 'Teasing the toddlers' (interaction with student), (6) 'Tv talent show' (interaction with host mother), (7) 'History homework' (interaction with school friends), (8) 'Chocolate bar' (interaction with host mother), (9) 'Chocolate bar' (interaction with student), (10) 'Food allergies' (interaction with host mother), (11) 'Kissing students' (interaction with school friends), and (12) 'Physics test' (interaction with school friends).

Of the twelve questionnaire scenarios, ten were intended to elicit agreements and disagreements, while two (Scenarios 9 and 10) were distractors scenarios. To obtain speech act utterances that reflected EFL learners' own opinion and therefore a more authentic response than for example a forced disagreement utterance, learners were not prompted how to respond (i.e., instead of 'you disagree' or 'you agree', the prompt simply stated 'you say'). One of the aims of the research project was to examine how EFL learners of the different year groups would respond to the scenarios and whether – even without explicit prompting – certain speech act preferences would emerge. Table 6.1 shows how the two learner groups responded to the individual scenarios and which of the scenarios[3] were then subsequently analysed as agreement or disagreement scenarios.

6.3.4   *Input and Output: Framework*

I will first provide definitions for agreements and disagreements that were used for this study and will then present an overview of the agreement and disagreement strategies that were employed in this study. For the purpose of this investigation, agreements will be defined as utterances that indicate to the interlocutor(s) that the speaker agrees with their previous evaluation / assertion.

Examples:

Evaluation / Assertion	Agreement
S1: 'It's a lovely day today.'	S2: 'Yes, it is.'
S1: 'I don't like him.'	S2: 'Me neither. He is awful.'

Disagreements are defined as utterances that indicate to the interlocutor(s) that the speaker does not agree with their previous evaluation / assertion.

Examples:

Evaluation / Assertion	Disagreement
S1: 'It's a lovely day today.'	S2: 'I prefer cooler temperatures. It's far too hot for me.'
S1: 'I don't like him.'	S2: 'I do. I think he's lovely.'

---

[3] Once a scenario had been clearly classified as an agreement or disagreement scenario based on the majority of learners' utterances, only the utterances of those learners that corresponded to the classification (i.e. disagreements in scenarios that were categorised as disagreement scenarios) were analysed.

Table 6.1 *EFL learners' (dis)agreement utterances in the individual questionnaire scenario*

	S1	S2	S3	S4	S5	S6	S7	S8	S11	S12
Y8										
Agree	27	0	24	10	1	19	20	11	0	23
Disagree	0	27	2	3	25	4	2	5	23	1
Unclear	1	1	2	5	2	5	6	12	5	4
Neutral	0	0	0	10	0	0	0	0	0	0
Y10										
Agree	29	1	27	10	1	20	20	7	4	23
Disagree	0	28	3	3	24	8	2	13	21	3
Unclear	2	2	1	2	6	3	9	11	6	5
Neutral	0	0	0	16	0	0	0	0	0	0
Total	59	59	59	59	59	59	59	59	59	59
Majority	**A**	**D**	**A**	**N/A**	**D**	**A**	**A**	**N/A**	**D**	**A**

Notes: In the majority utterance row, 'A' signifies a majority for 'agreements', while 'D' signifies a majority for 'disagreements'. If no clear majority could be determined, 'N/A' for not applicable is used. The category 'unclear' includes both utterances that could not be understood (often as a result of a language issue) and opt outs.

Consequently, positive or negative replies to questions / requests for information (e.g., S1: 'Is Mum here?' S2: 'Yes, she is'), suggestions (e.g., S1: 'Let's go to the cinema.' S2: 'Great idea!') and offers (e.g., S1: 'I can help you with that.' S2: 'Great! That would be brilliant!') are therefore not investigated.

All examples in the tables detailing the (dis)agreement strategies are taken from the EFL learner data and are accompanied by the individual learner id code. The code includes the following components: 'S' (for student data), followed by year ID in the format Y8 or Y10, followed by the gender identifier 'M' for males, 'F' for females, 'D' for diverse[4], and finally the individual learner number. The agreement strategies are presented in Table 6.2.

As the examples in the Table 6.2 have shown, learners may use more than one agreement strategy in an agreement utterance, for example, 'Yes, I think so.' (S-Y10F-ID1005, Scenario 12) was coded as Agreement token + Knowledge marker.

---

[4] According to a recent change in German law, three genders are now distinguished, male, female and diverse.

Table 6.2 *Agreement strategies*

Strategy name	Definition	Example
Agreement token[1]	This includes short words or formulaic expressions that show agreement, such as *yes, yeah, I agree, [that's]/ [you're] right.*	A: 'Ooh …, look who is there. The neighbours' new dog is soo cute, isn't he?' B: 'Ooh *yes* the dog is so cute.' (S-Y10F-ID1005, Scenario 3)
Same evaluation[2]	The speaker produces an utterance that shows the interlocutor that they evaluate the issue similarly.	A: 'Look, the sun is shining! Isn't it a beautiful day today?' B: 'Yes, *it is wounderful* [sic].' (S-Y8M-ID827, Scenario 1)
Downgraded evaluation[3]	Although the speaker shows agreement with the interlocutor, the force of agreement is weaker than the interlocutor's force (this strategy is on the end of the agreement scale close and can be close to disagreements)	A: 'What an awful test! Physics is the most awful subject ever!' B: 'Yes, it's difficult.' (S-Y8M-ID820, Scenario 12)
Upgraded evaluation[4]	The speaker's assessment is more positive or negative than the original evaluation of their interlocutor	A: 'The neighbour's new dog is soo cute, isn't he?' B: 'Yeah, it's maybe *the cutest thing I ever saw.*' (S-Y10F-ID1006, Scenario 3)
Topic expander[5]	The speaker expands on their agreement by making additional statements that are in-line with the agreed proposition.	A: 'Look, the sun is shining! Isn't it a beautiful day today?' B: 'Yes, it's a beautiful day today. *I think I wear a T-shirt.*' (S-Y10F-ID1011, Scenario 1)
Perspective change	While the speaker is in agreement with the interlocutor, they highlight further aspects related to the topic that provide a different perspective on the issue.	A: 'Mr. Atkins must be crazy!! 5 pages about the Second World War in 3 days, this is absolutely impossible!' B: 'Yes, it is. But in Germany our teacher gave us bigger homeworks [sic] than Mr. Atkins gave.' (S-Y10F-ID1020, scenario 7)
Rhetorical Question	A rhetorical question is asked that is in-line with the agreed proposition.	A: 'Mr. Atkins must be crazy!! 5 pages about the Second World War in 3 days, this is absolutely impossible!' B: 'How long does it takes? 3 hours? I don't want to do this homework.' (S-Y10F-ID1003, Scenario 7)
Knowledge marker[6]	'Where the responder agrees by laying claim to the same knowledge or belief as the giver of the assessment, by saying "I know", or "I think so"' (Johnson, 2006: 51)	A: 'What an awful test! Physics is really the most horrible subject ever!' B: 'Yes, *I think so.*' (S-Y10F-ID1005, Scenario 12)

Notes: 1, 2, 3, 4 cf.) and Johnson (2006); 5 this is similar to Johnson's (2006) topic developer; 6 cf. Johnson (2006).

Table 6.3 *Disagreement strategies*

Strategy name	Definition	Example
Disagreement token[1]	This includes words or formulaic expressions that show a speaker's or writer's disagreement, such as *no, that's wrong, I don't agree.*	A: 'I think I have heard that German people don't like barbecues.' B: '*No*, Germans love barbecues.' (S-Y8M-ID819, Scenario 2) B: '*That's wrong.* I like barbecues.' (S-Y8F-ID814, Scenario 2)
Hedged negation	The producer of the utterance conveys their disagreement more indirectly with the use of hedges, e.g., *I don't think so.*	A: 'I think I have heard that German people don't like barbecues.' B: 'Oh, *I don't think so.* My friends and I like barbecues.' (S-Y10F-ID1002, Scenario 2)
Contradiction[4]	The speaker or writer produces an utterance that clearly conveys to their interlocutor that they do not share the interlocutor's view. This can be done by (partially) repeating the preceding utterance and taking the opposite stance.	A: 'That was fun, wasn't it? Teasing the toddlers [Kleinkinder] is the best!' B: 'No! *It is not funny!*' (S-Y10F-ID1017, Scenario 5)
General statement	A general statement is made that shows disagreement with the interlocutor's previous utterance.	A: 'Yuck! [Igitt!] Can't they do that in private? This is so inappropriate!' B: 'Oh no *love is something nice.*' (S-Y10M-ID1030, Scenario 11)
Attack – rhetorical question	The interlocutor's view is attacked by asking a rhetorical question that attacks their face	A: 'That was fun, wasn't it? Teasing the toddlers [Kleinkinder] is the best!' B: '*Are you dumb?* That wasn't nice the poor kid.' (S-Y10M-ID1023, Scenario 5)
Attack – statement	The interlocutor's utterance is attacked by the use of face-threatening statements or names.	A: 'That was fun, wasn't it? Teasing the toddlers [Kleinkinder] is the best!' B: '*You are a moron.*' (S-Y8F-ID813, Scenario 5)
Challenge[5]	The interlocutor's view is challenged by a direct utterance that shows disagreement and may also convey aggression.	A: 'I think I have heard that German people don't like barbecues.' B: 'That isn't right. *who say that?* We often have a barbecue in summer and we have the "rost bratwurst" which is very delicious.' (S-Y10M-ID1023, Scenario 2)
Command[6]	The speaker forcefully tells the interlocutor to do or not do something.	A: 'Yuck! [Igitt!] Can't they do that in private? This is so inappropriate!' B: 'They are just in love. *Leave them alone.* You don't have to look at it.' (S-Y10F-ID1007, Scenario 11)

Table 6.3 *(cont.)*

Strategy name	Definition	Example
Question	The speaker indicates that they either doubt the interlocutor's utterance and/ or that they would like more information.	A: 'Yuck! [Igitt!] Can't they do that in private? This is so inappropriate!' B: '*Why it is so problematic for you?* If they want to do this here they can do it here. As long as they don't do more here.' (S-Y10M-ID1027, Scenario 11)
Sympathy	The producer of the utterance shows sympathy towards a third person that has been negatively affected by the interlocutor's actions.	A: 'That was fun, wasn't it? Teasing the toddlers [Kleinkinder] is the best!' B: 'Are you dumb? That wasn't nice *the poor kid.*' (S-Y10M-ID1023, Scenario 5)
Consequence	The producer of the utterance makes the interlocutor aware of the (potential) consequences of their actions.	A: 'That was fun, wasn't it? Teasing the toddlers [Kleinkinder] is the best!' B: 'No that's wrong. It wasn't funny – *He ist [sic] dirty and he has hurt.*' (S-Y10F-ID1011, Scenario 5)
Perspective change	The producer of the utterance makes the interlocutor aware of a different perspective by asking them to consider being in a different position or being the recipient of the interlocutor's actions.	A: 'That was fun, wasn't it? Teasing the toddlers [Kleinkinder] is the best!' B: 'It isn't funny to teasing the toddlers. I think *you also want not that some others people teasing you.*' (S-Y10F-ID1001, Scenario 5)
Grounder[7]	The speaker provides an explanation for their disagreement.	A: 'That was fun, wasn't it? Teasing the toddlers [Kleinkinder] is the best!' B: 'No, I think it's very unfair *because you are stronger as he.* We have to protect them.' (S-Y8F-ID809, Scenario 5)

Notes: 1) confer Pomerantz's 1984 negation and Glaser's (2014) negating adverb,
2) 2, 3, 4, 5, 6) confer Glaser (2014)
3) 7) confer Blum-Kulka, House and Kasper (1989).
Confer Brown and Levinson (1987) and Spencer-Oatey (2002, 2008) on conceptualisations of face.

Due to word count constraints, the analysis presented in this chapter will focus on (dis)agreement strategies only and will not address internal modifiers, such as exclamations or address terms, or other speech acts included in the (dis)agreement utterance, such as greetings. Table 6.3 presents the disagreement strategies.

As was the case for agreements, EFL learners also frequently used more than one disagreement strategy in their disagreement utterance, for example, 'No! It is not funny!' (S-Y10F-ID1017, Scenario 5) which was coded as Disagreement Token + Contradiction.

6.4   Results

In the following, I will first present and discuss the results of the materials analysis (input) and then move on to the findings from the EFL learners' (output).

6.4.1   Results: Input

I will first focus on the overall number of agreements and disagreements included in the teaching materials and will then analyse and discuss the agreement and disagreement strategies included in the textbooks and audio CDs.

6.4.1.1   Input: Overview of Agreement and Disagreement Instances   In total, 135 agreements and 136 disagreements instances[5] were included in the Lighthouse materials that I analysed. This means that the representation of agreements and disagreements in the input materials is even, suggesting that the materials give learners options and do not show bias towards an overly conciliatory or overly contentious stance. However, when the number of agreement and disagreement instances in the individual material types – as shown in Figure 6.1 – are compared, it is evident that there are considerable differences in the number of (dis)agreement instances included in the two material types. For example, while the total number of agreement and disagreement instances in the materials for Lighthouse 1 is again even (forty-five for both speech acts), the distribution of these instances across the materials differs very much: nine agreements in book 1, thirty-six agreements in audio CD1, twenty-four disagreements in book 1, twenty-one disagreements in audio 1.

Although it needs to be acknowledged that the distribution of (dis)agreement instances is also even/similar in some years, for example, agreements in year 3 with ten instances each in the textbook and the audio material or disagreements in year 5 with thirteen instances in the book and eleven in the audio materials, in four cases (i.e., agreements year 1, disagreements year 3, disagreements year 4, disagreements year 6), the number of (dis)agreement instances in the two material types is markedly different. The question is what impact this uneven distribution may have. Is it better for learners to encounter speech acts in textbooks or in audio materials?

While EFL learners working with the Lighthouse series will typically have access to their textbooks and would be allowed to take them home, access to

---

[5] For the present study, instances are defined as an occurrence of an agreement or disagreement utterance that corresponds to what is called a turn in conversation analysis. A single agreement or disagreement instance can contain more than one strategy, e.g., two different disagreement tokens (no, that's wrong).

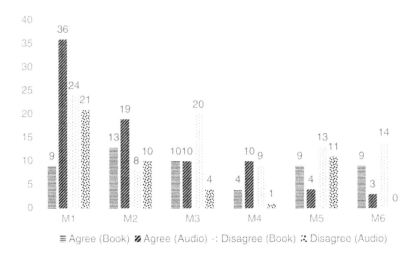

Figure 6.1   Agreement and disagreement instances in the input materials

accompanying audio CDs is likely to be more limited, since parents or guardians would need to purchase them. As discussed in Schauer (2020), listening to speech acts, especially if teachers make good and frequent use of the audio materials, may also be highly beneficial for EFL learners but we simply do not know enough about the acquisition of speech acts with the help of different material types yet.

This is an area that future interlanguage pragmatics research should explore, as to date the majority of studies that examine interlanguage pragmatics and teaching materials tend to focus almost exclusively on textbook input (but see Jernigan, 2012, Bardovi-Harlig, Mossman, and Vellenga, 2015; Nguyen, 2011; Glaser, 2020; Halenko, 2021 for different approaches).

It is also interesting that the total number of agreement and disagreement instances in the two material types differ within and across the speech acts as presented in Figure 6.2.

Of the 136 agreements included in the Lighthouse materials examined, fifty-four are featured in the textbooks and eighty-two in the audio materials, while the inverse is the case for disagreements, since eighty-eight instances of this speech act are included in the textbook, while forty-seven are presented in the audio materials. It is unclear whether this mirror image presentation of the two speech acts was intended or not but it could be usefully employed for future studies that focus on EFL classrooms in which the Lighthouse series is used that wish to explore the impact of different pragmatic input types on EFL learners' speech act competence.

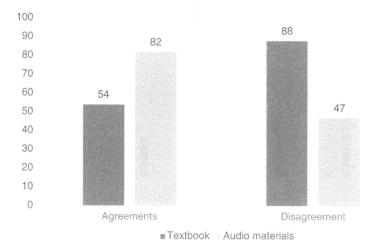

Figure 6.2 Total number of agreements and disagreements according to teaching material type

6.4.1.2 Input: Agreement Strategies   As Section 6.4.2.1 will also show, the input materials investigated included a lower number of agreement strategies than the EFL learners used in their output. This is interesting and could be the result of (a combination of) different factors: (1) learners may be transferring agreement norms from their L1s to their L2s; (2) additional teaching materials available in the Lighthouse series but not investigated here may include additional agreement strategies that learners have acquired; (3) teaching staff at the school may have placed emphasis on discussion tasks and taught additional agreement strategies over the years; and (4) learners may have acquired different strategies by listening to music, watching TV or films, or by being otherwise exposed to the target language. As Figure 6.3 illustrates, there is not much variety with regard to agreement strategies in the input materials.

The results show that EFL learners using Lighthouse will encounter a considerable number of agreement tokens in their first two years of learning English at secondary school, while also being exposed to same evaluation and topic expander strategies. In the subsequent years, the frequency with which these strategies are included decreases but learners still regularly encounter strategies that are used to agree with another person. This needs to be acknowledged since other studies have shown that some speech acts tend to be very infrequently presented – if at all in other textbook series (cf. Vellenga, 2004; Nguyen, 2011; Schauer, 2019). Somewhat surprisingly, the only instances of

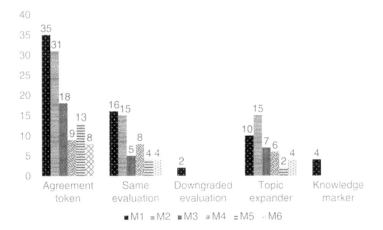

Figure 6.3 Agreement strategies in the input materials

knowledge markers and downgraded evaluation are found in the materials for year 1. Here, a repetition of these strategies in the subsequent years would have been helpful.

Since the strategy agreement token subsumes a number of different words and formulaic expressions that would enable even beginner level learners to show their agreement with their interlocutors and could therefore be considered the building blocks of agreements, it is worth taking a closer look at the different options included in the input materials, which are presented in Figure 6.4.

In total, the input materials included the following numbers of agreement tokens: *yes* (19), *yeah* (32), *yup* (1), agreement tokens involving an utterance with the word *agree* (17), expressions including *right* (31), expressions including *true* (9), *point* (2), *sure* (2). As Figure 6.4 shows, some agreement tokens are introduced and repeated rather frequently (e.g., *yeah*), while others only occur rarely in the input materials (e.g., *yup*). Overall, however, EFL learners are exposed to a variety of different agreement tokens over the years and thus should have frequent opportunity to acquire the most frequently included ones therefore enabling them to express their agreements with interlocutors in their L2.

6.4.1.3 Input: Disagreement Strategies As Figure 6.5 shows, the presentation of disagreement strategies in the input materials appears rather different than the presentation of agreement strategies in the same materials. While in the case of agreements, EFL learners were presented with more than thirty agreement tokens in the materials for years 1 and 2, there is a

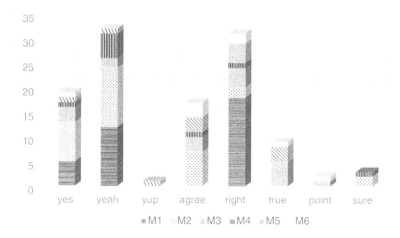

Figure 6.4 Agreement tokens in the input materials

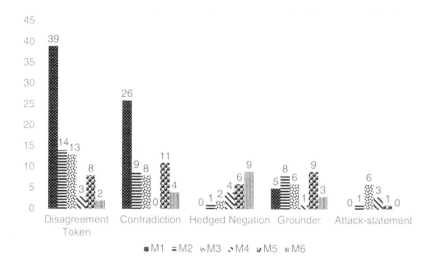

Figure 6.5 Disagreement strategies in the input materials

sharp drop in the number of disagreement tokens from year one to year 2. In addition, the number of contradictions included also decreases considerably from twenty-six to nine from year 1 to year 2. In contrast, the number of hedged negations steadily increase from zero in year 1 to nine in year 6. This could suggest a move away from more direct disagreement utterance towards more indirect utterances – a development that would be in line with developmental interlanguage pragmatic studies, which have shown a move from more direct to more indirect expressions in English (e.g., Rose, 2000, 2009). It also needs to be noted that disagreement tokens such as *no* are multi-functional and not solely restricted to the speech act of disagreement as defined in this study. *No* can also occur as response to a request and thus be part of a refusal, for example, A: 'Can you lend me these books?' B: 'No.', or an answer to a question for information, for example, A: 'Do you have a sister?', B: 'No', thus learners are likely to come across different utterances including *no* in their textbooks where *no* is not a disagreement token.

Another finding that needs to be addressed is the number of attack statements found in the teaching materials. While it may be somewhat unexpected to also encounter utterances that are likely to be considered impolite such as expressions that indicate doubt about an interlocutor's intelligence or belong to the taboo category, the inclusion of these items is in line with calls for teaching impoliteness in order ensure L2 learners' safety and expose them to authentic language (e.g., Mugford, 2008; Pizziconi & Locher, 2015). Attack statements may therefore provide EFL teachers and learners with valuable opportunities to discuss polite and appropriate language use in the L2. It also needs to be noted that the input materials include twice the amount of hedged negations (twenty-two) than attack statements (eleven) and that the materials in the final years focus more on hedged negations and less on attack statements, which means that the weighting in the input materials is clearly balanced towards the more indirect and polite disagreement strategies.

Similar to the discussion of input materials and agreements above, I will also address the individual disagreement tokens included in the teaching materials which are presented in Figure 6.6. The most striking finding here is the high number of disagreement tokens featuring *wrong* in the materials for year 1. In total, there are thirty-four disagreement instances included in the year 1 materials that contain the token *wrong*, which suggests that the textbook writers or the publishing house have placed much emphasis on teaching disagreements that contain this word. A possible explanation could be that the authors wanted to ensure that even beginner-level learners have the linguistic means to express their disagreement with something and deliberately included a very high number of these disagreement tokens in order to ensure that the learners have ample opportunity to acquire them.

The inclusion of *yes* may also be somewhat puzzling at first glance. However, when an individual disagrees with a negative utterance made by their interlocutor, then *yes* can also have the function of a disagreement token, for example, A: '*No, she can't.*' B: '*Yes, she can.*' Overall, the number of disagreement tokens included in the materials is smaller than the number of agreement tokens, seventy-nine and 114 respectively.

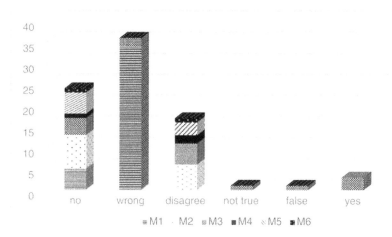

Figure 6.6 Disagreement tokens in the input materials

6.4.2   Results: Output

6.4.2.1 Output: Agreements   The agreement strategies used by the two groups of EFL learners in the individual scenarios are presented in Table 6.4. The results reveal that the overall number of strategies used in each individual scenario by members of the two groups are not drastically different in most cases, for example, in Scenario 1, members of year 8 employed sixty-four strategies, while members of year 10 employed sixty-seven strategies. In addition, the results show that members of both groups tended to use more than one strategy per scenario (cf. Table 6.1 for the total number of EFL learners in each group that provided agreements or disagreements in the individual scenarios).

Also, as already mentioned in Section 6.4.1.2, the EFL learners used a greater variety of agreement strategies than were provided in the input materials investigated. While the materials had only featured five agreement strategies (agreement tokens, same evaluation, downgraded evaluation, topic expander, knowledge marker), the EFL learners also used upgraded evaluations, rhetorical questions and perspective changes. This could indicate transfer from their L1 or a particular instructional focus not related to the textbook and audio materials. Concerning the agreement markers, it is interesting to note that both learner groups used the more formal *yes* considerably more frequently than the more informal *yeah*: (*yes*: year 8 (seventy-two instances), year 10 (seventy-three instances), *yeah*: year 8 (two instances), year 10 (six instances). This is

Table 6.4 *Output: agreement strategies used by the EFL learner groups*

Agree	S1Y8	S1Y10	S3Y8	S3Y10	S6Y8	S6Y10	S7Y8	S7Y10	S12Y8	S12Y10	TOTAL Y8	TOTAL Y10
AGT	29	26	22	25	19	20	10	10	20	27	**100**	**108**
Yes	*25*	*23*	*21*	*20*	*7*	*9*	*8*	*6*	*11*	*15*	*72*	*73*
Yeah	*1*	*1*	*1*	*3*	*0*	*1*	*0*	*0*	*0*	*1*	*2*	*6*
agree	*0*	*0*	*0*	*0*	*4*	*3*	*1*	*2*	*3*	*4*	*8*	*9*
True	*0*	*0*	*0*	*0*	*0*	*0*	*0*	*0*	*0*	*1*	*0*	*1*
Right	*3*	*2*	*0*	*2*	*8*	*7*	*1*	*2*	*6*	*6*	*18*	*19*
Same Eval.	18	28	17	24	16	10	19	20	22	15	**92**	**97**
Down. Eval.	0	0	3	1	0	2	0	0	2	1	**5**	**2**
Up. Eval	1	2	0	1	1	2	2	0	0	0	**4**	**5**
Topic ex.	14	11	19	18	3	3	14	8	1	5	**51**	**45**
Persp. c.	0	0	0	0	3	1	0	3	0	1	**3**	**5**
Rhet. q.	0	0	0	1	0	0	1	3	0	0	**1**	**4**
Know. m.	2	0	0	0	0	4	0	0	0	3	**2**	**7**
TOTAL	**64**	**67**	**61**	**70**	**42**	**40**	**46**	**44**	**45**	**52**	**258**	**273**

Notes: The total number of agreement tokens per year group is presented in the first line called Agreement tokens (AGT). The scenarios are abbreviated according to their number and year group, e.g., S2Y8 refers to scenario 2 completed by EFL learners in year 8. The different agreement strategies are abbreviated as follows: same evaluation (Same eval.), downgraded evaluation (Down. eval.), upgraded evaluation (Up. eval.), topic expander (Topic ex.), perspective change (Persp. c.), rhetorical question (Rhet. q.), knowledge marker (Know. m.).

interesting because the teaching materials feature a higher number of the informal *yeah* (thirty-two instances) than *yes* (nineteen instances).

A possible explanation for the higher use of the formal agreement token could be that EFL teachers may prefer formal over more informal options because they consider them more polite and thus emphasise them more when teaching. As a recent study (Schauer, 2019) on EFL teachers' reported use of pragmatic routines in primary EFL classrooms has shown, the more formal expression of gratitude *thank you* was used often by 93 per cent of the teachers, while only 36 per cent of them used *thanks* often. The same applied to *goodbye* (used often by 77 per cent of the teachers) compared to *bye* (used often by 38 per cent of the teachers). Since the more formal expressions tend to be appropriate and acceptable in a wide variety of situations and with a wide variety of interlocutors, emphasising them over the more informal options in the EFL classrooms has merit.

While there is no great difference in the agreement strategies used by the EFL learners, this does not mean that the actual agreement utterances of the two year groups do not show an increased L2 competence for the learners in the higher grade. The utterances produced by the year 8 learners tend to be shorter and less syntactically complex. In addition, they also often contain grammatical infelicities. The utterances by the year 10 learners often show a greater maturity and more advanced L2 competence. The following four examples from Scenario 3 ('Dog') representing female and male learners' responses from each group illustrate these points:

> *Yes, he is. I love dog.* (Y8F-ID805)
> *Yes, we have a lithel biger dog.* (Y8M-ID819)
>
> *Oh my god, what's your name? You're very beautiful dog. But sorry, you can't have a Sausage.* (Y10F-ID1012)
> *Ohh yeah! He's really cute. He looks a bit like my friends Dog Merlin.* (Y10M-ID1029)

Unfortunately, it is not possible to discuss the complexities of the different agreement utterances with regard to internal modification, grammatical correctness and idiomatic language here. However, what should be borne in mind is that while the use of strategy types is important in that it tells us something about learners' ability to employ different strategies to achieve their speech act aims, the overall effect an utterance has on an interlocutor may also be determined by a producer's grammatical and lexical/idiomatic competence. Thus, the interrelationship of L2 learners' productive competences in the areas of grammar and pragmatics should be researched in more depth in future studies (cf. Bardovi-Harlig, 2003).

Concerning the link between input and output materials, the data seem to show quite clearly that in the case of individual agreement tokens a low frequency with which individual tokens are presented is likely to result in limited or no use by the EFL learners. For example, none of the learners used an agreement token based on a 'point' expression, such as *good point*, and only one learner in year 10 used an agreement token that contained the word *true*. Both of these agreement tokens feature rarely in Lighthouse, with both only being introduced in year three and featuring two and nine times respectively in the whole series. A somewhat higher number of instances in the teaching materials could have resulted in a more varied use of agreement tokens by the EFL learners.

6.4.2.2 Output: Disagreements   As was the case for the EFL groups' strategy use in the agreement scenarios, there does not tend to be a great difference in the EFL groups' use of disagreement strategies as shown in Table 6.5. However, in contrast to the agreement strategies, the disagreement strategy results suggest that there are differences in the EFL learners' strategy choices that could be related to their respective proficiency levels in the L2. For example, grounders were used considerably more frequently by EFL learners in year 10 compared to EFL learners in year 8 (twenty-two and seven respectively).

In addition, year 10 learners used more questions than year 8 learners (twelve compared to three), and some strategies were only used by the year 10 learners: sympathy, perspective change, and consequence. These results may be related to the increasing grammatical complexity of the utterances that were produced by the learners in the higher grade. The interplay of grammatical and pragmatic competence can be seen in the following responses to Scenario 11 ('Kissing students'):

> *It isn't not bad. Let they do did.* (Y8F-ID803)
> *You are from yesterday? This is normaly okay.* (Y8F-ID815)
> *not so yuck* (Y8M-ID822)
> *Are you from yesterday* (Y8M-ID826)

> *Why so mad? They are in love. Let them kiss. It's not really a crime.* (Y10F-ID1004)
> *No they are in love. It's not inappropriate.* (Y10F-ID1016)
> *It's not Yuck it's Love laiter you now what i mean* (Y10M-ID1024)
> *Why it is so problematic for you? If they want to do this here they can do it here. As long as they don't do more here.* (Y10M-ID1027)

The utterances show that learners in year 8 are generally able to convey their opinions to their interlocutors, even if they struggle with some aspects related to grammar, which means that if their interlocutors are willing to overlook grammatical infelicities, the learners will be able to partake in conversations and exchange views. What is striking in the disagreement utterances produced by

Table 6.5 *Output: disagreement strategies used by the EFL learner groups*

Disagree	S2Y8	S2Y10	S5Y8	S5Y10	S11Y8	S11Y10	TOTAL Y8	TOTAL Y10
Disagreement Token	24	20	9	11	1	2	**34**	**33**
no	*11*	*11*	*9*	*10*	*1*	*2*	*21*	*23*
wrong	*9*	*4*	*0*	*1*	*0*	*0*	*9*	*5*
disagree	*4*	*0*	*0*	*0*	*0*	*0*	*4*	*0*
not true	*0*	*2*	*0*	*0*	*0*	*0*	*0*	*2*
false	*0*	*0*	*0*	*0*	*0*	*0*	*0*	*0*
not right	*0*	*3*	*0*	*0*	*0*	*0*	*0*	*3*
Contradiction	30	27	22	14	15	9	**67**	**50**
Hedged negation	1	3	4	1	1	5	**6**	**9**
Grounder	1	10	4	3	2	9	**7**	**22**
Attack Statement	1	0	4	5	1	0	**6**	**5**
General Statement	2	2	2	3	2	4	**6**	**9**
Attack-rhetorical question	0	2	0	2	4	0	**4**	**4**
Challenge	0	0	0	0	0	0	**0**	**0**
Command	1	0	8	4	6	7	**15**	**11**
Question	1	1	0	4	2	7	**3**	**12**
Sympathy	0	0	0	2	0	0	**0**	**2**
Consequence	0	0	0	1	0	0	**0**	**1**
Perspective change	0	0	0	5	0	0	**0**	**5**
TOTAL STRATEGIES	**61**	**65**	**53**	**55**	**34**	**43**	**148**	**163**

Notes: The total number of disagreement tokens per year group is presented in the first line called Disagreement tokens. The scenarios are abbreviated according to their number and year group, e.g., S2Y8 refers to Scenario 2 completed by EFL learners in year 8.

the year 8 learners in response to Scenario 11 is the use of some version of 'are you from yesterday', which was employed by four of the twenty-three learners that produced a disagreement in this scenario. None of the learners in year 10 used this expression and the expression was also only used by the year 8 learners in this scenario. It is likely that the learners translated the German expression *bist du / sind Sie von gestern?* – which can be a rather aggressive attack question – into English and thus made a negative transfer from their L1 to their L2. The fact that this expression was used by four learners, three females and one male, from this group suggests that this is an expression that is fashionable among the teenagers in this year group but not among the teenagers in year 10.

Concerning the interrelationship between the input from the Lighthouse materials and EFL learners' output, it is noticeable that the overall variety of disagreement tokens used by the EFL learners in both groups is rather small. This, however, is not surprising when the teaching materials are considered, since the tokens that are rather low or not present in the learner data, for example, *not true* (used by two learners in year 10) and *false* (not used by any learner), are also very rarely presented in the teaching materials: both feature once in year 3. Thus, formulaic disagreement token expressions, similar to formulaic agreement tokens expressions discussed in Section 6.4.2.1 should be focussed on more in the instructional materials.

6.5   Conclusion

The analysis of the EFL Lighthouse teaching materials for years 1–6 of German intermediate secondary school learners has shown that they consistently contain agreement and disagreement strategies and therefore enable L2 learners to encounter them repeatedly throughout their secondary school years. This is a good result. In addition, the materials also provided learners with examples of impolite disagreement utterances thereby answering the call to expose L2 learners to a wide variety of authentic language options, including options that may be considered taboo in order to prepare them for real-life communication situations. While the overall number of agreement and disagreement strategies was very similar, it was surprising that there was an inverse presentation of agreement and disagreement strategies in the two material types investigated: the textbooks contained 88 disagreement instances but only fifty-four agreement instances. In contrast, the audio materials contained only forty-seven disagreement instances but eighty-two agreement instances. It would be interesting to further investigate how this difference concerning number of instances in the materials is addressed in classrooms.

Somewhat disappointingly, the Lighthouse materials contained only a limited repertoire of (dis)agreement tokens, which meant that although EFL learners will encounter the two speech act types frequently, they may not acquire a very varied repertoire of formulaic expressions.

The benefit of teaching formulaic expressions is apparent when looking at the (dis)agreement utterances produced by the lower intermediate learners in year 8, which show that these learners still tend to struggle with producing grammatically correct utterances. Having analysed the data of this and also my recent study on teaching EFL in primary school (Schauer, 2019), my impression is that especially beginner and lower intermediate learners would benefit very much from formulaic sequences as those would enable them to better achieve their communicative goals without being weighed down by trying to process and assemble grammatically correct utterances. Focussed and easily processable language chunks could help learners produce more idiomatic output that enables them to express themselves better (see also Schauer &

Adolphs, 2006; Bardovi-Harlig, Mossman, & Vellenga, 2015; Bardovi-Harlig, 2019). That lower intermediate learners are potentially quite happy to work with set expressions seems clear from their negative transfer of the *are you from yesterday* expression in the disagreement scenarios. This willingness is something that materials writers and teachers could use to their advantage.

I also think that we need to involve in-service teachers more in interlanguage pragmatics research (cf. Cohen, 2018; Schauer, 2019). This is evident when looking at the findings of the cross-sectional developmental study and the EFL learners' (dis)agreement responses. Here it would have been enlightening to have had teachers' views on (dis)agreements, especially on their perceptions concerning teaching direct versus indirect and formal versus informal expressions.

Also, it would be helpful to learn more about the distribution of speech acts across different teaching materials that are available from state or commercial publishing houses. While some recent studies (e.g., Nguyen, 2011; Glaser, 2020; Schauer, 2020) have employed a textbook + approach (i.e., have analysed additional materials and not solely focussed on textbooks), this should be done more widely and connected to in-service teachers' actual use of different teaching materials in different classroom settings (e.g., primary, secondary, tertiary / adult) to explore what role textbooks and other materials play in different contexts. In addition, it would also be worthwhile to explore teacher's books and other materials made solely available to teachers to examine how pragmatic content is addressed there as done recently by Glaser (2020).

Moreover, it would also be interesting to learn more about L2 learners own use and evaluation of their teaching materials. For example, are certain texts revisited after they have been covered in the classroom because they were interesting or funny? Do jokes[6] and funny illustrations exemplifying certain language issues remain in learners' memory for a long time and are reactivated whenever learners encounter the language item thus making them useful for L2 learning? Are songs produced for learning the L2 that are included on audio CDs perceived as enjoyable and therefore sung in learners' spare time or perceived as rather tacky and embarrassing and never revisited? Are apps/digital resources available that accompany the materials – and if so, are they enjoyable, challenging but not too difficult and attractively designed, as well as affordable and easily available?

The link between the pragmatic input provided in instructional materials and L2 learners' output is not always clear-cut. In some instances, the link seems clearer when learners are not using certain strategies that are very infrequently presented than when they are actually using high-frequency strategies

---

[6] Whenever I hear the word *become* in English, I am reminded of a joke accompanied by a funny restaurant illustration in one of my secondary school English textbooks: A person in a restaurant asks the waiter 'When can I become my steak?' and the waiter replies 'I hope never, Sir!'. This short text illustrated the false friend relationship between the German verb *bekommen* [obtain, receive, get] and the English verb *become* well.

that can also easily be transferred from their L1 to their L2, such as *ja-yes* and *richtig-right*.

However, while transfer may play a role in L2 learners' use of strategies and expressions, the findings of the present investigation also show that the possibility of positive transfer combined with little/no representation of the transferable feature in the teaching materials tends to result in L2 learners not using the transferable feature. This is exemplified by the disagreement tokens *falsch/false* and *nicht richtig/not right* that would be good candidates for positive transfer. However, *false* was not used by any of the L2 learners, even though it would be easy to transfer from their L1 and *not right* was only used by three learners in year 10, although it again would have been easy to transfer. In the input materials *false* only features once and *not right* not at all. In contrast, *wrong* features thirty-four times in the teaching materials for year one and twice in the teaching materials for year 3. It was used by nine learners in year 8 and five learners in year 10 – this could be interpreted as suggesting a link between input and output also highlighting the importance of regular repetitions since the disagreement token was used more frequently by learners who had more recently encountered it.

Overall, I would argue that if we truly want to promote pragmatics as a key skill in L2 learners' communicative and intercultural competence, we need to obtain a better picture of what actually goes on in L2 classrooms and work more closely with in-service teachers and people / institutions in charge of curriculum development. In addition, if we want to help materials developers in making teaching materials as attractive and useful as possible, we also need to engage with L2 learners more to find out what their needs and preferences are.

Acknowledgements

I am grateful to D. Böhm for his assistance in this research project and the EFL learners who completed the questionnaires.

Dis(agreement) Questionnaire Scenarios

[due to copyright restrictions, the images accompanying the individual scenarios have not been included]

1) It's 6.40 in the morning. You go into the kitchen to have breakfast. Mrs. Miller is already in the kitchen and is putting food on the table. She wishes you good morning, then points towards the window and says: 'Look, the sun is shining! Isn't it a beautiful day today?'. You say: …

2) You are having a barbecue with your host family and a few friends from school. Everybody is eating and drinking and having fun. Then Mr. Miller says: 'I think I have heard that German people don't like barbecues.' You say: …

3) Half an hour later …. Attracted by the good smell of the sausages, the neighbours' new dog comes to the fence. Your host sister Lory says: 'Ooh …, look who is there. The neighbours' new dog is soo cute, isn't he?' You say: …

4) One hour later … Everybody is eating, there are Burgers, sausages, grilled corncobs, dips and salads. One of your friends from school turns to you and says: 'You know, I visited Germany with my family last year and I just loved the food there. I think it's MUCH better than the British food. Don't you think so, too?' You say: …

5) It is lunchbreak at school. You are outside with Emily, Sarah and Patrick, who are your classmates. You are just standing there eating your sandwich when Patrick starts teasing a younger boy. He calls him 'moron' [Idiot] and pushes him into a puddle [Pfütze]. Then he comes back to you and says: 'That was fun, wasn't it? Teasing the toddlers [Kleinkinder] is the best!' You: …

6) In the evening, you are watching *Britain's Got Talent* on TV [The British version of 'Das Supertalent']. Following a young girl's performance, Mrs. Miller says: 'Oh, my gosh! That girl sound terrible! She'll never make it to the next round!' You: …

7) After school, you walk to the bus stop with your friends Terry and Emily. You talk about your history teacher, Mr. Atkins, and about the homework he gave you. Terry says: 'Mr. Atkins must be crazy!! 5 pages about the Second World War in 3 days, this is absolutely impossible!' You say: …

8) One of your classmates stole a chocolate bar out of your schoolbag. At home, you tell Mrs. Miller about it. She gets very angry and says: Stealing from classmates is completely unacceptable! I will call your teacher straight away. Mr. Atkins will need to sort this out and inform the parents of the boy who did this!" You say: …

9) One day later, at school, the same boy comes to you during the break. He brought a chocolate bar for you and says: 'Hi, I want to apologise. Stealing your chocolate bar was wrong. Here, I brought a new one for you because I think we should rather be friends.' You say: …

10) It's 3 o'clock in the afternoon and you have just come home. You are very hungry, because you could not eat the sandwiches that Mrs. Miller prepared for your lunch (they had peanut butter on them and you are allergic to peanuts). When she realizes that, she says: 'Oh, my god! I totally forgot that. I'm sorry. I am so stupid. You must believe I'm a terrible host mother.' You say: …

11) A few days later, together with your friends you walk across the school yard. At the ping pong tables you see a boy and a girl from your parallel class

kissing. One of your friends says: 'Yuck! [Igitt!] Can't they do that in private? This is so inappropriate!' You say: …

12) After a very difficult physics test, you are standing in the corridor and talking with Emily, Sarah and Terry. Sarah says: 'What an awful test! Physics is really the most horrible subject ever!' You say: …

References

Alcón-Soler, E. (2005). Does instruction work for learning pragmatics in the EFL context? *System*, 33(3), 417–435.

Angouri, J., & Locher, M. (2012). Theorising disagreement. *Journal of Pragmatics*, 44(12), 1549–1553.

Bardovi-Harlig, K. (2001). Evaluating the empirical evidence. Grounds for instruction in pragmatics. In K. Rose & G. Kasper (eds.), *Pragmatics and Language Teaching*. Cambridge: Cambridge University Press, pp. 13–32.

Bardovi-Harlig, K. (2003). Understanding the role of grammar in the acquisition of L2 pragmatics. In A. Martinez-Flor, E. Usó Juan, & A. Fernandez Guerra (eds.), *Pragmatic Competence in Foreign Language Teaching* (pp. 25–44). Castelló de la Plana: Universitat Jaume I.

Bardovi-Harlig, I. (2019). Formulaic language in second language pragmatics research. In A. Siyanova-Chanturia & A. Pellicér-Sanchez (eds.), *Understanding Formulaic Language: A Second Language Acquisition Perspective*. Abingdon: Routledge, pp. 97–114.

Bardovi-Harlig, K., Mossman, S., & Vellenga, H. (2015). The effect of instruction on pragmatic routines in academic discussions. *Language Teaching Research*, 19(3), 324–350.

Barron, A. (2016). Developing pragmatic competence using EFL textbooks: Focus on requests. *Literacy Information and Computer Education Journal*, 7(1), 2172–2179.

Blum-Kulka, S., House, J., & Kasper, G. (1989). *Cross-Cultural Pragmatics: Requests and Apologies*. Norwood, NJ: Ablex.

Brown, P., & Levinson, S. C. (1987). *Politeness: Some Universals in Language Usage*. Cambridge: Cambridge University Press.

Cohen, A. D. (2018). *Learning Pragmatics from Native and Non-Native Language Teachers*. Bristol: Multilingual Matters.

Diepenbroek, L., & Derwing, T. (2013). To what extent do popular ESL textbooks incorporate oral fluency and pragmatic development? *TESL Canada Journal* 30(7), 1–20.

Ekin, M. T. Y. (2013). Do current EFL coursebooks work for the development of L2 pragmatic competence? The case of suggestions. *Procedia – Social and Behavioural Sciences*, 93, 1306–1311.

Ellis, G. (2014). 'Young learners' – clarifying our terms. *English Language Teaching Journal*, 68(1), 75–78.

Félix-Brasdefer, C. (2007). Pragmatic development in the Spanish FL classroom: A cross-sectional study of learner requests. *Intercultural Pragmatics*, 4(2), 253–286.

Fordyce, K. (2014). The differential effects of explicit and implicit instruction on EFL learners' use of epistemic stance. *Applied Linguistics*, 35(1), 6–28.

Glaser, K. (2014). *Inductive or Deductive? The Impact of Method of Instruction on the Acquisition of Pragmatic Competence in EFL.* Newcastle upon Tyne: Cambridge Scholars Publishing.

Glaser, K. (2020). Pragmatikvermittlung im Englischunterricht der Primarstufe: Der Sprechakt Begrüßen in Lehrplänen und Lehrwerken. In K. Glaser, & H. Limberg (eds.), *Pragmatische Kompetenzen im schulischen Fremdsprachenunterricht.* Frankfurt: Peter Lang Verlag, pp. 199–248.

House, J. (1996). Developing pragmatic fluency in English as a foreign language: Routines and metapragmatic awareness. *Studies in Second Language Acquisition*, 18, 225–252.

Halenko, N. (2021). *Teaching Pragmatics and Instructed Second Language Learning: Study Abroad and Technology-Enhanced Teaching.* London: Bloomsbury.

Jernigan, J. (2012). Output and English as a second language pragmatic development: The effectiveness of output-focused video-based instruction. *English Language Teaching*, 5(4), 2–14.

Johnson, F. (2006). Agreement and disagreement: A cross-cultural comparison. *BISAL*, 1, 41–76.

KMK (2003). *Beschlüsse der Kultusministerkonferenz: Bildungsstandards für die erste Fremdsprache (Englisch/Französisch) für den Mittleren Schulabschluss.* Sekretariat der Ständigen Konferenz der Kultusminister der Länder in der Bundesrepublik Deutschland. www.kmk.org/fileadmin/veroeffentlichungen_beschluesse/2003/2003_12_04-BS-erste-Fremdsprache.pdf.

Limberg, H. (2015). Teaching how to apologise: EFL textbooks and pragmatic input. *Language Teaching Research.*

Liew, S. T. (2016). Comparison of agreement and disagreement expressions between Malaysian and New Headway coursebooks. *Malaysian Journal of ELT Research*,12(1), 20–36.

Martinez Flor, A., & Alcón-Soler, E. (2007). Developing pragmatic awareness of suggestions in the EFL classroom: A focus on instructional effects. *Canadian Journal of Applied Linguistics*, 10(1), 47–76.

Mugford, G. (2008). How rude! Teaching impoliteness in the second language classroom. *ELT Journal*, 62(4), 375–384.

Nguyen, M. T. T. (2011). Learning to communicate in a globalised world: To what extent do school textbooks facilitate the development of intercultural pragmatic competence. *RELC Journal*, 42(1), 17–30.

Nguyen, M. T. T., Pham, T. H., & Pham, M. T. (2012). The relative effects of explicit and implicit form-focuses instruction on the development of L2 pragmatic competence. *Journal of Pragmatics*, 44(4), 416–434.

Ogiermann, E. (2010). Teaching politeness with Green Line New? In M. Engelhardt & W. Gehring (eds.), *Fremdsprachendidaktik: Neue Aspekte in Forschung und Lehre.* Oldenburg: BIS Verlag, pp. 117–134

Pizziconi, B., & Locher, M. (2015). *Teaching and Learning (Im)Politeness.* Berlin: De Gruyter Mouton.

Pomerantz, A. (1984). Agreeing and disagreeing with assessments: Some features of preferred /dispreferred turn shapes. In J. Maxwell Atkinson & J. Heritage (eds.), *Structures of Social Action.* Cambridge: Cambridge University Press, pp. 57–101

Ren, W., & Han, Z. (2016). The representation of pragmatic knowledge in recent ELT textbooks. *ELT Journal*, 70(4), 424–434.

Rose, K. R. (2000). An exploratory cross-sectional study of interlanguage pragmatic development. *Studies in Second Language Acquisition*, 22, 27–67.

Rose, K. R. (2009) Interlanguage pragmatic development in Hong Kong, phase 2. *Journal of Pragmatics*, 41, 2345–2364.

Sadeghidizaj, S. (2014). The Contribution of Explicit Instruction vs. Implicit Instruction to the Acquisition of Requests and Request Responses by EFL Students in Iran. Unpublished Doctoral Dissertation, Lancaster University.

Schauer, G. A. (2019). *Teaching and Learning English in the Primary School: Interlanguage Pragmatics in the EFL Context*. Cham: Springer.

Schauer, G. A. (2020). Lehrmaterialien für Sekundarschulschüler*innen mit speziellem Förderbedarf: eine kontrastive pragmatische Studie von Sprechakten in zwei Lehrwerken. In K. Glaser & H. Limberg (eds.), *Pragmatische Kompetenzen im schulischen Fremdsprachenunterricht*. Frankfurt: Peter Lang Verlag, pp. 249–275.

Schauer, G. A., & Adolphs, S. (2006). Expressions of gratitude in corpus and DCT data: Vocabulary, formulaic sequences, and pedagogy. *System*, 34(1), 119–134.

Schulportal Thüringen (n.d.). Englisch Grundschule. www.schulportal-thueringen.de/bildungbis10jahre/grundschule/englisch.

Seto, A. (2009). 'I Agree with You' – a corpus-based study of agreement. *3L: The Southeast Asian Journal of English Language Studies*, 15, 41–67.

Spencer-Oatey, H. (2002). Managing rapport in talk: Using rapport sensitive incidents to explore the motivational concerns underlying the management of relations. *Journal of Pragmatics*, 34, 529–545.

Spencer-Oatey, H. (2008). Face, (im)politeness and rapport. In H. Spencer-Oatey (ed.), *Culturally Speaking: Culture, Communication and Politeness Theory*. London: Continuum, pp. 11–47.

Uso-Juan, E. (2007). The presentation and practice of the communicative act of requesting in textbooks: Focusing on modifiers. In E. Alcón-Soler & M. P. Safont Jorda (eds.), *Intercultural Language Use and Language Learning*. Dordrecht: Springer, pp. 223–243.

Vellenga, H. (2004). Learning pragmatics from ESL & EFL textbooks: How likely? *TESL EJ*, 8(2).

Warga, M. (2004). *Pragmatische Entwicklung in der Fremdsprache: Der Sprechakt 'Aufforderung' im Französischen*. Tübingen: Gunter Narr.

7 'Learning to Say "No" in Different Ways'

Tracking EFL Learner Performance and Perceptions of Pragmatics Instruction in Mexico

Elizabeth Flores-Salgado and Nicola Halenko

7.1 Introduction

Like other speech acts, refusals are sensitive to a range of social variables such as gender, age, level of education, power, and social distance, but empirical studies on refusals appear less frequently than other speech acts such as requests, for instance. Refusal strategies are selected and deployed based upon cultural norms and values which may differ across languages. A refusal considered polite and appropriate in one language may be completely unacceptable or even insulting in another. Due to the nature of this speech act, the potential risk of threatening the addressee's face can increase if linguistic devices are not used appropriately. The production of refusals, therefore, requires high levels of both pragmalinguistic and sociopragmatic expertise on the part of the speaker, in order to accomplish a successful interaction and avoid unwelcome effects on the hearer. Examining and understanding potential causes of L2 miscommunication has important consequences for teaching learners how to avert unintended offence and communication breakdown in the L2.

This quasi-experimental study originates from a larger project focussing on the benefits of technology for teaching speech acts in the classroom (Halenko & Flores Salgado, 2019). This chapter analyses the subset of refusal data to examine to what extent explicit instruction enhances L2 English learners' production of refusal strategies and modification devices. The following research questions frame this investigation:

1. Is there a difference in refusal production as a result of an explicit instructional intervention?
2. What are the participants' perceptions of the pragmatics training for producing refusals in English?

Since politeness is an important variable to successfully deploying refusals but notions of politeness have also been shown to vary cross-culturally, the refusal data in this study are examined against notions of politeness theory based on Scollon and Scollon (2001). In more recent times, L2 pragmatics research is increasingly situated within notions of interactional and intercultural competencies which better reflect the shared goals, social actions and co-constructed understanding of modern-day language users. Similar developments highlighting the importance of the interaction process can also be found in politeness research. The discursive approach, for instance, aims to recognise the complexities of operationalising politeness, accounting for participant interaction and interlocutor interpretations of what actually constitutes politeness in particular communicative encounters, as opposed to pre-determined theoretical views (Van Der Bom & Mills, 2015). While the authors in the present study acknowledge these developments, this study adopts the more traditional view of politeness as a more suitable fit for measuring instructional effects in a pre-test/post-test design. In this way, established taxonomies of refusal moves provide a useful pedagogical template for instruction, against which the presence or absence of these linguistic features can be measured to determine instructional effects. Section 7.2, therefore, first considers some of the well-established theoretical concepts and empirical research related to this more traditional view of politeness, as relevant to the Mexican culture within which this study is based.

7.2   Background to Research

7.2.1   *Theoretical Framework: Politeness*

Empirical research on Mexican Spanish politeness has re-examined the notion of face. Some perspectives question Brown and Levinson's (1987) universal vision of politeness and face and propose that the cultural aspects of societies have not been fully considered. Based on Scollon and Scollon's (2001) two notions of face involvement (the need to be considered as a supporting member of a group) and independence (the need to emphasise the individuality of participants), Félix-Brasdefer (2009) claims that, in Mexican culture, involvement and independence have two sociopragmatic manifestations: *respeto* (respect) and *confianza* (trust). Respect, as a manifestation of independence, is associated with the recognition of the speaker's hierarchy and the social distance involved in order to indicate the formality of the situation (Covarrubias, 2002). Respect is shown by using indirect strategies, making minimal assumptions, giving options to the interlocutor, and using formal names, titles and the pronoun *usted* (the formal form of you). These forms are commonly found in asymmetric situations (in which either the speaker or interlocutor has more authority) and deference-symmetric situations (featuring a distant relationship between interlocutors). Meanwhile, face involvement shows *confianza* manifests in familiarity, freedom of action, and frankness, and is realised by such discourse strategies as paying attention to others, claiming group membership, using first names or nicknames, and using the pronoun *tu* (the informal form of you). Both aspects of face, *respeto* and *confianza*, are governed by the external and internal situational factors involved in the interaction, and by the cultural expectations established by the members of a particular culture. The present study examines the refusal data against Félix-Brasdefer's (2009) concepts of *respeto* and *confianza* because they specifically link to the Mexican participant community recruited for this study.

7.2.2 Refusals

The speech act of refusing is of interest in pragmatics study due to its notorious face-threatening nature (Brown & Levinson, 1987). A refusal is classified as a commissive speech act because the speaker commits himself not to carry out the action proposed by the interlocutor (Searle, 1969). It is part of an adjacency pair that consists of two sequences. The first part of the sequence can be an invitation, an offering, a suggestion, or a request (Gass & Houck, 1999, Martínez-Flor & Usó-Juan, 2010). The second part is a response that can be an acceptance, which is the preferred act (Pomerantz, 1984) or a refusal which is the dispreferred act. Unlike acceptances, refusals are both high-risk and face-threatening acts. Refusals contradict the hearer's expectations (Allami & Naeimi, 2011; Goffman, 1967) and threaten the hearer's positive face because the negative response may indicate that the speaker does not care about his/ her wants (Brown & Levinson, 1987). In addition, for spoken communication, as the refusal is a second pair part of a conversation sequence, extensive planning is not an option. Therefore, refusals are complex speech acts that include various strategies to carry out different levels of directness, indirectness and degrees of politeness. The main communicative purposes of refusals are to avoid offending one's interlocutors, to negotiate a satisfactory outcome, and to save each other's face (Gass & Houck, 1999; Eslami, 2010).

Refusals are speech acts that can be realised by selecting one or multiple strategies. Beebe, Takahashi, and Uliss-Weltz's (1990) identification of different refusal strategy types still remains the most used and cited taxonomy (Bella, 2014; Félix-Brasdefer, 2008a; Gass & Houck, 1999; Nelson et al., 2002). Following this scheme, refusals are grouped into two main categories with accompanying subcategories: direct (characterised by means of negative propositions) or indirect (the use of forms that can be contextually identified as refusals). Direct refusals encompass two substrategies: flat 'No' or negation (e.g., 'Sorry, I can't go'). Indirect refusals, on the other hand, comprise ten different substrategies: mitigated refusal (e.g., 'I don't think I can'), reason/explanation (e.g., 'I already have plans'), indefinite reply (e.g., 'I can't promise anything'), promise to comply (e.g., 'I promise I'll make it up to you'), regret/apology (e.g., 'I'm sorry'), alternative (e.g., 'Maybe we can go next week?'), postponement (e.g., 'Do you mind if we go another time?'), set condition for future acceptance (e.g., 'We'll have to do something later'), set condition for past acceptance (e.g., 'I wish you would've told me earlier'), or request for additional information (e.g., 'Have you bought the tickets already?').

A refusal can also be modified to mitigate or weaken its illocutionary force by expressing subjectivity, tentativeness, hesitation, or lack of commitment. Modifications items are optional and can be embedded within the refusal. Internal modification devices are classified as lexical/phrasal expressions: understaters, subjectivisers, downtoners, cajolers, appealers, and solidarity markers (Félix-Brasdefer, 2008b). On the other hand, adjuncts to refusals (strategies that cannot be recognised as refusals, but they can downgrade the force of this face threatening act by expressing involvement with the interlocutor) are modifiers located outside the refusal head acts. These external modifiers can be considered supportive moves and are classified into four substrategies: positive opinion, willingness, expression of gratitude, and agreement (Beebe et al., 1990; Bella, 2014).

Refusals have been empirically examined by a number of cross-cultural studies across a range of languages: Japanese (Beebe et al., 1990; Kondo, 2008), Mandarin (Liao & Bresnahan, 1996), Iranian (Allami & Naeimi, 2011), Spanish (Félix-Brasdefer, 2008b), Egyptian Arabic (Nelson et al., 2002), Korean (Kwon, 2004), English (Turnbull, 2001; Turnbull & Saxton, 1997). These studies have examined the linguistic resources required for formulating a refusal in a particular language and the contextual and sociocultural variables that govern the selection of a certain pragmalinguistic choice appropriate to a particular speech situation.

To date, empirical research has shown that the degree of directness, the selection and content of refusal strategies, and the sensitivity of social variables can vary from culture to culture. As an example of cross-cultural variation between L1 Mexican and L1 American cultures, Félix-Brasdefer (2008b) found much variation in the trends of refusal behaviour. L1 Mexican Spanish speakers showed a preference for lengthy negotiations and elaborate responses in formal interactions. Similarly, greater attempts at negotiation, in the form of post-refusals to soften negative effects of the undesirable response, were more common in his L1 Spanish data. By contrast, L1 American English speakers typically employed most of their polite refusal strategies in informal interactions, producing fewer polite strategies with status-unequals. Pre-refusals, to delay the main refusal act and avoid a direct confrontation with the interlocutor, were also more frequent in the L1 English data. The data confirmed differing perceptions of social status between the two cultures when interacting with status unequals, intimates and strangers. While L1 Mexican Spanish speakers preferred to use indirectness (greater respect) with a person of higher status (+P) and use directness with an equal speaker (-SD), L1 American English speakers had a strong preference for directness in both face systems and with a person of equal and higher status.

The acquisition of refusals by language learners has also been analysed by several interlanguage (Beebe et al., 1990; Bella, 2011; Gass & Houck, 1999; Félix-Brasdefer, 2003) and developmental studies (Allami & Naeimi, 2011; Bardovi-Harlig & Hartford, 1993; Bella, 2014; Félix-Brasdefer, 2008b; Takahashi & Beebe, 1987). These studies have demonstrated that the production of refusals can be a challenge for language learners due to lack of linguistic resources, sociocultural knowledge and pragmatic ability in the target language (Martínez-Flor & Usó-Juan, 2010). The performance of this speech act requires the learners to reach a stage at which they are able to negotiate a refusal by selecting the appropriate semantic formulae and employing different degrees of politeness appropriate to a particular situation (Eslami, 2010). Pedagogical intervention has been repeatedly recommended to help learners overcome such challenges, as examined in the Section 7.2.3.

7.2.3   Teaching L2 Refusals

The teaching of L2 refusals can be enhanced by taking into consideration findings from cross-cultural and developmental pragmatics. Pragmatic instruction can be planned based on understanding the learners' existing knowledge derived from their first language, and through understanding that not all students follow the same path towards achieving appropriate language use. To our knowledge, intervention studies of this kind with Latin American (specifically, Mexican) learners of English have yet to be explored. In the absence of such data, what follows is a review of the limited number of intervention studies which have focussed on enhancing refusal production of (peninsular) Spanish-speaking learners of English. Such studies offer insights into common challenges when mapping L1 knowledge to L2 practices and provide evidence-based suggestions as to how refusals can be best taught. In this way, practitioners can effectively maximise limited class time to advance learners' pragmatic awareness and production of this highly frequent, but notoriously complex, speech act.

Analysing the underexplored area of cognitive processes, Alcón Soler and Guzmán-Pitarch (2010) employed individual retrospective verbal reports to ascertain instructional effects of refusals. Learners received twelve hours of spaced, explicit instruction which was contextualised through scenes from the American TV series *Stargate*. Before and after instruction, ninety-two Spanish university students completed an oral interview task requiring the production of a refusal to a request. In subsequent verbal reports, learners were asked to explain and give reasons behind the planning and execution of the refusal during these tasks. The authors deemed the awareness-raising approach adopted in the explicit instruction to be a success as measured by the cognitive changes in behaviour pre-test and post-test. Specifically, the verbal reports indicated the learners attended to broader pragmalinguistic and sociopragmatic issues post-instruction but showed less concern for linguistic issues such as grammar, vocabulary, and pronunciation.

Employing the same dataset, Alcón Soler and Guzmán-Pitarch (2013) measured the learners' use of refusal strategies and changes in success of negotiating refusals pre- and post-instruction. Results showed the positive influence of instruction as indicated by the statistically significant changes across all measures. At the pre-test, direct refusal strategies and avoidance strategies were the most common options but by the post-test stage, a trend towards indirectness, and a reduction of avoidance and directness could be observed. Learners produced more varied and frequent indirect refusal strategies post-instruction, in addition to embedding a greater range and number of adjuncts to accommodate the non-compliant nature of refusals.

Usó-Juan's (2013) intervention study with ten low-intermediate Spanish EFL university students also reported similar learning outcomes following six hours of explicit instruction on refusals. An interactive written discourse completion task (DCT) captured post-test decreases in directness and increases in the use and variety of indirect refusal strategies and adjuncts.

Since none of these studies employed a non-instructed control group, however, the true effectiveness of these interventions cannot be entirely verified. The present study adopted a Control group to measure evidence of gains more accurately, in addition to including a qualitative dimension through participant interviews (see also Chapter 2, this volume). A full account of the study design is outlined in the Section 7.3.

7.3   Method

7.3.1   *Participants*

Thirty Mexican Spanish language learners of English (19–22 years of age) participated in the study. Participants were native speakers of Mexican Spanish and natives of the state of Puebla, Mexico. They were low-intermediate undergraduate students (approximate TOEFL score 510) studying in their second year of English Teaching as a Foreign Language at the Benemérita Universidad Autónoma de Puebla, Mexico. The participants were divided into an Experimental (n=15) and Control (n=15) group for comparison purposes. The former received ten hours of explicit instruction on English refusals, while the latter received only general EFL instruction. Both groups participated voluntarily and were offered the opportunity to gain extra credit on their midterm exams.

7.3.2   Data Collection Instruments

At the start of the study, a background questionnaire collected personal data to examine group homogeneity. Following this, the main instructional phase consisted of ten hours of explicit instruction over a four-week period. The study adopted a pre-test-post-test design to analyse the extent of instructional gains within and between the two groups. Finally, individual participant interviews were conducted post-instruction to ascertain learners' perceptions of the pragmatics training for enhancing their ability to produce refusals in L2 English. The three research instruments (background questionnaire, oral production tasks, and semi-structured participant interviews), in addition to the instructional procedure, are summarised below.

7.3.2.1 Background Questionnaire   All the English language participants completed an initial background questionnaire. The purpose was to ensure group homogeneity and to achieve optimum comparability among the groups so that differences could not be attributed to variables other than those being studied. The survey of twelve questions, presented in the mother tongue of the language learners (Spanish), elicited personal and educational information, L2 linguistic proficiency and previous study abroad experience. The two groups of learners did not differ significantly in any of the variables, contained individuals from both urban and suburban areas, and males and females were equally represented in each group. Gender was not a variable examined in this study.

7.3.2.2 Oral Production Tasks (Pre-Test and Post-Test)   A computer-animated production task (CAPT) collected the data at the pre-test (before instruction), and post-test (after instruction) stages. The success of the CAPT for teaching and testing L2 pragmatics has been established in previous studies (Economidou-Kogetsidis & Halenko, 2022; Halenko, 2018, 2021; Halenko & Jones, 2017; Halenko et al., 2019). The CAPT analysed the oral productive pragmatic ability of the learners and utilised an interactive computerised presentation format that offers similar advantages to role plays. A role play involves the presence and participation of two interlocutors, most commonly a learner and a second person. In the case of the CAPT, one is a virtual (animated) participant and the other is the learner. The CAPT included four refusal situations that were especially designed for the college participants in this study and represented different social situations focussing on this speech event: (1) refusing a friend's request to borrow a car; (2) refusing an employer's request to work extra hours; (3) refusing a classmate's request for study help; (4) refusing a professor's request to change a scheduled appointment.

Each situation in the CAPT was presented through a series of animated slides that provided rich audio and visual contextual information (Figure 7.1). The test

Situation 2

Your boss asks you if you can work extra hours this weekend but you have already made plans.

You say?

Figure 7.1 An example refusal scenario on the computer-animated production task (CAPT)

followed a read, listen, and speak process. Each slide contained a brief description of the situation written in English that explained the setting, the social distance between the interlocutors, and their relative status. This information allowed an opportunity for the respondents to understand the context to be able to provide an appropriate response in English. In addition, it ensured the adequate comprehension of the task and scenarios. According to Schauer (2009), it is important to give participants time to think about what they are going to say because this is something that we commonly do in a real-life situation. The slides also included an audiovisual element in the form of a virtual interlocutor who initiated the conversation. Respondents were asked to imagine themselves interacting in the prescribed scenario and respond to the interlocutor's preceding turn. The expectation was for the learners to supply an appropriate refusal to each situation.

The social situations represented in the scenarios took into account the two variables *power* and *distance* which have been shown to be important in determining speech act performance (Brown & Levinson, 1987; Byon, 2004; Félix-Brasdefer, 2008b; Rose, 2000). Distance was treated as binary-valued; either they knew one another or did not know one another (acquaintances [A], or strangers [S]). The social power also considered two possible values: status equal [=] or speaker dominant [SD]. Gender of speakers in the initial turns was considered and varied randomly across all situations. However, the purpose of the study was not to investigate this variable.

7.3.2.3 Participant Interviews Oral interviews were included to corroborate the findings of the production data and to ascertain the learners' perceptions of and motivation for pragmatics instruction. The interviews with the Experimental group took place immediately after the completion of the post-test. The researchers focussed on three aspects (language production, language instruction, and materials) and posed ten fixed questions presented in the mother tongue of the language learners (Spanish) to guide the activity. Sample questions related to evaluating the ease or difficulty of producing refusals during the tests (language production), identifying the most memorable aspects of the explicit input (language instruction) and assessing the usefulness of the online activities for language practice (language materials). All interviews were recorded and transcribed for analysis.

7.3.3   Instructional Phase

In order to analyse the extent of instructional gains, only the Experimental group participated in the ten hours of pragmatics training. Usó-Juan's (2010) teaching framework guided the planning of the online activities which include a five-step phase of L1 exploration, L2 exploration, awareness-raising, language practice and learner feedback. Four online activities were specifically designed to reflect this teaching framework (see Halenko & Flores-Salgado, 2019 for more detail). Firstly, scenes from two films, *Me before You* and *The King's Speech*, were employed to demonstrate how refusals were employed by native speakers of English. Post-observational discussions then facilitated a comparison of learners' L1 and target language pragmatic norms. Secondly, matching column exercises were used to identify common L2 refusal strategies. The strategies used in the exercises were based on the refusal taxonomy proposed by Beebe et al. (1990). By using the free software Hot potatoes, three exercises for refusals were created for language practice which involved learners matching semantic descriptions with refusal expressions. As a third activity type, using the Hot potatoes software again, eight multiple choice refusal situations were designed to raise learners' pragmatic awareness by addressing comprehension of several refusal expressions. In both cases, immediate feedback was provided by clicking the 'check' button. As a final activity, eight open role plays were employed to practise the refusal strategies. Here, learners worked collaboratively to focus on form and meaning in their selection of situationally appropriate refusal strategies. The activity also allowed the learners to consolidate what they had already learned, and instructor feedback was provided.

7.3.4   Data Collection Procedure

Prior to instruction, the Experimental and Control groups completed the background questionnaire and attended a short training session on using the CAPT. Following this, both groups participated in the pre-test which acted as a baseline indicator of their current ability to produce appropriate refusals in English. All tests were supervised and involved learners recording their oral responses on their mobile phones and emailing these to the researcher immediately following the test. The Experimental group then participated in ten hours of explicit instruction on formulating refusals in English, as well as understanding the relevant cross-cultural differences which may influence language choice. The thirty-minute classes were delivered five days a week over a four-week period.

Following instruction (a month after the pre-test), the Experimental and Control groups completed a post-test version of the CAPT which contained the same situations, for comparison purposes, but were presented in a different order to avoid test effects. Only the Experimental group participated in an interview following the post-test to capture their thoughts on the learning experience. All the oral responses were transcribed for analysis.

7.3.5   Data Analysis

The data were subject to a linguistic analysis of the refusal formulaic sequences employed and were classified according to a modified version of Beebe et al.'s (1990) and Félix-Brasdefer's (2008a) taxonomy of refusal strategies (direct refusals, indirect refusals, and adjuncts to refusals). Responses of twenty native speakers of English in a relevant study (Félix-Brasdefer, 2008a) were reviewed for evidence of common components of speech act sets to establish a set of baseline responses.

Descriptive statistics in SPSS were used to compute the frequency of semantic formulas (direct, indirect, and adjuncts) to address the first research question. The statistical tests used to examine the data were one-way ANOVAs since the data were normally distributed. For all analyses in the study, the alpha level was set at 0.05. Besides the researchers, the data were coded by a third coder, a native English-speaking postgraduate student from the language Department in Mexico. A 96 per cent match was achieved between the third coder and that of the researchers. The discrepancies noted were discussed by the coders and a consensus was reached. The qualitative interview data were thematically analysed according to the second research question on participants' perceptions of the pragmatics training. Both sets of results are presented in the following section.

7.4   Results

This section first presents the results for research question 1 concerning the degree of change in refusal production based on the pragmatics-focussed instruction. These findings are presented quantitatively in regard to frequency, distribution, and strategy use (direct strategies, indirect strategies, and adjuncts). This is followed by examining the results for research question

Table 7.1 *Refusal strategies employed by the Control and the Experimental groups*

Strategies	Control (n=15)		Experimental (n=15)	
Direct	Pre-Test	Post-Test	Pre-Test	Post-Test
Flat	0 (0%)	0 (0%)	2 (1.1%)	0 (0%)
Negation of a proposition	11 (7%)	10 (6.1%)	13 (7.5%)	12 (5.1%)
Negative ability	21 (13.4%)	18 (11%)	25 (14.4%)	22 9.3%)
Total direct	**32 (20.4%)**	**28 (17.2%)**	**40 (23%)**	**34 (14.4%)**
Indirect				
Mitigated refusal	13 (8%)	13 (8.3%)	18 (10.3%)	38 (16.1%)
Explanations	41 (26.1%)	47 (28.8%)	45 (25.9)	69 (29.2%)
Indefinite reply	1 (0.6%)	4 (2.5%)	1 (0.6%)	2 (0.8)
Promise to comply	2 (1.3%)	1 (0.6%)	2 (1.1%)	0 (0%)
Regret/apology	36 (22.9%)	34 (20.9%)	41 (23.6%)	41 (17.4%)
Alternative	26 (16.6%)	24 (14.7%)	17 (9.8%)	17 (7.2%)
Postponement	0 (0%)	2 (1.2%)	0 (0%)	0 (0%)
Set condition for future acceptance	0 (0%)	1 (0.6%)	0 (0%)	4 (1.7%)
Set condition for past acceptance	1 (0.6%)	0 (0%)	0 (0%)	1 (0.4%)
Request for additional information	0 (0%)	1 (0.6%)	1 (0.6%)	5 (2.1%)
Total indirect	**120 (76.4%)**	**127 (77.9%)**	**125 (71.8%)**	**177 (75%)**
Adjuncts				
Positive opinion	1 (0.6%)	1 (0.6%)	2 (1.1%)	5 (2.1%)
Willingness	3 (1.9%)	3 (1.8%)	4 (2.3%)	11 (4.7%)
Gratitude	0 (0%)	1 (0.6%)	0 (0%)	0 (0%)
Empathy	0 (0%)	1 (0.6%)	1 (0.6%)	3 (1.3%)
Request for clarification	1 (0.6%)	0 (0%)	2 (1.1%)	5 (2.1%)
Agreement	0 (0%)	2 (1.2%)	0 (0%)	1 (0.4%)
Total adjuncts	**5 (3.2%)**	**8 (4.9%)**	**9 (5.2%)**	**25 (10.6)**
Total strategies	**157 (100%)**	**163 (100%)**	**174 (100%)**	**236 (100%)**

2 concerning the learners' perceptions of pragmatics study and tools used. The learner interview data is presented qualitatively and ascertains their perceptions of which activities were helpful in understanding refusals in English.

7.4.1   Refusals: Direct Strategies, Indirect Strategies, and Adjuncts (RQ1)

The distribution of direct strategies, indirect strategies, and adjuncts between the Experimental and Control groups across the different situations in the pretest and post-test stages is displayed in Table 7.1. The number of strategies or semantic formulae were distributed across twenty-one coding strategies.

Table 7.2 *Experimental and Control groups' pre-test and post-test variance of refusal strategies*

Source of Variation	SS	df	MS	F	P-value	F crit
Between Groups	124.3214	1	124.3214	8.55606	0.007054	4.225201
Within Groups	377.7857	26	14.53022			
Total	**502.1071**	**27**				

As Table 7.1 shows, the Experimental group in the post-test displayed the highest number of strategies (n=236) while the Control group in the pre-test exhibited the lowest number (n=157). Based on the results in Table 7.1, it can be observed that indirect strategies and mainly adjuncts were employed more by the Experimental group in the post-test than the Control group in the same test.

Table 7.2 presents the means and standard deviations for the use of these strategies in the four different situations. Analyses of variance were used to detect the effects of instruction on the subjects' choice of refusal strategies. Table 7.2 displays the results for all speakers' overall performance of these strategies.

As shown in Table 7.2, the Experimental and the Control group used refusal strategies differently (F=8.55, $p<0.0070$). Post hoc Tukey tests indicated that the Experimental group used significantly more strategies in the post-test than in the pre-test and more than the Control group in the pre-test and post-test.

The performance of the Experimental and Control groups on the four refusal situations in the pre-test and post-test can be observed in Table 7.3 and Figure 7.2.

Table 7.3 indicates a significant effect of improvement of the Experimental group from the pre-test (M=12.43) to the post-test (M=16.86). However, no significant improvement of the Control group was attested between the pre-test (M=11.21) and the post-test (M=11.64) who employed similar frequencies of strategies in both tests.

Figure 7.2 shows that the number and variety of refusal strategies used by the Experimental group in the post-test increased with respect to the pre-test. On the contrary, no significant differences were exhibited by the Control group between the pre-test and post-test. Figure 7.2 displays some differences between the two groups in regard to the distribution of strategies across the four situations. The Experimental group participants were able to distribute their strategies evenly in the various episodes in the post-test. In other words, they were able to use a bigger number and variety of strategies in different situations in the post-test. This distribution is represented in Figure 7.2. Therefore, it seems that only the Experimental group showed a significant effect of improvement over time in pragmatic performance.

Table 7.3 *Descriptive statistics of students' test performances*

Strategies	Control				Experimental			
	Pre-Test		Post-Test		Pre-Test		Post-Test	
	M	SD	M	SD	M	SD	M	SD
Direct	2.29	1.62	2.00	1.07	2.86	1.42	2.43	1.44
Indirect	8.57	2.47	9.07	2.34	8.93	4.09	12.64	5.68
Adjunct	0.36	0.72	0.57	0.62	0.64	0.93	1.79	1.58
Total	**11.21**	**2.68**	**11.64**	**3.11**	**12.43**	**5.00**	**16.86**	**7.29**

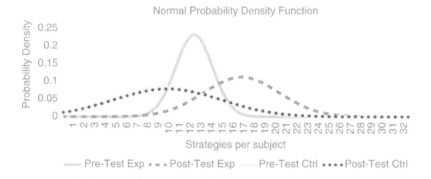

Figure 7.2 Performance of the Control and Experimental group in the pre-test and post-test

As shown in Table 7.1, very few instances of direct strategies were employed by the two groups. No significant differences were calculated between the Experimental and Control group in the pre-test and post-test (F= (0.052), $p <.819$). However, differences in preference for strategy use can be noticed at each level of formality (status-equal and status-unequal). The two informal situations: Borrowing the car (Situation 1) and Student help (Situation 3) involved a solidarity politeness system. The structure of the refusals differed in the two groups in the post-test. Whereas the Experimental group produced a higher proportion of more target-like direct strategies in these two situations of informal status (Example 1), the Control group employed direct strategies in formal and informal status situations (Example 2). This result is in line with Félix-Brasdefer's (2008b) study in which English speakers had a strong preference for directness in equal status situations. It is also important to mention that participants of both groups preferred the negative ability strategy (I can't go) as can be observed in the following examples.

(1) Sorry my friend, but I guess I can't borrow my car because I will use it (2EW, Situation 1 -D-P[1])

(2) Err, am sorry tutor bu' I have afraid I cannot do that. Err, can we rearrange it, erm, another day or … something like that if you … if you want to? (15CM, Situation 4, +D+P[2])

Turning now to indirect strategies, the Experimental group used significantly more than the Control group (F= (5.02), p <0.033). An increase in the number and the variety of indirect strategies was attested by the Experimental group, particularly in the two formal unequal Situations 2 and 4 (where a person of lower status (employee, students) performed a refusal to a person of higher status (boss, tutor)). While the Control group employed significantly less indirectness than the Experimental group for Situation 2 (work meeting during lunch time) (M=2) and for Situation 4 (tutor meeting) (M=2.5), the Experimental group used more indirect strategies for situation 2 (M=9.14) and for situation 4 (M=3). Important differences emerged in regard to the type of indirect strategies employed by the two groups. Specifically, in Situation 2, the results showed that when refusing a boss's request, the Experimental group used more target-like mitigated refusal and explanations/reasons strategies (Example 3) than the Control group (Example 4), while in Situation 4, the same group employed more explanations/reasons and regret/apology strategies (Example 5) than the Control group (Example 6) in the post-test. This result lends support to Beebe et al.'s (1990) finding that English speakers preferred to offer an explanation when they used a refusal.

(3) I'mm … ssss-sorry but I don't think that I could go. Err … erm I'm really sorry, I guess. I don't think I could go. Sorry. (13EM, Situation 2)

(4) Erm, I don't know. I think it's a bad idea to a meeting in the lunch hour. Err … we need to eat an' we need energy to work, so maybe you can change the hour to arrange the meeting an' … maybe we will available. (7CW, Situation 2)

(5) I am really sorry professor but I have another class, so I, it cannot happen in this class because I have going to, err, to do my exam. (1EM, Situation 4)

(6) Err, I don't have free time to 'rerange' your schedule. Err … I, I have, I have many classes and I … I, I, I have to go home in a hurry. I don't think, that I can. (13CW, Situation 4)

In addition, the Experimental group showed more post-test contextual sensitivity. This increased awareness was evident in their selection of different

[1] Participant 2, Experimental group, female, Situation 1, -Distance -Power.
[2] Participant 15, Control group, male, Situation 4, +Distance +Power.

strategies according to different situation variables. The following strategies were all employed more frequently in the post-test stage: Situation 1 (borrowing the car), explanations (M=21); Situation 2 (work meeting), mitigated refusals (M=47); Situation 3 (refusing a classmate's request for study help), increased regrets/apologies (M=15); and Situation 4 (tutor meeting) increased explanations (M=15). In contrast, the Control group relied almost exclusively on reasons/explanations and apologies as mitigators in all situations. It is worth noting, however, that no frequent use of set condition of future acceptance or set condition of past acceptance was attested in the performance of either group. The lack of frequency of these strategies was probably due to the low-level proficiency of the participants. Bella's (2014) study showed that these two strategies appeared at the advanced level.

Finally, four qualitative differences in respect to the content and phrasing of certain indirect strategies were observed. First, the findings showed that both groups relied on reasons/explanations and apologies in all situations. However, the Experimental group used the expression of regret 'I'm sorry' that sometimes they upgraded with one or more adverbial intensifiers or repeated it more than once to upgrade the remorse. Second, although reasons/explanations were the most frequent strategy in the data of the two groups in all situations in both tests, a marked difference involved the content of the Experimental group as compared to the Control group's explanations in Situation 4 (+P,+D). While learners in the Experimental group employed various reasons/explanations for not being able to attend to the tutorial meeting ('I have another class', 'I have plans'), the Control group opted more for explanations concerning family issues ('I have a family emergency', 'I have to go home in a hurry'). Third, as mentioned before, the distribution and selection of indirect strategies depended on the contextual situations. The Experimental group opted more for explanations and alternatives in Situations 1 and 3 (-P,-D), whereas they used explanations and mitigated refusals in 2 and 4 (+P,+D). Fourth, the Experimental group's explanations were found to be more specific, elaborate, and appropriate than those of the Control group in all situations. The latter group's explanations and contributions turned out to be vague and often blunt in certain circumstances, specifically in Situations 2 and 4 where participants of this group opted for expressions such as 'I think it is a bad idea', 'I disagree ...', that are direct, and thus giving an impression of abruptness and disrespect in these contextual circumstances. These findings have certain implications for both the sociopragmatic and the general interlanguage development of the learners.

In regard to adjuncts, the Experimental group were the highest performing group, using adjuncts significantly more frequently in all situations: (M=.3) for Situation 1 (borrow car), (M=.78) for Situation 2 (lunch meeting), (M=.64) for Situation 3 (student help), and (M=.5) for Situation 4 (tutor meeting). It is important to mention that the number of adjuncts employed by the Experimental group increased from the pre-test (M=.64) to the post-test (M=1.79), whereas in the Control group the use of adjuncts remained almost the same in the pre-test (M=.36) and post-test (M=.57). The most common strategies employed to initiate a refusal by the Experimental group included various adjuncts (willingness, positive opinion, empathy) that could reflect the desire of the speaker to protect his/her face and the other's face (solidarity strategies). Moreover, this group made frequent use of adjuncts, especially in Situations 3 (-P,-D) and 4 (+P.+D). For example,

(7) Sorry, **I'd like** to help you but I really can't because I don't have enough time to help you because I have other work to do. (9EW, Situation 3)

(8) Umm **that's a good idea** but for me, it could be a little difficult because I have plans for that time so, I didn't know about to do the meeting at this time, so I'm sorry. (8EW, Situation 2)

(9) **I really want to** borrow my car, but I need it this weekend. (12 EW, Situation 1)

(10) Professor, you know **I would love** to rearrange the meeting but it's not possible for me because I have to do certain things at that time tomorrow (11EW, Situation 4)

There were some differences in regard to the content and phrasing of adjuncts. The most marked one concerned the realisation of the Willingness strategy. The Experimental group expressed willingness employing the subjunctive 'I would like' in Situations 3 and 4, whereas in Situation 1, they used the present tense 'I really want to …'. Very few instances of this phrasing appeared in the Control's group data. Another difference concerned the realisation of the request for additional information strategy. In all the cases that the Experimental group employed it, the learners phrased it by means of questions such as 'What do you say about that?' or 'What do you think?'.

7.4.2   *Participant Perceptions of Pragmatics Instruction (RQ2)*

This section analyses the Experimental group's perceptions of the pragmatics instruction. The perceptions were analysed according to the subjects' responses to the interview questions with respect to the following parameters: (1) the degree of difficulty responding to the situations in the pre-test, (2) the degree of difficulty and appropriateness of their own answers in the post-test, (3) the cross-linguistic influence when responding to the situations, (4) the differences of the main features of refusals between English and Spanish, (5) the degree of effectiveness of pragmatic instruction for the post-test, and (6) whether the instruction time was sufficient to be able to produce English refusals.

The question employed as a prompt to elicit the learners' perceptions of task difficulty in the pre-test was: 'From 1 to 5 where 1 is very difficult and 5 very easy, how difficult did you find it to answer the situations in the first test?'. 46.6 per cent (seven out of fifteen) of the participants considered that it was number 1 (very difficult) and 60 per cent (nine out of fifteen) chose number 2 (difficult). Overall, they reported that the four situations presented great difficulties for them at the pre-test stage, emphasising that they did not possess the strategies to respond appropriately in each situation. Examples 1–2 are representative of the Experimental group's comments:

(1) Un 2, yo diría un 2, si nada que ver ahorita porque uno tiene un cierto vocabulario, una cierta manera de decir las cosas, pero obviamente entre más vas descubriendo más vas aprendiendo. Adquieres un poquito de conocimiento en cuestión como son ellos como es su cultura como son ellos y por lo tanto tú te tienes que adaptar un poquito a ellos, en ese aspecto, así que yo creo que si antes fue un poquito más difícil que ahora. (Participant 3)

    Two, I would say two, nothing to do right now because one has a certain vocabulary, a certain way of saying things, but obviously the more you discover, the more you learn. You acquire a little knowledge about how they are, how their culture is, how they are and therefore you have to adapt a little to them, in that aspect, so I think that last time it was a little more difficult than now.

(2) Creo que un 2, fue más complicado porque sabía como rechazar en español pero no es lo mismo en inglés. (Participant 7)

    I think 2, it was more complicated because I knew how to refuse in Spanish but it is not the same in English.

With respect to the second question, eliciting the learners' perceptions of task difficulty in the post-test, 20 per cent (three out of fifteen) selected number 3, reporting that it was not so difficult to provide an answer to the situations, 60 per cent (nine out of fifteen) chose number 4 because it was easy and they knew what to say in each situation (Example 4), and 20 per cent (three out of fifteen) opted for number 5, considering that it was easy for them to realise a refusal because they knew the strategies (Example 3). These results seem to corroborate the positive effects of instruction found in the quantitative data.

(3) 5 porque con la información que hemos visto, fue más fácil identificar o saber como rechazar en una situación. (Participant 9)

    5 because with the information we have seen, it was easier to identify or know how to perform a refusal in a situation.

(4) Pues 4 porque de acuerdo con las estrategias que vimos, sabemos como responder de acuerdo con la persona y su relación con los demás. (Participant 12)

Well 4 because according to the strategies we saw, we know how to respond according to the person and their relationship with others.

In exploring the learners' awareness of cross-linguistic influence, the prompt was the question 'At the moment of responding to a situation, did you use English or Spanish refusal strategies?' The majority of the learners (66.6 per cent or ten out of fifteen) considered that they try to use English strategies, based on the instruction that they received in class (Example 6), 20 per cent (three out of fifteen) mentioned that they employed both Spanish and English because there were some strategies that were similar in both languages (Example 5). Finally, 20 per cent (three out of fifteen) responded that they thought about their responses in Spanish and then, they looked for the words in English.

(5) Creo que fue un poco de las dos, las que conozco, en español y las que vimos en clase. (Participant 2)
    I think it was a bit of both, the ones I know in Spanish and the ones we saw in class.
(6) yo diría que la de inglés porque por lo mismo estoy estudiando este idioma estoy adaptándome a su cultura prácticamente tengo que pensar como ellos y sentirme como un nativo como tal para tratar de entrar a su contexto. (Participant 13)
    I would say that English because for the same reason I am studying this language I am adapting to their culture I practically have to think like them and feel like a native as such to try to enter their context.

The basic prompt for the elicitation of the refusal strategies differences between English and Spanish was the question 'What are the main features of refusals which you find the most different in English compared to Spanish?'. All the English learners agreed that there are clear differences between English and Spanish. For instance, many commented that Spanish refusals were less direct since the aim of refusals was not to offend the interlocutor (Example 7). Students were also more aware that English is clearer and more direct but that using fewer strategies, does not mean that they are being rude (Example 8).

(7) Si, bueno en español tratamos de no ser tan directos y ser formales con la respuesta que damos, pero en inglés es más directo más claro y creo que menos redundante como en el español. (Participant 1)
    Yes, well in Spanish we try not to be so direct and to be formal with the answer we give, but in English it is more direct, clearer and I think less redundant than in Spanish.
(8) Si, creo que son más directos las que se utilizan en inglés porque vas a un punto en el que rechazan las cosas y en español como que buscamos muchas alternativas o excusas. (Participant 8)

Yes, I think the ones used in English are more direct because you go to a point where they reject things and in Spanish we look for many alternatives or excuses.

Regarding the fifth question, which assessed the degree of effectiveness of pragmatic instruction to realise refusals in the post-test, 86.6 per cent (thirteen out of fifteen) of participants considered that the pragmatic input was very helpful in understanding the different strategies that can be used depending on the contextual circumstances (Example 9). They added that the information was not only useful to complete the test, but also for the future, if they had an opportunity to interact in a real situation (Example 10).

(9) Ok, bueno creo que sería 5 creo que me ayudo bastante porque hay muchas estrategias que no conocía las cuales ahora puedo aplicar mejor tal vez no pueda acordarme de todas, pero ahora es más fácil para mi decirle a alguien no de diferentes maneras. (Participant 15)

Ok, well I think it would be 5 I think it helped me a lot because there are many strategies that I did not know which now I can better use. Maybe I cannot remember all of them, but now it is easier for me to tell someone no in different ways.

(10) Pues 5, por ejemplo ahorita me ayudo y en algún momento lo voy a volver a utilizar, así que sirvió. (Participant 6)

Well 5, for example, right now it will help me and at some point I will use it again, so it worked.

With respect to the last question, surveying the length of instruction, 60 per cent (nine out of fifteen) of the learners considered that the sessions that they had were sufficient to learn to carry out a refusal in the target language (Example 11), meanwhile 46.6 per cent (seven out of fifteen) mentioned that even though the material was interesting, more time was needed to practise in class (Example 12).

(11) Si, creo que fue suficiente porque no teníamos una idea de como hacer un rechazo y ahora con las explicaciones y las actividades que tuvimos, nos dio una idea más clara sobre que hacer y como responder a una situación. (Participant 14)

Yes, I think it was enough because we didn't have an idea of how to carry out a refusal and now with the explanations and the activities that we had, it gave us a clearer idea about what to do and how to respond to a situation.

(12) No, no, yo creo que necesitábamos más tiempo para practicar un poco más. (Participant 5)

No, no, I think we needed more time to practise a little bit more.

To sum up, the following general conclusions can be drawn from the participants' interview: (1) Language learners from the Experimental group reported improved use of refusals following pragmatic instruction. For them, it was much easier to respond to the situations in the post-test than in the pre-test. (2) All learners seemed to have a greater awareness of the different strategies to realise a refusal in English and in Spanish. (3) However, some of them, considered that they still used some words and phrases of the L1 to respond in the L2, mainly due to the lack of vocabulary and linguistic structures in the target language. (4) They showed sociopragmatic awareness and considered that contextual variables such as degree of intimacy and status are important factors in selecting what to say. (5) The explanations and activities given in class helped them to raise awareness and provided them with opportunities to practise. These conclusions are taken into consideration in Section 7.5.

7.5   Discussion

With respect to the first question on the efficacy of instruction on refusals, the data provided evidence of a pragmalinguistic improvement in the amount and type of refusals. The group of learners that received the four-week instruction performed significantly better, whereas the Control group showed no gains over the same period. Specifically, the Control group appeared to continue to attend to the L1 notions of *confianza* and *respeto* to inform their choice and realisation of refusals by safeguarding the addressee's face and relying on indirect strategies, even in status-equal refusals. Mexican polite behaviour is said to be contingent on creating solidarity by placing the interlocutor at the centre of the interaction while placing the self on the periphery (Félix-Brasdefer, 2009). This seems to have been the case for the Control group. By contrast, the Experimental group were better able to differentiate between direct and indirect refusal situations following instruction and showed a greater control and variety of mitigated indirectness.

All in all, these findings lend support to previous studies showing the positive benefits of instruction to foster learners' pragmatic knowledge (Alcón Soler, 2012; Bardovi-Harlig, 2017; Eslami-Rasekh & Mardani, 2010; Martínez-Flor, 2016; Plonsky & Zhuang, 2019; Taguchi, 2015; see also Chapter 8, this volume, for the benefits of self-access instructional material). The explicit pragmatic instruction helped them to produce realisations that were pragmalinguistically and sociopragmatically appropriate to the contextual circumstances. In this respect, Ishihara (2010) pointed out that 'explicit teaching appears to heighten learners' attention to specific linguistic features and an understanding of how these features relate to contextual factors' (p. 103). This study included audiovisual materials (scenes from two films) to present contextual input that provided examples of refusals in interaction. In addition, learners received a series of awareness-raising activities (post-observational discussion, matching, and multiple-choice exercises) to attend to this input, as well as production tasks (role plays) to use the acquired refusal formulas in contextualised communicative situations. These production tasks also had a consciousness-raising function by helping learners to notice gaps in their output: a now well-established technique which has proved effective in other studies (Taguchi, 2015). Finally, learners had the opportunity to receive feedback from their peers and teachers when pragmatic failure was committed. According to Martínez-Flor and Usó-Juan (2010) appropriate input presentation, meaningful output practice and feedback are the necessary conditions so that pragmatic learning can take place. These conditions were met in the present study.

With respect to the number and variety of strategies, the Experimental group selected and employed more than one strategy in their refusals. Differences in preference for strategy use were also found at each level of formality. It can be observed that indirect strategies and mainly adjuncts were employed more by the Experimental group in the post-test than the Control group in the same test. Whereas the Experimental group produced a higher proportion of strategies in situations of formal rather than informal status, the Control group showed the opposite behaviour, with more strategies in informal status and fewer in situations of formal status. A similar finding is reported in Alcón Soler (2012) in regard to the positive effect of pragmatic instruction on learners' metapragmatic awareness of refusals, in which learners showed a wider range of linguistic resources in refusing an invitation and changes in the way they mitigated refusals. Another important result is that the content of the refusal varied between the Control and the Experimental groups in the post-test. The refusals of the Experimental group used more solidarity politeness strategies. The refusals of the Control group were sometimes plainly spoken and the participants expressed their feelings by means of various independence politeness strategies such as self-centred justifications ('I'm going to tell you the truth. I don't trust you.', 'I think that you are not responsible'). The Experimental group produced more elaborate responses attending to the sociopragmatic aspects involved in the different situations. Similar findings were found in the refusal studies by Alcón-Soler and Guzmán-Pitarch (2010, 2013) and Alcón-Soler (2012). As all these learners decreased the use of direct strategies and increased the use and variety of indirect strategies and adjuncts, their performance when refusing was appropriate in the scenarios. The authors indicated that learners' pragmalinguistic and sociopragmatic awareness improved after receiving pragmatic instruction.

The results of research question two shed light on students' perceptions of pragmatics instruction. The participants' responses alluded to three specific instructional aspects considered to be particularly beneficial. First, the use of online multiple choice and matching exercises, together with the explicit instruction of refusals, helped the language learners to comprehend the prag-malinguistic strategies and sociocultural differences between their L1 and their L2 with respect to the use of this speech act. The online activities facilitated self-paced, systematic language practice, promoted autonomous learning, and provided immediate, individualised feedback. These factors seemed to gener-ate a dynamic and motivating learning environment, as seen in other studies (see Taguchi & Sykes, 2013). Ishihara and Cohen (2010) state that the use of awareness-raising tasks provide information about what norms are appropriate in one culture but may vary in another, thereby facilitating an examination of L1-L2 differences. This exercise may then result in preventing learners from transferring L1 pragmatics norms into the target language and helping them to avoid pragmatic failure. In the same way, explicit instruction of L2 pragmatics norms also allows learners to examine the differences between the L1 and L2 norms. This analysis provides learners with an insider view of the L2 to avoid misconceptions, possible conflicts, negative judgements, and negative stereo-types towards the target culture. Ishihara (2010) considers that knowing the cultural reasoning behind language use could help language learners to make informed pragmatic choices.

Second, exposure to metapragmatic information in class, analysed in terms of social status, social distance, and degree of imposition, appears to have heightened an awareness of the importance of selecting refusal strategies according to contextual factors. In this study, learners were exposed to extracts from two films *The King's Speech* and *You before Me*. After watching them, the teacher and the learners engaged in critical reflection. This task facilitated learners' noticing and understanding of the form-context relationship within highly accessible and informative conversational models of language which learners may not encounter outside of the classroom (Bardovi-Harlig, 2015). The learners had the opportunity to identify the refusal strategies and analyse the use of directness, politeness, and formality in an interaction. Similar results were obtained in the research carried out by Derakhshan and Eslami-Rasekh (2015), which made use of audiovisual material to raise awareness of apology strategies, and Abrams (2014) who also found films to be rich in contextual-ised discourse-length language samples which allowed for pragmatic scaffold-ing. Growing evidence suggests films can help develop both pragmatic and intercultural competencies (Martínez-Flor, 2011) and should continue to be explored as a valuable resource.

Finally, the learners highlighted the benefits of the different production tasks which provided interactional opportunities to use the pragmalinguistic rules learned in class. Almost half of the learners also commented that addi-tional time to consolidate learning would have been useful, suggesting not only instructional length should be considered (Bardovi-Harlig, 2015) but also situ-ated practice time. The practice phase is widely advocated as being particularly valuable in intervention studies (e.g., Ishihara & Cohen, 2010; Martínez-Flor & Usó-Juan, 2010) but optimum timing has yet to be the subject of empirical inquiry. The practice tasks facilitated learners' noticing of pragmatic norms and forms that they did not know while they tried to communicate the intended meaning in the target language. In the production activities, learners could use the taught forms, receive corrective feedback from their teacher and gain control over these new pragmalinguistic structures. Thus, learners had the opportunity for input noticing and using language in a meaningful way. Ishihara (2010) states that not only noticing and attention are necessary to acquire a L2, but also output and interactional opportunities are likely to contribute to learners' acquisition. In addition, this interaction allows learners to negotiate meaning with their peers and receive feedback from them as well as from their teacher.

7.6   Conclusions

This study investigated the effects of explicit pragmatic instruction on English refusals among Mexican Spanish EFL learners, and the learners' perception of this instruction. Results showed that the types of indirect refusal strategies (explanations/reasons, mitigated refusal, apologies, and alternatives) produced by the Experimental group differed significantly from those produced in the post-test by the Control group. In addition, findings from this study also illustrated that adjuncts increased after the treatment. This positive trend indicated that the Experimental group produced more elaborate refusal responses and showed increased sensitivity to the sociopragmatic aspects involved in the different situations. Consequently, the results obtained in the study seem to demonstrate that the instruction positively affected the refusal performance of the Experimental group, in terms of both frequency and variety of indirect strategies and adjuncts. Regarding, learners' perceptions, they considered that the pragmatic instruction received in class helped them to be aware not only of the pragmatic differences between their mother tongue and the target language, but also of the pragmalinguistic and sociopragmatic aspects to produce English refusals appropriately according to the social norms of both languages. The participant interviews enhanced the results obtained in the study. The analysis of the learners' responses provided information about their cognitive processes when carrying out the tasks. It also showed the learners' planning and thought processes when performing refusals were different before and after receiving instruction. Specifically, their comments showed the attended aspects when uttering the strategies and the improvement learners had in the post-test.

The current study is subject to some limitations that need to be addressed in future research. One limitation concerns the particular population of learners involved in this study. It consisted of thirty male and female university students with a lower-intermediate level of proficiency in English divided into two groups (Experimental and Control); therefore, each group was formed by a small sample of fifteen learners. Thus, the number of participants taking part in the study and their specific individual variables may have influenced the results. Another limitation related to the research methodology is that it was not possible to carry out a delayed post-test that could examine the longevity of the instructional gains or whether the long-lasting effects may have been influenced by other factors such as the opportunity to hear and use refusals in communication. Martínez-Flor's (2016) results of a delayed post-test show that learners maintained the use of a variety of strategies when apologising five months after instruction. By contrast, Halenko and Jones (2011) found only minimal delayed effects six weeks after instruction on spoken requests. Therefore, paying attention to the durability of pragmatics teaching, and how this affects different speech acts, and learner groups, is an issue that warrants more attention.

The present study can contribute to increase the growing body of L2 pragmatics research and allows us to see the positive effects of instruction in foreign language learning settings. As the research field moves forward, more work needs to be done on how pragmatics instruction is operationalised such as length of instruction, intensive or spaced input, frequency and length of practice stages, and the kinds of materials and language samples which can provide effective classroom models. Such efforts are particularly valuable in English as a foreign language contexts because these language learners do not have opportunities to hear and use the language as employed authentically in a target community. Therefore, the instruction and the material used in the classroom can provide important models for pragmatic use within an L2 community. In addition, these learners do not have opportunities to use the target language outside the classroom, thus, focussed production activities can offer meaningful opportunities to practice the language in the classroom and facilitate the acquisition of the L2 pragmatic rules. Studies like this go some way to addressing these gaps but much more work is needed in these areas.

References

Abrams, Z. (2014). Using film to provide a context for teaching L2 pragmatics. *System*, 46, 55–64.

Alcón Soler, E. (2012). Teachability and bilingualism effects on third language learners' pragmatic knowledge. *Intercultural Pragmatics*, 9, 511–541.

Alcón Soler, E., & Guzmán-Pitarch, J. (2010). The effect of instruction on learners' pragmatic awareness: A focus on refusals. *International Journal of English Studies*, 10, 65–80.

Alcón-Soler, E., & Guzmán-Pitarch, J. (2013). The effect of instruction on learners' use and negotiation of refusals. *Utrecht Studies in Language & Communication*, 25, 41–63.

Allami, H., & Naeimi, A. (2011) A cross-linguistic study of refusals: An analysis of pragmatic competence development in Iranian EFL learners. *Journal of Pragmatics*, 43(1), 385–406.

Bardovi-Harlig, K. (2015). Designing instructional effect studies for L2 pragmatics: A guide for teachers and researchers. In S. Gesuato, F. Bianchi, & W. Cheng (eds.), *Teaching, Learning and Investigating Pragmatics: Principles, Methods and Practices*. Newcastle upon Tyne: Cambridge Scholars Publishing, pp. 135–164.

Bardovi-Harlig, K. (2017). Acquisition of L2 pragmatics. In S. Loewen & M. Sato (eds.), *Routledge Handbook of Instructed Second Language Acquisition*. New York: Routledge, pp. 224–245.

Bardovi Harlig, K., & Hartford, B. (1993). Learning the rules of academic talk: A longitudinal study of pragmatic change. *Studies in Second Language Acquisition*, 15, 279–304.

Beebe, L., Takahashi, T., & Uliss-Weltz, R. (1990). Pragmatic transfer in ESL refusals. In R. Scarcella, E. Andersen, & S. Krashen (eds.), *Developing Communicative Competence in a Second Language*. New York: Newbury House, pp. 55–73.

Bella, S. (2011). Mitigation and politeness in Greek invitation refusals: effects of length of residence in the target community and intensity of interaction on non-native speakers' performance. *Journal of Pragmatics*, 43, 1718–1740.

Bella, S. (2014). Developing the ability to refuse: A cross-sectional study of Greek FL refusals. *Journal of Pragmatics*, 61, 35–62.

Brown, P., & Levinson, S. (1987). *Politeness: Some Universals of Language Use*. Cambridge: Cambridge University Press.

Byon, A. S. (2004). Sociopragmatic analysis of Korean requests: Pedagogical settings. *Journal of Pragmatics*, 36, 1673–1704.

Covarrubias, P. (2002). *Culture, Communication, and Communication: Interpersonal Relations and Pronominal Address in a Mexican Organization*. Lanham, MD: Rowman & Littlefield.

Derakhshan, A., & Eslami-Rasekh, Z. (2015). The effect of consciousness-raising instruction on the pragmatic development of apology and request. *TESLEJ*, 18, 1–24.

Economidou-Kogetsidis, M., & Halenko, N. (2022). Developing spoken requests during UK study abroad: A longitudinal look at Japanese learners of English. *Study Abroad Research in Second Language Acquisition and International Education*, 7(1), 23–53. Eslami, Z. R. (2010). Refusals: How to develop appropriate refusal strategies. In A. Martínez- Flor & E. Usó-Juan (eds.), *Speech Act Performance: Theoretical, Empirical and Methodological Issues*. Amsterdam and Philadelphia: John Benjamins, pp. 217–237.

Eslami-Rasekh, A., & Mardani, M. (2010). Investigating the effects of teaching apology speech act, with a focus on intensifying strategies, on pragmatic development of EFL learners: The Iranian context. *The International Journal of Language Society and Culture*, 30, 96–103.

Félix-Brasdefer, C. (2003). Validity in data collection methods in pragmatics research. In P. Kempehinsky & C. E. Piñeros (eds.), *Theory, Practice, and Acquisition. Papers from the 6th Hispanic Linguistic Symposium and the 5th Conference on the Acquisition of Spanish and Portuguese*. Somerville, MA: Cascadilla Press, pp. 239–257.

Félix-Brasdefer, C. (2008a). *Politeness in Mexico and the United States: A Contrastive Study of the Realizations and Perceptions of Refusals*. Amsterdam: John Benjamins.

Félix-Brasdefer, C. (2008b). Perceptions of refusals to invitations: exploring the minds of foreign language learners. *Language Awareness*, 17, 195–211.

Félix-Brasdefer, C. (2009). Estado de la cuestión sobre el discurso de la (des) cortesía y la imagen social en México. In L. Alfano Rodríguez (ed.), *La (des) cortesía y la imagen social en México: Estudios semiótico discursivos desde varios enfoques analíticos. Universidad Autónoma de Nuevo León.* Monterrey: Universidad de Nuevo León, pp. 15–46.

Gass, S. M., & Houck, N. (1999). *Interlanguage Refusals: A Cross-Cultural Study of Japanese-English.* New York: De Gruyter Mouton.

Goffman, E. (1967). *Interactional Ritual: Essays on Face-to-face Behavior.* Garden City, NY: Anchor Books.

Halenko, N. (2018). Using computer-assisted language learning (CALL) tools to enhance output practice. In C. Jones (ed.), *Practice in Second Language Learning.* Cambridge: Cambridge University Press, pp. 137–163.

Halenko, N. (2021). *Teaching Pragmatics and Instructed Second Language Acquisition.* London: Bloomsbury.

Halenko, N., & Flores-Salgado, E. (2019). Embedding ICT to teach and assess the pragmatic targets of refusals and disagreements in spoken English. *British Council ELT Research Papers*, 19(3), 1–21.

Halenko, N., & Jones, C. (2011). Teaching pragmatic awareness of spoken requests to Chinese EAP learners in the UK: Is explicit instruction effective? *System*, 39, 240–250.

Halenko, N., & Jones, C. (2017). Explicit instruction of spoken requests: an examination of pre-departure instruction and L2 contact in the study abroad environment. *System* 68, 26–37.

Halenko, N., Jones, C., Davies, L., & Davies, J. (2019). Surveying pragmatic performance during a study abroad stay: A cross-sectional look at the language of spoken requests. *Intercultural Communication Education*, 2(2), 71–87.

Ishihara, N. (2010). Incorporating technology into pragmatics-focused instruction. In N. Ishihara & A. D. Cohen (eds.), *Teaching and Learning Pragmatics: Where Language and Culture Meet.* London: Routledge, pp. 244–263.

Ishihara, N., & Cohen, A. D. (2010). *Teaching and Learning Pragmatics: Where Language and Culture Meet.* London: Routledge.

Kondo, S. (2008). Effects on pragmatic development through awareness-raising instruction: Refusals by Japanese EFL learners. In E. Alcón Soler & A. Martínez-Flor (eds.), *Investigating Pragmatics in Foreign Language Learning, Teaching and Testing.* Bristol: Multilingual Matters, pp. 153–178.

Kwon, J. (2004). Expressing refusals in Korean and in American English. *Multilingua*, 23(4), 339–364.

Liao, Ch., & Bresnahan, M. (1996). A contrastive pragmatic study on American English and Mandarin refusal strategies. *Language Sciences*, 18(3–4), 703–727.

Martínez-Flor, A. (2011). Analysing request modification devices in films: Implications for pragmatic learning in instructed foreign language contexts. In E. Alcón Soler & M. P. Safont Jordà (eds.), *Intercultural Language Use and Language Learning.* Dordrecht: Springer, pp. 245–280.

Martínez-Flor, A. (2016). Teaching apology formulas at the discourse Level: Are instructional effects maintained over time? *ELIA*, 16, 13–48.

Martínez-Flor, A., & Usó-Juan, E. (2010). *Speech Act Performance: Theoretical, Empirical and Methodological Issues*. Amsterdam and Philadelphia: John Benjamins.

Nelson, G., Carson, J., Al Batal, M., & El Bakary, W. (2002). Cross-cultural pragmatics: Strategy use in Egyptian Arabic and American English refusals. *Applied Linguistics*, 23(2), 163–189.

Plonsky, L., & Zhuang, J. (2019). A meta-analysis of L2 pragmatics instruction. In N. Taguchi (ed.), *The Routledge Handbook of SLA and Pragmatics*. New York: Routledge, pp. 297–307.

Pomerantz, A. (1984). Agreeing and disagreeing with assessments: Some features of preferred/dispreferred turn shapes. In J. M. Atkinson & J. Heritage (eds.), *Structures of Social Action*. Cambridge: Cambridge University Press, pp. 57–101.

Rose, K. (2000). An exploratory cross-sectional study of interlanguage pragmatic development. *Studies in Second Language Acquisition*, 22(1), 27–67.

Schauer, G. (2009). *Interlanguage Pragmatic Development: The Study Abroad Context*. London: Continuum.

Searle, J. R. (1969). *Speech Acts: An Essay in the Philosophy of Language*. Cambridge: Cambridge University Press.

Scollon, R., & Scollon, S. W. (2001). *Intercultural Communication*, 2nd ed. Malden, MA: Blackwell.

Taguchi, N. (2015). Instructed pragmatics at a glance: Where instructional studies were, are, and should be going. *Language Teaching*, 48, 1–50.

Taguchi, N., & Sykes, J. M. (2013). *Technology in Interlanguage Pragmatics Research and Teaching*. Amsterdam and Philadelphia: John Benjamins.

Takahashi, T., & Beebe, L.M. (1987). The development of pragmatic competence by Japanese learners of English. *JALT Journal*, 8, 131–155.

Turnbull, W. (2001). An appraisal of pragmatic elicitation techniques for the social psychological study of talk: The case of request refusals. *Journal of Pragmatics*, 11(1), 31–61.

Turnbull, W., & Saxton, K. (1997). Modal expressions as facework in refusals to comply with requests: I think I should say 'no' right now. *Journal of Pragmatics*, 27, 145–181.

Usó-Juan, E. (2010). Requests: A sociopragmatic approach. In A. Martínez-Flor & E. Usó-Juan (eds.), *Speech Act Performance: Theoretical, Empirical and Methodological Issues*. Amsterdam and Philadelphia: John Benjamins, pp. 237–256.

Usó-Juan, E. (2013). Effects of metapragmatic instruction on EFL learners' production of refusals. In O. Martí-Arandiz & P. Salazar Campillo (eds.), *Refusals in Instructional Contexts and Beyond*. Amsterdam: Rodopi, pp. 65–101.

Van Der Bom, I., & Mills, S. (2015). A discursive approach to the analysis of politeness data. *Journal of Politeness Research*, 11(2), 179–206.

8 Using Self-Access Materials to Learn Pragmatics in the US Academic Setting
What Do Indonesian EFL Learners Pick Up?

Ananda Astrini Muhammad

8.1 Introduction

Pragmatic competence has been broadly defined by Taguchi (2009: 1) as 'the ability to use language appropriately in a social context'. What constitutes appropriate use of language in a social context varies very much from language to language. Unfortunately, English as a foreign language (EFL) learners typically do not have adequate opportunity to be exposed to pragmatic input from their surrounding environment. Their development of pragmatic competence relies heavily on classroom learning (Kim & Hall, 2002), in which EFL teachers may depend on textbooks for language learning activities in the classroom. Studies analysing EFL textbooks have indicated that textbooks are not an adequate source of pragmatic input because language is often taught in a decontextualised manner (McConachy & Hata, 2013; Meihami & Khanlarzadeh, 2015; Ren & Han, 2016; Vellenga, 2004; see also Chapter 6, this volume).

In order to address this learner need, the current chapter aims to explore the use of self-access language learning (SALL) materials designed specifically for current and prospective US international students who are looking to develop their pragmatic competence in the US academic setting. Materials that are presented in self-access format will enable both prospective and current international students to use the materials whenever and wherever they decide to. Finally, SALL can offer learners a low-stakes learning opportunity as they are not graded by an instructor, which could open up the opportunity for learners to engage in pragmatics language learning that is free of consequences. Through the use of self-access materials specifically designed to help these EFL students develop their pragmatic competence, learners can obtain contextualised pragmatic input that they otherwise may not have obtained in their formal education.

8.2 Teaching Second Language Pragmatics through an Online Learning Platform

Literature on communicative language ability has identified pragmatic competence as a crucial aspect of second language (L2) communicative language ability (see Chapter 1, this volume). However, pragmatic competence has been difficult to operationalise in language teaching and assessment due to two main problems. Firstly, although there has been a lot of work on pragmatics, the definition of pragmatic competence employed in studies is varied, prompting Eslami-Rasekh (2005) to state that there is no clear and generally accepted definition of the term itself. In relation to this, there has been little effort to synthesise pragmatics studies in order to come up with a comprehensive list of components that comprise pragmatic competence (Timpe-Laughlin, Wain, & Schmidgall, 2015), which is essential if we are to operationalise the construct of pragmatic competence in learning materials. Thus, there is a need to create a more comprehensive operationalisation of the construct.

Researchers from the Educational Testing Service have undertaken this endeavour. Timpe-Laughlin, Wain, and Schmidgall (2015) conducted a systematic literature review of many different models, principles, and theories of pragmatics. Their aim was to 'propose a construct definition of pragmatic competence for the development of future assessment and learning tools' (p. 1). Based on their synthesis of literature on pragmatic competence, they defined pragmatic competence as 'mastery of strategically relating linguistic and nonlinguistic contextual information in order to generate meaning beyond the grammatical level in oral, written, or a hybrid mode of communication' (Timpe-Laughlin, Wain, & Schmidgall, 2015: 19). They also posit that pragmatic competence consists of five distinct but interrelated dimensions of knowledge, namely sociocultural knowledge, pragmatic-functional knowledge, grammatical knowledge, discourse knowledge, and strategic knowledge. Sociocultural knowledge refers to the knowledge that language users require to 'tailor their speech intentions and utterance(s) to the characteristics of the situational context' (Timpe-Laughlin, Wain, & Schmidgall, 2015: 18). Sociocultural knowledge consists of knowledge of factors such as topic, role of participants, setting, norms of conventions and interaction, power relations, gender, and age. Pragmatic-functional knowledge pertains to knowledge required to make connections between form and meaning. Grammatical knowledge pertains to knowledge of lexis and rules of morphology, syntax, semantics, phonology, and graphology. Discourse knowledge is required for cohesion and coherence. Finally, strategic knowledge is represented as knowledge that acts as a support system when there is insufficient knowledge and/or communicative breakdown. However, in the case of the current study, strategic knowledge is conceptualised as the knowledge acquired from learning about other people's experiences and reflecting on the knowledge of their own culture, while simultaneously comparing it with the culture (in this case of making requests) of the target language. The rest of the dimensions of pragmatic knowledge follow the definitions of Timpe-Laughlin, Wain, and Schmidgall (2015).

Utilising this construct of pragmatic competence, Timpe-Laughlin, Wain, and Schmidgall (2015) set to conceptualise the teaching of pragmatics within the context of an online learning platform. Their proposal centred around creating materials and tasks that would promote the development of learners' pragmatic awareness using goal-oriented tasks that reflect real-life target language use (TLU) in a specific domain. In their paper, they used the workplace as their TLU domain. They then outlined two example modules, one focussing on making spoken requests, the other focussing on making requests in emails. The proposed modules were then adopted in this study but with the US academic setting as the TLU domain.

8.2.1   Self-Access Language Learning Materials

Self-access materials have been defined as 'materials that are designed and organised in such a way that students can select and work on tasks on their own … and obtain feedback on their performance, for example by comparing their answers to a key which accompanies the material' (Sheerin, 1991: 143). In the context of SALL materials, they are nowadays typically found in a digital format (e.g., software packages, web resources), and easily accessible through the use of a computer or other electronic devices. Besides ease of access, SALL materials are now also commonly found free online (e.g., Duolingo, Coursera, LiveMocha, BBC Languages). Moreover, self-access materials have been said to promote 'independent and learner-centered learning' (Ishihara and Cohen, 2010: 204). In other words, using SALL materials can lead to greater learner autonomy, which will benefit international students. Not only this, but such materials can relieve the pressures on classroom time for the teacher and learner.

In terms of currently available SALL materials for L2 pragmatics learning, the number is scarce, and none seem to be addressing pragmatics in the context of US academic settings. Currently available materials include resources hosted by the Centre for Advanced Research on Language Acquisition (CARLA) at the University of Minnesota, namely Strategies for Learning Speech Acts in Japanese and Dancing with Words: Strategies for Learning Pragmatics in Spanish, both of which are web-based. These online SALL materials offer instructional input related to speech act strategies in textual, visual, and audiovisual modes; provide practise opportunities in various forms including multiple-choice, fill-in-the-blanks, and discourse completion tasks; and invite users of the materials to reflect on their learning through self-reflection activities. These two valuable resources are, to the best of the author's knowledge, the most widely used publicly available SALL materials that are geared towards helping language learners develop their L2 pragmatic competence. Therefore, there is a clear need for more accessible SALL materials that are more focussed towards providing L2 pragmatic input and opportunities for practise to EFL learners who are in L2 pragmatics instruction deprived settings.

To investigate Indonesian EFL learners' use of the self-access learning materials to learn how to make requests in a US academic setting, two research questions frame this study:

1. To what extent do participants incorporate the request strategies introduced in the materials into their productions of spoken and email requests?
2. What reported knowledge gains did participants identify in their self-evaluation and feedback?

8.3   Methods

8.3.1   Participants

The participants in the present study were twenty-one Indonesian EFL learners[1] (fourteen males, seven females). They were interested in studying in the US, and some of them were actively seeking scholarships to pursue their graduate education in US universities. Participants were recruited with the help of the researcher's acquaintances in Indonesia, as well as contacted directly by the researcher, who maintains a blog that caters to individuals who would like to continue their studies in the US. They were 18 to 34 years old with a range of professional backgrounds but were mainly people who work in education or were currently studying at a university. Most of the participants had never lived in an English-speaking country. Those who had resided in an English-speaking country (US, UK, Australia, Singapore) did not stay for a substantial length of time (i.e., less than two months). However, there were exceptions to this; two participants had been in the UK for over a year. Regarding their English language learning experience, all participants noted that they had been studying English for at least three years with most indicating that they had been learning English for more than seven years. Besides formal settings, most participants had taken up additional English learning opportunities in places such as English conversation clubs and supplementary language schools.

---

[1] The twenty-one Indonesian EFL learners were part of a larger research study (Muhammad, 2017).

8.3.2   Self-Access Language Learning Materials Developed

The videos and tasks used in this study were hosted on Moodle (Version 3.1.3+; Moodle, 2017),[2] an open-source learning platform. The overall layout of the Moodle course was largely based upon the course design proposed by Timpe-Laughlin, Wain, and Schmidgall (2015). They suggested five parts for each learning unit: Part 1: Introduction and Outline; Part 2: Pre-Instruction Assessment; Part 3: Instruction; Part 4: Instructional Content Review; and Part 5: Application. An additional section – Part 6: Strategies – was created for the current course. The Moodle course was divided into two units, one focussed on making requests in spoken communication, and the other focussed on requests in email communication. Learners moved through each part in a unit in the order that they appear at their own pace. Table 8.1 shows the breakdown of parts in Unit 1 and Unit 2. Overall, participants managed to complete the course in one month. The following sections briefly describe the components of the course.

8.3.2.1   Part 1: Introduction and Outline   The goal of Unit 1-Part 1 on spoken requests is to provide learners with background information regarding the speech act of making requests through a video. The video elaborated on three topics: (1) important terms and definitions learners will encounter in the video and throughout the first unit, (2) three important contextual factors that one must consider when making requests (power relationships, social distance, and degree of imposition), and (3) four types of people that they will communicate with in a US academic setting and who they will 'see' in the unit (professors, teaching assistants, classmates, and writing centre consultants). The material on contextual factors was based on politeness theory information from an online pragmatics learning website, Dancing with Words, designed and created by Julie Sykes under the direction of Andrew Cohen (2006) to teach the pragmatics of several speech acts. This information is important to raise learners' awareness of the contextual factors that come into play when formulating requests.

In Unit 2-Part 1 on email requests, learners were also provided with a video that served to explain the importance of email communication in academic life in the US. The video highlighted that learners will only communicate with professors, TAs, and classmates in the unit. This is because learners do not usually communicate through email with writing centre consultants.

---

[2] The materials were developed as part of a larger research study on the creation and evaluation of multimedia materials to promote development of international students' pragmatic competence in the US academic setting (Muhammad, 2017).

Table 8.1 *Overview of the sequence of the self-access language learning materials*

Part	Description of Task(s)	Approximate Completion Time
Unit 1 – Making Requests in Spoken Communication	Learners will …	3 hours
Part 1: Introduction and Outline	View a unit introduction video.	10 minutes
Part 2: Pre-Instruction Assessment	• View a video presenting four requesting scenarios. • Formulate a request for each scenario.	20 minutes
Part 3: Instruction	View a video showing the request scenarios introduced in Part 2 play out, followed by explanation of different request strategies, and an analysis of the request strategies used.	20 minutes
Part 4: Instructional Content Review	Complete a quiz consisting of audiovisual situational judgement tasks (SJTs).	20 minutes
Part 5: Application	Complete a self-evaluation, view a video presenting four new requesting scenarios, and practice formulating requests.	30 minutes
Part 6: Strategies	• View a video showing two international students share their spoken request-making experience. • Complete a self-reflection task.	30 minutes
Questionnaire for Unit 1: Making Requests in Spoken Communication	Provide feedback on the usefulness of the materials in Unit 1. This online questionnaire signals the end of Unit 1.	30 minutes
Unit 2 – Making Requests in Written Communication	Learners will …	3 hours
Part 1: Introduction and Outline	View a unit introduction video.	5 minutes
Part 2: Pre-Instruction Assessment	Complete a quiz on identifying the correct order of information in an email and the request statement in the emails presented.	30 minutes
Part 3: Instruction	View a video explaining the essential components of an email and reviews the construction of the emails shown in Part 2.	15 minutes
Part 4: Instructional Content Review	Complete a quiz that requires them to correct an email.	30 minutes
Part 5: Application	Practice writing their own emails based on email request scenarios.	30 minutes
Part 6: Strategies	• View a video showing two international students share their email request-making experience. • Complete a self-reflection task.	20 minutes
Questionnaire for Unit 2: Making Requests in Written Communication	Provide feedback on the usefulness of the materials in Unit 2. This online questionnaire signals the end of Unit 2.	30 minutes

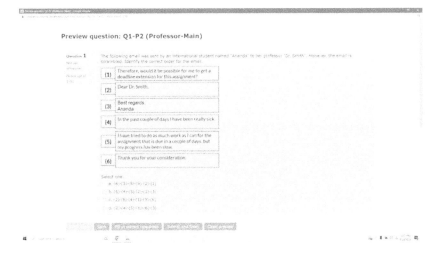

Figure 8.1 Example of a scrambled email task

8.3.2.2 *Part 2: Pre-Instruction Assessment* The goal of Unit 1-Part 2 on spoken requests was to give learners the opportunity to produce output prior to viewing the main instructional content. For this study, it was useful for the researcher to see whether the learners' pre-instruction requests were different in terms of the strategies and politeness features that they chose compared to the requests that they made in post-instruction tasks. The video showed four request scenarios presented in the form of static images to highlight the context of the scenarios. Their task was to formulate a request that best fits each scenario. Learners were provided two choices to record their requests, using audio or text.

Unit 2-Part 2 on email requests involved an activity that aimed to determine learners' pre-instructional knowledge of making requests in email communication. The activity consisted of three scenarios and two types of tasks for each scenario. The first task required learners to identify the correct order of a scrambled email (Figure 8.1).

This task was intended to measure learners' knowledge of the structure of an email. No explicit feedback was provided, though the correct order of the scrambled email was shown. Learners were notified that they would learn the order of the email elements in Part 3. The second task required learners to identify the request in the email, and to describe why they identified it as a request. Timpe-Laughlin, Wain, and Schmidgall (2015) stated that learner's explanation 'could provide teachers with insights into a learner's pragmatic awareness' (p. 28). Additionally, learners also review their knowledge of request strategies from Unit 1. For the second task, the type of request in each email was provided as delayed feedback.

8.3.2.3 Part 3: Instruction In Unit 1-Part 3 on spoken requests, the aim of the video provided was twofold. Firstly, to review the scenarios presented in Part 2 by showing how the request scenarios actually played out. Secondly, to explicitly teach different request strategies and politeness features that learners can use which were based on Trosborg (1995). The explanation focussed on helping learners make connections between the form of the requests and its meaning. While they viewed the scenarios, the learners were instructed to compare the requests made by the student and the requests that they produced in Part 2. The idea was that using the information that they have learned in Part 1 about contextual factors in an interaction and the request strategies in Part 3, learners could self-evaluate their performance and identify areas in which they could improve. They were also directed to pay attention to the student's intonation, pronunciation, and body language during the interactions.

In Unit 2-Part 3 on email requests, the main goal of the video was to explain the structure of an email. The video discussed four topics: (1) important terms and definitions, (2) distinction between email communication and text messaging, (3) elements of an email, and (4) review of the email scenarios in Part 2. The subject of email elements was important because completeness of the email elements is a crucial aspect of e-politeness, particularly in the academic setting (e.g., a request email sent to a professor without adequate background information as to why the request is being made). The term e-politeness refers to the notion of politeness in computer-mediated communication (CMC) such as email communication that is 'characterised by features that reflect greater formality' (Biesenbach-Lucas, 2007: 60) especially in emails to faculty. An email that does not have complete email elements (e.g., a subject line) could potentially be understood by the recipient as the sender's lack of interest in or knowledge of writing the email.

8.3.2.4 Part 4: Instructional Content Review In Unit 1 on spoken requests, Part 4 aimed to review learners' understanding of the instructional video in Part 3. One type of assessment that Timpe-Laughlin, Wain, and Schmidgall (2015) suggested for this section was audiovisual situational judgement tasks (SJTs). In audiovisual SJTs, learners are provided with multiple detailed scenarios and their task is to choose the most appropriate request. Four scenarios were presented in the form of multiple choice questions. Each option was in the form of videos. The options demonstrated request forms at differing levels. Figure 8.2 shows the layout of the first question in the SJT. After learners submitted their answer, they were given feedback as shown in Figure 8.3.

In Unit 2 on email requests, Part 4 aimed to review learners' understanding of the email structure and request strategies through asking them to correct

Figure 8.2 Partial view of an example situational judgement task (SJT) question

Figure 8.3 Two different types of feedback for the audiovisual SJT

three emails. The emails were to be corrected in terms of their approximations of the expected email elements and the appropriateness of the request in each email. Learners were provided with feedback after submitting the corrections to all three email requests, which included the missing email elements appropriateness of the elements, and the request strategies used. Additionally, an example corrected email was also provided.

Figure 8.4 Example email writing scenario and feedback

8.3.2.5 Part 5: Application In Unit 1 on spoken requests, Part 5 aimed to provide learners with more opportunities to practise producing requests. Before they practised, learners self-evaluated their output from Part 2 by accessing the audio or text file that they had submitted. Their self-evaluation was guided by the following open-ended questions:

1. How did your requests in Part 2 differ from the requests that you chose in Part 4?
2. Do you think the requests that you chose in Part 4 reflected what you had learned from Part 3 (Instruction)?
3. After completing this self-evaluation, you will do some more practice. What do you think you will need to pay attention to more in order to improve your requests?

After completing the self-evaluation task, learners were shown video scenarios similar to Part 2 but with different requesting situations and asked to record their responses via audio or text. Example request responses are provided in video format after they complete the practice task.

In Unit 2 on email requests, Part 5 aimed to provide learners the chance to further apply their knowledge. They were tasked to write an email based on several scenarios. After the learners submitted all their email responses, they received feedback in the form of an example email response appropriate to each scenario (Figure 8.4).

8.3.2.6 Part 6: Strategies The goal of Unit 1-Part 6 was to provide strategies to make spoken requests in academic settings through the lens of international

Figure 8.5 Linguistic form and type of request highlighted in the video

students with high English language proficiency currently in the US. In the video, two international students gave some of the request strategies that they had used in the past. They also described some of the more difficult situations in which they had to make requests. As the international students narrated their experience, the forms of the request and the types of request strategies used were highlighted on the video (Figure 8.5).

After viewing the two international students sharing their experiences, learners were tasked with self-reflection. Learners wrote their reflections in English and were given as much time as they needed to complete the task. In their self-reflection, they were asked to compare spoken request strategies in academic settings within the US and their home country. This self-reflection was important because it can be considered a part of strategic knowledge, knowledge that acts as a support system when there is insufficient information and/ or communicative breakdown (Timpe-Laughlin, Wain, & Schmidgall, 2015). Unit 2-Part 6 was structured the same way as Unit 1-Part 6 but focussed on requests in email communication.

8.3.3   Data Collection

To emulate the use of self-access materials in the real world, participants were given as much time as they needed to view the instructional materials and complete the tasks. They were also under no pressure to complete all tasks in the course, although they were instructed to try to complete the course in a linear manner. After completing Units 1 and 2, participants completed a feedback questionnaire for each unit. The question from the feedback questionnaire that

Table 8.2 *Number of participants who completed the tasks and feedback question in each unit*

Task	Unit 1	Unit 2
Part 2: Pre-Instruction Assessment	18	12
Part 5: Application	13	9
Feedback Question	16	11

Note: The Pre-Instruction Assessment in Unit 2 is not included in the data analysis in the present study because the learners did not produce any requests in the task. Each number represented in the table is out of twenty-one possible participants.

Table 8.3 *Scenarios for pre- and post-instruction tasks in Units 1 and 2*

	Professor	Teaching Assistant (TA)	Classmate	Writing Centre Consultant
Unit 1-Part 2 (Spoken Requests, Pre-Instruction)	**Advising session.** Request information on some elective course.	**Consultation session.** Request clarification for feedback on an essay assignment.	**Classroom.** Request for help with a topic that was covered in class.	**Consultation session.** Request to focus on the grammar of a paper.
Unit 1-Part 5 (Spoken Requests, Post-Instruction)	**Office hours.** Request further explanation for concepts introduced in class.	**Consultation session.** Request clarification of an assignment instruction.	**Classroom.** Request to work together for a group assignment.	**Consultation session.** Request help with the overall structure of a research paper.
Unit 2-Part 5 (Email Requests, Post-Instruction)	Request for a letter of recommendation for a scholarship.	Request for a way to possibly improve your current grade.	Request that the classmate submit the assignment by the deadline.	-

was analysed for this chapter was 'Did your knowledge of making requests improve from using this unit? Why or why not?'.

Of the twenty-one participants, five participants did not complete any unit, sixteen participants completed the first unit, and eleven participants completed both units. Although some did not complete all the tasks in the units and did not submit the questionnaires (Table 8.2), all participant answers were still saved and used in the data analysis.

Table 8.3 summarises the scenarios and interlocutors introduced in Part 2 in Unit 1, and Part 5 in Units 1 and 2.

8.3.4 Data Analysis

To answer the first research question (To what extent do participants incorporate the request strategies introduced in the materials into their productions of

Table 8.4 *Coding of learners' request strategies in the production tasks*

Strategy		Example Linguistic Realisation
Indirect request	Str 1. Hints	*Do I need to add information about figures who develop economics?*
Conventionally indirect (hearer-oriented conditions)	Str 2. Ability	*Can you help explain what those mean?*
	Willingness	*... would you mind giving me suggestion about elective courses that I should take?*
	Permission	*May I take your time?*
	Str 3. Suggestory Formulae	*Since it require a teamwork to fulfill, why don't we working together?*
Conventionally indirect (speaker-based conditions)	Str 4. Wishes	*I would like to consult on the grammar of my paper ...*
	Str 5. Desires/needs	*... I think I need some assistance in the last topic.*
Direct requests	Str 6. Obligation	*We have to move fast.*
	Str 7. Performatives	*But for improvement, I want you to analyse some examples I made regarding direct and indirect request in my assignment.*
	Str 8. Imperatives	*Please give me some advice.*

spoken and email requests?), the researcher focussed on analysing data collected from pre-instruction (Unit 1-Part 2: Pre-Instruction Assessment) and post-instruction (Unit 1 and Unit 2-Part 5: Application) production tasks. The learner responses in the Pre-Instruction Assessment and Application that were in the form of audio files were transcribed. The transcribed responses and those that were already in text format were then coded using the request strategies framework by Trosborg (1995). Table 8.4 illustrates this framework using example linguistic realisations from learner responses. The request strategies were counted to calculate the raw frequencies and percentages.

To answer the second research question (What reported knowledge gains did participants identify in their self-evaluation and feedback?), participants' responses to the self-evaluation prompt in Unit 1-Part 5 and an open-ended question (Did your knowledge of making requests improve from using this unit? Why or why not?) in both feedback questionnaires were deductively coded using Timpe-Laughlin, Wain, and Schmidgall's (2015) knowledge components of pragmatic competence. Table 8.5 shows example comments and the type of knowledge that it represents.

Table 8.5 *Coding of learners' reported knowledge gains (adapted from Timpe-Laughlin, Wain, & Schmidgall, 2015)*

Knowledge	Definition	Example Comments
Sociocultural	Knowledge of factors such as topic, role of participants, setting, norms of conventions and interaction, power relations, gender, and age.	*[I learned] how to choose the request in polite terms.*
Pragmatic-functional	Knowledge required to make connections between form and meaning.	*I can use more variety making requests strategies.*
Grammatical	Knowledge of lexis and rules of morphology, syntax, semantics, phonology, and graphology.	*I did not know what words that needs to be used whenever we speak, even I did not care what words coming out of my mouth. so, I think I feel improved after taking this unit.*
Discourse	Knowledge required to create cohesion and coherence.	*My response to this scenario wasn't flowing appropriately, I probably could formulate my request by questioning the hearer's ability to provide information before asking my purpose.*
Strategic	Knowledge acquired from learning about other people's experiences and reflecting on the knowledge of their own culture.	No examples found

8.4   Findings and Discussion

8.4.1   *Incorporation of Request Strategies in Participants' Productions of Requests*

To examine participants' use of request strategies before and after viewing the instructional materials in the course, their request responses were manually coded using Trosborg's (1995) framework of request strategy types.

8.4.1.1 Spoken Request Strategies Table 8.6 summarises the request strategies used by learners in Unit 1 Part 2, regardless of the request scenario in which it was produced.

From this frequency data, it is important to note that the participants seem to already be using indirect and conventionally indirect (hearer-oriented) request strategies prior to viewing the main instructional video in Unit 1-Part 3. Approximately 70.7 per cent were indirect and conventionally indirect

Table 8.6 *Overall request strategies produced by learners in Unit 1-Part 2: Pre-instruction assessment (N=18)*

Strategy		Raw Frequency	Percentage (%)
Indirect request	Str 1. Hints	2	2.06
Conventionally indirect (hearer-oriented conditions)	Str 2. Ability	33	33.33
	Str 2. Willingness	15	15.15
	Str 2. Permission	20	20.20
	Str 3. Suggestory Formulae	0	0.00
Conventionally indirect (speaker-based conditions)	Str 4. Wishes	5	5.05
	Str 5. Desires/Needs	18	18.18
Direct requests	Str 6. Obligation	0	0.00
	Str 7. Performatives	0	0.00
	Str 8. Imperatives	6	6.06
Total		99	100.00

(hearer-oriented) request strategies with the remaining being conventionally indirect (speaker-based) and direct request strategies. When this aggregated request strategy data is broken down based on the scenario in which it was produced, a different pattern can be seen. Figure 8.6 shows that the participants generally tend to question the ability of the hearer to make their requests. This strategy was more commonly used in the TA, classmate, and writing centre consultant scenarios. On the other hand, participants frequently used the willingness strategy in the professor scenario. Additionally, the conventionally indirect (speaker-based) and direct request strategies only account for 29.29 per cent of the request strategies produced, with participants favouring expressions of desires or needs.

A closer look at the actual linguistic realisations further revealed some interesting request realisations. In the first scenario, participants were asked to request information about elective courses from a professor, because they were unsure which courses were interesting. The scenario's imposition is quite low (-R), but the power relationship (+P) and social distance (+SD) can still be considered quite big. Though participants favoured the use of hearer-oriented strategies (ability and willingness), they tended to use only *can/could you* or *will/would you* request forms. In fact, of the 6 ability and 7 willingness request strategies produced in response to the first scenario, 12 of those were in the form of *can/could* and *will/would you* request with minimal internal or external modifiers. The findings are reminiscent of Wang and Halenko's study in this volume. They found that the Chinese L2 users of English who were studying abroad in England tended to use *can/could* with limited internal modification, though with a lot more external modification, in their email requests to faculty.

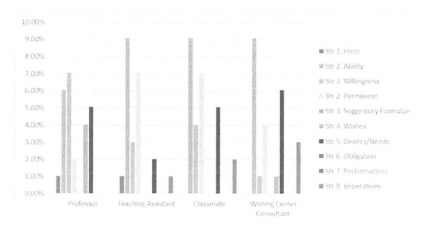

Figure 8.6 Breakdown of request strategies used by scenario type in the Unit 1 Part 2: Pre-instruction assessment

Furthermore, despite using indirect requests, the linguistics realisations demonstrated instances of pragmatic failure. Examples 1 and 2 illustrates this.

(1) Would you like to give me some recommendation, please?
(2) I just want to remind you that today is our appointment for advising me about my concern with the elective courses that I should take based on my research interest. Did you remember professor?

In Example 1, the request produced sounds quite unnatural and a misuse of the willingness query. This is because the request can possibly be understood as the participant placing the burden of offering the recommendation to the professor. On the other hand, Example 2 was coded as a hinting strategy. However, in the context of the scenario, using the hinting strategy would not be particularly helpful in helping achieve the request goal as the utterances produced places an emphasis on the professor's ability to remember the advising appointment.

Additionally, there were also instances in which participants used speaker-oriented strategies, specifically expressions of desires or needs which can be quite direct without appropriate modifications. Examples of these desire/needs request strategy are illustrated in Examples 3 to 5. These requests can come off as very demanding considering the student-professor power relationship.

(3) **I want** to know your opinion and **I wish** you could give me some advice.
(4) **I need** your advice to choose which course is suitable for me?
(5) Do you have any advice and suggestions? **I'd like** to hear it.

Aside from these pragmatic failures, some potential L1 pragmatic transfers were also observed in the supporting moves of the requests. In one instance, a participant used the phrase *Assalamu alaikum* as a greeting prior to making their request. This is a commonly used Arabic greeting used by Indonesians as Indonesia has one of the largest Muslim populations in the world. The reference term *Ma'am* or *Mam* was also used by the participants. In fact, this reference term was used by the participants in other scenarios. The use of this formal reference term can be quite out of place in a US academic setting. However, such terms are favoured in the Indonesian academic setting as a way to show reverence to people of higher power.

The second scenario was a situation in which participants were asked to request explanation about feedback on an essay assignment from a TA. Similar to the professor scenario, the imposition is low due to the fact that it is the expected duty of a TA to address any student concerns regarding their feedback. However, two participants used request strategies that can be construed as a demand. Their request realisations are shown in Examples 6 and 7.

(6) i wanna ask you about my essay? so what do you think? **Could** [sic] **you like** to tell me?

(7) **I need** a help from you to give some suggestions in order to enrich my essay assignment.

(8) **Please tell me** how to improve this essay.

Though participants who produced the requests in Examples 7 and 8 may have understood the goal of the request (to ask clarification about feedback they received on an assignment), it appears that they were not able to use the appropriate linguistic expressions to ask for clarification. It may also be that the participants chose to use these request strategies because the direct translation to the Indonesian language does not sound as face-threatening as it does in English.

The third scenario was a situation in which participants asked a classmate for help with a topic that was covered in class, but that they wanted to understand more. Similar to other scenarios, participants also used request strategies that can sound very demanding, especially because the request in this situation is particularly face-threatening due to the fact that the classmate is not someone that the requester has often talked to (this particular contextual information was made available to students prior to their completion of the task). Moreover, the request is of quite a high degree of imposition. One particularly demanding request produced is shown in Example 9.

(9) **I would like to** understand more about a topic that was covered in our class. If you don't mind, **teach me the topic**, please?

Table 8.7 *Overall request strategies produced by learners in Unit 1-Part 5: Application (N=11)*

Strategy		Raw Frequency	Percentage (%)
Indirect request	Str 1. Hints	1	2.08
Conventionally indirect (hearer-oriented conditions)	Str 2. Ability	13	27.08
	Str 2. Willingness	15	31.25
	Str 2. Permission	11	22.92
	Str3. Suggestory Formulae	1	2.08
Conventionally indirect (speaker-based conditions)	Str 4. Wishes	2	4.17
	Str 5. Desires/needs	5	10.42
Direct requests	Str 6. Obligation	0	0.00
	Str 7. Performatives	0	0.00
	Str 8. Imperatives	0	0.00
Total		48	100.00

Note: While thirteen participants completed this part, two participants misunderstood the prompt. Therefore, their responses were excluded from the analysis.

In Example 9, the expression of the speaker's own desire has already highlighted the speaker-orientation of the request, which became even more direct after the participant followed it by using the imperative *teach me the topic.* As can be seen, the addition of *If you don't mind* and *please* attempts to mitigate the directness of the request, which could be considered as an impolite request. However, the phrase *Kalau Anda tidak keberatan (If you don't mind)* and *Tolong (Please)* in Indonesian can be adequate politeness markers.

The fourth scenario that participants responded to was a situation in which they asked a writing centre consultant to focus on the grammar of a paper that they brought to a consultation session. This is a fairly low-imposition request, because of the nature of the interaction between a student and a writing consultant in a writing centre. The most demanding request produced was in the form of a *want*-statement as shown in Example 10.

(10) **I want you** to correct the grammar of my paper to focus on the grammar because I think that there are a lot of mistakes of my paper that I've made about the grammar. So I think **I need you** to correct them to become better.

Not only did the participant initiate their request using a *want*-statement, but the request is also followed by a need-statement. This further highlighted the speaker-orientation of the overall request.

Table 8.7 summarises the request strategies produced by learners in Part 5: Application of Unit 1. The number of indirect and conventionally indirect

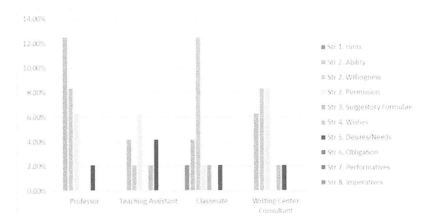

Figure 8.7 Breakdown of request strategies used by scenario type in the
Unit 1-Part 5: Application

(hearer-orientation) requests rose to approximately 85 per cent. In fact, compared to the requests produced in the pre-instruction, participants overwhelmingly used conventionally indirect strategies (97.92 per cent) with no direct requests observed in the post-instruction. Moreover, the suggestory formulae strategy also occurred in participants' production in the post-instruction task which was not observed in the pre-instruction.

As shown in Figure 8.7, a breakdown of request strategies by scenario type shows a similar pattern of requests produced in the pre-instruction. The frequency data suggests that participants still use more conventionally indirect strategies across the different scenarios. However, whereas participants used more willingness, ability, and desires/needs strategies in the professor scenario in the pre-instruction, in the post-instruction participants leaned towards using ability, willingness, and permission strategies. This is quite a safe approach, perhaps influenced by the discussion of power relationship and social distance in the instructional video. It is also possible that since the closeness of the participant and the professor was not specified, participants chose to be more polite. The sole conventionally indirect speaker-based strategy was a *need*-statement but was followed by an ability request type which made the *need*-statement quite appropriate (Example 11).

(11) Well, I have read from some sources explained about the definition of performative and imperatives but **I need** more clarity especially the difference between them, **could you** please give me further explanation?

In the TA scenario, learners were expected to request clarification of an assignment instruction. Surprisingly, three participants used direct questions as a request strategy. Since Trosborg's (1995) request framework does not consider direct questions as requests, these requests were not coded. However, Cunningham (2017) considers direct questions as a direct request type. In the context of the scenario, the questions should not be considered impolite as it is natural for learners to pose questions to their instructors.

In the classmate scenario, learners were expected to ask a classmate who they are friends with to work together for a group assignment. Examples 12 to 13 shows some instances of successful incorporation of willingness request strategies.

(12) … **do you mind** if we work together in a group assignment?
(13) **I was wondering if you'd be willing** to work together for a group assignment?
(14) … **would you mind** if we work it together?

Some participants also used request strategies that focussed on the 'wants' of the requestee, as opposed to the 'wants' of the requester.

(15) **… do you want to** work together with me?
(16) **Would you like to** become my partner?

Another interesting pattern occurred in the writing centre consultant scenario. In this scenario, participants were asked to request to a writing centre consultant for help with the overall structure of a research paper for a conference. In the pre-instruction, participants used a range of strategies, particularly ability and desires/needs strategies. However, in the post-instruction, participants overwhelmingly used conventionally indirect hearer-oriented request strategies, particularly permission and willingness strategies (16.66 per cent). Specifically, they frequently used *Could you/we* and *Can you/we* constructions that were introduced in the video materials whenever writing centre consultant scenarios were presented.

8.4.1.2 Email Request Strategies The other application task in the course was presented in Unit 2 which was specifically on making requests in email communication. Table 8.8 summarises the request strategies produced by learners in Unit 2-Part 5 on making requests in emails. Much like the distribution of strategies in Unit 1-Part 5, hearer-oriented strategies were frequent in participants' requesting emails making up 82.35per cent of the total requests produced. Similar findings were reported by Bou-Franch (2013), who found that the EFL participants in her study favoured using conventionally indirect request strategies in their emails.

Table 8.8 *Overall request strategies produced by learners in Unit 2-Part 5: Application (N=9)*

Strategy		Raw Frequency	Percentage (%)
Indirect request	Str 1. Hints	2	5.88
Conventionally indirect (hearer-oriented conditions)	Str 2. Ability	12	35.29
	Str 2. Willingness	9	26.47
	Str 2. Permission	5	14.71
	Str3. Suggestory Formulae	0	0.00
Conventionally indirect (speaker-based conditions)	Str 4. Wishes	2	5.88
	Str 5. Desires/needs	2	5.88
Direct requests	Str 6. Obligation	0	0.00
	Str 7. Performatives	1	2.94
	Str 8. Imperatives	1	2.94
Total		34	100.00

A breakdown of the request strategies used by scenario type can be seen in Figure 8.8. In the first scenario, learners were tasked to request a recommendation letter from their advisor. In general, participants were able to compose a coherent email with the corresponding appropriate request. The only request that stood out as particularly impolite is shown in Example 17 as the participant used the phrase *as soon as possible*, which is an intensifier (Blum-Kulka et al., 1989). Such an intensifier is inappropriate for this scenario because the request is directed to an advisor (+P) and it can be considered a high imposition (+R) one.

(17) May I get the letter of recommendation as soon as possible please?

The use of this intensifier was also observed in a corpus of EFL email requests to faculty collected by Economidou-Kogetsidis (2011). Native speaking lecturers who were asked to evaluate the appropriateness of the emails commented negatively on the use of the intensifier stating that the student 'failed to take the lecturer's time into consideration' (p. 3207).

In the TA scenario, learners needed to ask for a way to improve their grade. This can be quite a face-threatening situation. Overall, participants tended to choose one of two approaches: (1) request for a meeting with the TA to talk about their grade, or (2) asking whether it is possible to improve their grade. The first approach was surprising to see because the instructions were intended to result in the second approach. One explanation for this strategy is that, as opposed to making the request in an email, the participants were more comfortable communicating such a high imposition request in a face-to-face setting where they can observe the TAs responses.

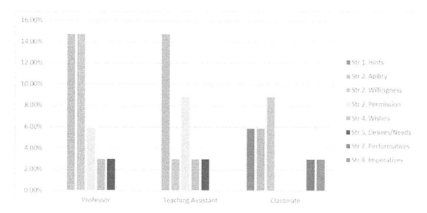

Figure 8.8 Breakdown of request strategies used by scenario type in the Unit 2-Part 5: Application

In the classmate scenario, participants wrote an email to a classmate who has not contributed to a group assignment, the task was to request that the classmate submit the assignment by the deadline. Learners were also informed that the classmate is a friend of theirs. Therefore, it seems that despite the relatively face-threatening potential of the situation, learners were comfortable enough to use a mix of hinting and desire/need strategies as illustrated in Examples 18 and 19.

(18) I noticed that you have not sent your part for our English Assignment.
      Do you have a problem with your parts? Would you like me to help you?
(19) **I would like** to remind you our assignment deadline is this Friday.

This is also perhaps due to the asynchronous nature of email communication which requires individuals to make clear their intended message in the initial email, especially in this scenario where there is a deadline looming. Economidou-Kogetsidis (2011) coded example responses such as the one in Example 19 as reminder requests, which can serve to highlight the addressee's unperformed duties.

Overall, compared to their performance in Unit 1: Pre-Instruction Assessment, most of the participants' performances in the post-instruction assessments seemed to suggest that they were able to some extent successfully incorporate the knowledge of request strategies that they obtained from the instructional materials.

8.4.2   Participants' Reported Knowledge Gains

To further explore how learners perceived their pragmatic competence, their self-evaluation entries and responses to an open-ended question in the feedback questionnaires were coded using Timpe-Laughlin, Wain, and Schmidgall's (2015) knowledge components of pragmatic competence. Overall, four of the five knowledge components were identified in the participants' comments. The first was sociocultural knowledge which was the most frequently reported learning gain. Comments that were coded as sociocultural knowledge mainly referred to participants' new-found awareness of power relationship, social distance, and degree of imposition as shown in Examples 20 to 24.

(20) I have a better picture of social relationship between several academic staffs and the students. Therefore, I could have simplified some of my requests.

(21) Same with two scenarios above, I used indirect request, but I am sure that I should modify my request to be more direct because I have same degree of level with the hearer which is my classmate.

(22) This course contains with some video demonstrations which showing users how to formulate request using various kind of ways in an academic setting, thus it makes me understand how to positioning myself appropriately when I make a request in a different situation.

(23) I was always composing my request email directly. but after this lesson, I find out that I have to make a strong reason for my request in order my request accepted.

(24) I know how to make request to someone like professor who's not too close to me.

Examples 20 to 23 are especially useful because participants were able to point out a specific outcome of their sociocultural awareness. In Example 20, the participant was aware that their requests tended to be lengthy and has now understood that having certain power relationships and social distance with different people in the US academic setting can affect the length of their request. Similarly, in Examples 21 and 22, the participants realised the importance of understanding their position as the requester relative to the position of the requestee to tailor their request. In the case of Example 21, the participant specifically noticed that they were using indirect requests regardless of the situational context, but having viewed the instructional video, now believed they can be more direct with classmates. In Example 23, the comment provided arguably seems as though the participant is referring to making direct requests in emails, but the following sentence suggests that they are referring to the notion of writing an email just by stating the request without supporting moves, such as a strong reason. This awareness is definitely a positive outcome as the instructional video in Unit 2 highlighted the importance of providing a reason especially for high imposition requests.

The second type of knowledge gain found was pragmatic-functional knowledge. Most participants' comments were not as specific as the ones coded as sociocultural knowledge as shown in Examples 25 and 26.

(25) I can use more variety making requests strategies.
(26) I used several phrases that do not suit the context. After learning the material in part 3, I know more about proper phrases or words that can be used in certain contexts.

But three participants were able to provide specific examples for what they had learned:

(27) ... I should also consider the use of Could and Would. All this time, I thought they are interchangeable. After watching the video, though, I realise using Could is preferable is [sic] some settings and using Would is better in the other.
(28) ... but sometimes i have to change can to may to be more polite.
(29) I have just realised that I can make a polite request not only by using 'could' or 'would', but also the combination between 'can' and 'please' will do.

Indeed, the instructional video in Unit 1-Part 3 discussed the differentiation between *could*, *would*, *can*, and *may* in making requests; modal verbs frequently taught to Indonesian learners. However, English language textbooks used in Indonesian schools rarely provide the contextual information needed to make subtle distinctions between words and phrases that can affect their pragmatic meaning (Muhammad, 2018). As such, it is not surprising to see participants' comments like Example 27 in which they stated they use words like *could* and *would* interchangeably.

The third type of knowledge gain perceived by learners was grammatical knowledge. There were only two instances of grammatical knowledge-related comments found. This particular type of knowledge gain was related to the knowledge of lexis and phonology (Timpe-Laughlin, Wain, & Schmidgall, 2015: 18) components of grammatical knowledge. Example 30 demonstrates knowledge of lexis, and Example 31 reflects knowledge of phonology.

(30) I did not know what words that needs to be used whenever we speak [in the context of making requests], even I did not care what words coming out of my mouth.
(31) Basically, I am used to making request in English when I was an undergraduate myself. However, I can improve the way I said itt[sic] to sound more natural.

Example 30 suggests that through viewing the instructional content and completing the tasks, the participant was able to obtain knowledge of words that they can use to deliberately form their utterances. On the other hand, Example 31 suggests that while the participant believed that they were already familiar with making requests in English, they can make the effort to make their speech sound more natural.

The fourth and final type of perceived knowledge gain found was discourse knowledge. There were only four instances of comments on this particular gain as shown in Examples 32 to 35.

(32) opening and ice breakers are needed to start a request.
(33) Now, I also know how to avoid making complex request when it's actually not necessary.
(34) My response to this scenario wasn't flowing appropriately, I probably could formulate my request by questioning the hearer's ability to provide information before asking my purpose.
(35) I got new knowledge about: – email structure.

Example 32 was notable in that the participant noted that before they go straight to the request, they need some background information as the absence of such information for a request often affects the politeness of the request. While Example 33 was coded as evidence of discourse knowledge, it is related to sociocultural knowledge. This is implied by the participant's statement ... *when it's actually not necessary*. This statement suggests that the participant was aware that certain requests should be more complex compared to others depending on the situational context. Example 34 was also particularly insightful because the participant noticed that the flow of their response was not quite appropriate for a particular scenario (requesting to a writing centre consultant to focus on the grammar of their paper). They continued by providing an alternative way to formulate their utterance, which made use of insights obtained from the instructional material (questioning the hearer's ability to provide information). Finally, Example 35 was seen as a positive outcome of teaching the email structure in Unit 2, indicating that the participant understood that there is a certain structure to email communication. While the use of email communication is particularly prevalent in the US academic setting, this is not necessarily true for the Indonesian academic setting. Based on a questionnaire completed by ninety-four Indonesian undergraduate and postgraduate students who have studied at Australian universities, Suryani (2007) found that students rarely sent emails to lecturers or tutors and that face-to-face communication was preferred over email communication. This is unsurprising as email communication is not the most popular medium of communication among Indonesian university students, with students preferring to communicate face-to-face, by phone call, or by text message with faculty members, TAs, classmates, and staff.

Interestingly, strategic knowledge was not found in any of the participants' comments. This may be because there was only one video in each unit (Part 6: Strategies) that served to help them obtain this knowledge, which may not be enough to make an impression on the participants. Regardless, the fact that four of the pragmatic competence knowledge components appeared in the participants' comments is a positive outcome. This is especially true with the many sociocultural knowledge-related comments. This finding is in line with previous literature on the outcome of explicit teaching of pragmatics, in that explicit instruction led to better gains in sociopragmatic knowledge (e.g., Rose & Ng, 2001; Chapter 7, this volume).

8.5   Conclusion

As with any study, some limitations emerged that needs to be addressed in future research. Firstly, the instructional videos, particularly those in the making requests in spoken communication unit, could delve deeper into the non-verbal communication part of pragmatics (e.g., prosody, body language, eye contact). The focus of the current video materials was very much verbal communication. Additionally, learners were not able to observe longer multi-turn exchanges that would potentially help them gain discourse knowledge. Not showing lengthier discourse can also skew their idea of what US academic discourse is like. In relation to this, the production tasks did not allow learners to do longer dialogues. In fact, some participants attempted to write a whole dialogue. Perhaps providing multi-turn discourse completion tasks (Nguyen, 2019) can help learners practise turn-taking. We also need to acknowledge that some participants opted to type their spoken requests as opposed to recording them. While the typing option was provided to give learners with slow internet access the opportunity to still participate in the task, some studies (e.g., Koike & Palmiere, 2011) have found that request strategies used in spoken versus written tasks differ.

Future expansion of the course should also include more opportunities for practise along with example possible answers, and robust informative feedback that learners can refer to when self-evaluating their learning performance. Providing extensive prepared feedback can address the limitation of SALL, that is, it is limited in providing more personalised feedback. As such, learners may pick up pragmatic knowledge in fragmented pieces. Specifically, for Unit 2's instructional video on email communication, it should elaborate on email etiquette, particularly in terms of communicating in a 'multi-party interaction' context (Skovholt & Svennevig, 2006), which the current materials were unable to address.

In conclusion, the present study adds to the body of literature on the use of SALL to teach pragmatics, specifically making requests in US academic settings. This is accomplished by elaborating on the design of the materials, investigating how participants perceived the usefulness of the SALL materials, and analysing how their performance in making requests differed between pre-instruction and post-instruction tasks. In order to accommodate the need for more SALL materials to help EFL learners develop their pragmatic competence, this study can and should be expanded on to include other speech acts that are identified to be most important in US academic settings.

References

Biesenbach-Lucas, S. (2007). Students writing emails to faculty: An examination of e-politeness among native and non-native speakers of English. *Language Learning & Technology*, 11(2), 59–81.

Blum-Kulka, S., House, J., & Kasper, G. (1989). The CCSARP coding manual. In S. Blum-Kulka, J. House, & G. Kasper (eds.), *Cross-Cultural Pragmatics: Requests and Apologies*. Norwood, NJ: Ablex, pp. 273–294.

Bou-Franch, P. (2013) EFL email writing: A focus on pragmatic transfer. In N. Estevez & B. Clavel (eds.), *La Adquisición de una Segunda Lengua en el Nuevo Espacio Europeo de Educación Superior*. Valencia: Universitat de València, pp. 39–55.

Cunningham, D. J. (2017). Methodological innovation for the study of request production in telecollaboration. *Language Learning & Technology*, 21(1), 75–98.

Economidou-Kogetsidis, M. (2011). 'Please answer me as soon as possible': Pragmatic failure in non-native speakers' e-mail requests to faculty. *Journal of Pragmatics*, 43(13), 3193–3215.

Eslami-Rasekh, Z. (2005). Raising the pragmatic awareness of language learners. *ELT Journal*, 59(3), 199–208.

Ishihara, N., & Cohen, A. (2010). *Teaching and Learning Pragmatics*, Harlow: Pearson.

Kim, D., & Hall, J. K. (2002). The role of an interactive book reading program in the development of second language pragmatic competence. *The Modern Language Journal*, 86(3), 332–348.

Koike, D. A., & Palmiere, D. T. (2011). First and second language pragmatics in third language oral and written modalities. *Foreign Language Annals*, 44(1), 80–104.

McConachy, T., & Hata, K. (2013). Addressing textbook representations of pragmatics and culture. *ELT Journal*, 67(3), 294–301.

Meihami, H., & Khanlarzadeh, M. (2015). Pragmatic content in global and local ELT textbooks: A micro analysis study. *SAGE Open*, 5(4), 1–10.

Muhammad, A. A. (2017). Creation and Evaluation of Multimedia Materials to Promote Development of Current and Prospective International Students' Pragmatic Competence in Academic Settings. Unpublished master's thesis, Iowa State University.

Muhammad, A. A. (2018). The Representation of Pragmatic Input in English Language Textbooks Used in Indonesian High Schools. 4th International Conference of the American Pragmatics Association. University at Albany, SUNY.

Nguyen, M. (2019). Data collection methods in L2 pragmatics research. In N. Taguchi (ed.), *The Routledge Handbook of Second Language Acquisition and Pragmatics*. New York: Routledge, pp. 195–211.

Ren, W., & Han, Z. (2016). The representation of pragmatic knowledge in recent ELT textbooks. *ELT Journal*, 70(4), 424–434.

Rose, K. R., & Ng, C. (2001). Inductive and deductive teaching of compliments and compliment responses. In K. R. Rose & G. Kasper (eds.), *Pragmatics in Language Teaching*. New York: Cambridge University Press, pp. 145–170.

Sheerin, S. (1991). Self-access. *Language Teaching*, 24(3), 143–157.

Skovholt, K., & Svennevig, J. (2006). Email copies in workplace interaction. *Journal of Computer-Mediated Communication*, 12(1), 42–65.

Suryani, A. (2007). *Exploring new media usage among Indonesian students in Australian universities.* 2007 ISANA International Conference 'Student success in international education'. Stamford Grand, Glenelg, Adelaide, Australia, ISANA. https://users.monash.edu/~hwatt/students/A%20Suryani_ISANA%20Conference_2007.pdf.

Sykes, J. M., & Cohen, A. (2006). Dancing with Words: Strategies for Learning Pragmatics in Spanish. www.carla.umn.edu/speechacts/sp_pragmatics/home.html.

Taguchi, N. (2009). Pragmatic competence in Japanese as a second language: An introduction. In N. Taguchi (ed.), *Pragmatic Competence.* Berlin and New York: Mouton De Gruyter, pp. 1–18.

Timpe-Laughlin, V., Wain, J., & Schmidgall, J. (2015). Defining and operationalizing the construct of pragmatic competence: Review and recommendations. ETS Research Report Series, 15.06. Princeton, NJ: ETS.

Trosborg, A. (1995). *Interlanguage Pragmatics: Requests, Complaints, and Apologies.* Berlin and New York: Mouton De Gruyter.

Vellenga, H. (2004). Learning pragmatics from ESL and EFL textbooks: How likely? *TESL-EJ*, 8(2), 1–18.

Conclusion

Jiayi Wang and Nicola Halenko

As the world's common language, English is widely perceived as a valuable skill in today's global community. The number of English learners is over 1 billion today and is only going to grow (Beare, 2020). For many years, English language learning and teaching has prioritised grammar and vocabulary. However, Thomas's (1983) seminal work brings home the point that even with well-developed grammar and vocabulary, learners could still fail in communication, and their pragmatic infelicities may not only reflect them as being less-than-proficient speakers but also poorly on them as individuals, thus causing more serious consequences. Interactants may display different levels of tolerance with regards pragmatic failure, however. Within English as a Lingua Franca (ELF) interactions, which involve the negotiation of intercultural discourse and behaviours, participants may be more forgiving of pragmatic failure, playing down or even ignoring infelicitous moves as they work towards their shared communicative goals. Interactions in educational or professional contexts, however, which are constrained by local norms, conventions and expectations (e.g., study abroad academic settings), may be less forgiving, meaning developing pragmatic competence remains an important issue in language teaching and learning (e.g., Chapters 2, 3, and 4, this volume).

As the emphasis is now rightly being placed on developing *intercultural* users of English, L2 pragmatics has a major role to play. Intercultural competence, defined as 'a complex of abilities needed to perform effectively and appropriately when interacting with linguistically and culturally different others' (Fantini, 2007: 9), is not an easy task to promote in the language classroom since it does not come with a standardised set of pedagogical techniques (Liddicoat, 2011; Wang & Halenko, 2022). Instead, practitioners should be led by a mutual understanding of what it means to teach language in an intercultural way in order to inform their own classroom practices. In terms of operationalising this intercultural understanding, Liddicoat and Scarino (2013) offer a useful starting point by encouraging the design of activities which engage learners to 'notice', 'compare', 'reflect', and 'interact' with language materials to explore and advance their own intercultural experiences. By initiating this sequence of steps, learning becomes meaningful, contextualised, thought-provoking, and personal. These four steps are not dissimilar to existing frameworks designed to support pragmatics instruction which further underline the existing interrelationship between intercultural and pragmatic competencies.

This book makes an original contribution to our knowledge of pragmatics in English language learning by, for the first time, bringing together different age groups (young and adult learners), international perspectives (Chinese, German, Greek, Indonesian, Italian, Mexican, and Norwegian learners), and modes, media, and contexts of learning (self-access online learning, and learning inside and outside the classroom with and without explicit instruction, in both at-home and study abroad settings). It incorporates instructional input, productive output, and evaluation. There are several common threads emerging from this collection of chapters. First, learners' pragmatic competence can be very slow to grow naturally, and moreover, it often does not grow in tandem with language proficiency, even in a native English-speaking environment (see Chapters 2 and 3, which tracked the pragmatic development of Chinese and Greek learners). While this observation is not new, it further underscores the importance of integrating pragmatics into the curriculum. Second, pragmatics tends to be overlooked in English language teaching and learning, and learners are often left to their own devices to muddle through, as illustrated in Chapter 4. There is still a clear need for more systematic approaches to pragmatics instruction (see Chapter 6 for an examination of EFL textbooks in Germany and Chapter 8 for the use of self-access online learning materials for Indonesian learners). Third, diversifying conceptual and methodological approaches to L2 pragmatics holds promise for future language learning, teaching, and research (see Chapter 7 for technology-enhanced instruction and assessment, and Chapter 5 for the use of visual and kinaesthetic tasks for young learners). Let us now consider the research and pedagogical implications of the book.

Research and Pedagogical Implications

This volume has four implications for research and pedagogy. First, *pragmatics in online and blended English language learning* warrants further research. As mentioned in Taguchi's opening chapter (Chapter 1), recent technological developments have given rise to new research areas which have advanced our investigation of pragmatics learning. The COVID-19 pandemic has fundamentally transformed the world of education. Online learning has become increasingly mainstream, bringing both challenges and opportunities. Schools, colleges, and universities around the world are reimagining learning and teaching. As a recent Joint Information Systems Committee (JISC) report shows, for example, universities are now less focussed on the either on-campus or

230 Jiayi Wang and Nicola Halenko

online debate: the future of higher education is blended (Maguire, Dale, & Pauli, 2020). In other words, blended learning in institutional settings is highly likely to be the new normal. Digital learning spaces are expanding the physical classroom as a learning site. Muhammad's study (Chapter 8) has proven the utility of self-access online learning. Online and blended learning in English teaching and learning is a relatively new area of study (Albiladi & Alshareef, 2019), and there is a clear need for more research.

Second, *young learners* (YLs) are a particularly underexplored learner population. Studies dedicated to YLs' pragmatics knowledge and development have been few and far between, partly due to the greater difficulty in gaining access and ethical approval and partly due to questioning whether children are able to understand the complexities involved in making socially and culturally informed language choices. Savić and Myrset's (Chapter 5) and Schauer's (Chapter 6) studies have shed light on the possibilities of working with YLs and adolescents in investigating their metapragmatic awareness and responses to input, but we call for more research on this under-investigated group of English learners.

Third, we recommend *diversifying conceptual and methodological approaches to inquiry*. Longitudinal studies which track learners over time such as the one by Wang and Halenko (Chapter 2) offer valuable insight, because the development of pragmatic competence is a long and often slow process, which does not typically follow a linear trajectory either. Mixed-methods research, which combines quantitative and qualitative data to gain a more holistic picture of learners' pragmatic development, as seen in Chapters 2, 5, and 7, is also needed on a much greater scale.

L2 pragmatics is more than learners' deployment of appropriate linguistic resources to express meanings, perception and evaluation are also important to consider. The recent conceptual development in the field of linguistic pragmatics has given growing attention to participant perspectives and interpretations, stressing that the very essence of language use lies in evaluation, because, for example, politeness only comes into existence through the evaluative moment (Spencer-Oatey & Kádár, 2021). Gesuato's (Chapter 4) and Savić and Myrset's (Chapter 5) contributions to this volume have adopted such lenses. Additionally, an L2 user is an inherently intercultural speaker with agency and L2 pragmatic development is layered and nuanced in nature (McConachy, 2019). Continuing the trend of drawing inspiration from other disciplines beyond second language acquisition (e.g., intercultural communication and psychology) would be useful to unpack the complexities of L2 pragmatic development, particularly in understanding the ways in which it is promoted and hindered.

Pedagogically, it is high time that we should consider how to *use online and blended learning to promote pragmatics teaching and learning and pragmatic development*, with the shifting landscape of educational change. We anticipate a surge of research activity in this area in the coming years. All the instructional chapters have once again shown that pragmatics is teachable and explicit instruction is usually beneficial. However, textbooks and classroom materials are well-known for lacking systematic and authentic pragmatics input (see for example Schauer's examination of secondary school textbooks and accompanying audio materials in Chapter 6). We acknowledge that not all teaching and learning settings have access to such resources but there is little doubt that digital integration gives flexible ways to redesign learning spaces and approaches to teaching.

In terms of where we head next with L2 pragmatic instruction, researchers would do well to consider some of these pertinent questions: (1) What is the turning point at which pragmatics gains as a result of instruction start to diminish? While (delayed) post-tests are a recommended feature of experimental studies, few adopt multiple post-test designs (Wang & Halenko, 2022); (2) Does intensive or spaced instruction offer better opportunities for pragmatics learning and retention? Though investigations with L2 learners have considered the distribution of instruction in the acquisition of grammar and vocabulary, it has yet to be directly applied to L2 pragmatics; (3) How do teachers in FL contexts maximise exposure to authentic L2 language? Since the classroom is typically the sole or major source of L2 input and exposure in FL settings, we need to empirically evaluate the effectiveness of resources which can offer access to the target language. Audiovisual materials such as films and TV shows, as well as corpus databases, have shown promise so far. Drawing on the studies in this volume, these questions are just some of the areas which have yet to be empirically validated on a wider scale.

Concluding Comments

Finally, we would like to thank you, the reader, for exploring some of the key issues in pragmatics and English language learning with us. English is more than a tool for communication, because language is power. It can open up new doors of opportunities, see new options, and build relationships across cultures. With contributions from some world-leading experts in this field, we hope that our book has highlighted the challenges and opportunities that have emerged across the different countries, as well as the various modes and contexts of learning. We hope this volume will stimulate reflection and inspiration for future research in L2 pragmatics.

References

Albiladi, W. S., & Alshareef, K. K. (2019). Blended learning in English teaching and learning: A review of the current literature. *Journal of Language Teaching and Research*, 10(2), 232–238.

Beare, K. (2020). How Many People Learn English?, ThoughtCo, 27 August, www .thoughtco.com/how-many-people-learn-english-globally-1210367.

Fantini, A. E. (2007). *Exploring and Assessing Intercultural Competence: Research Report*. Brattleboro, VT: Federation of the Experiment in International Living.

Liddicoat, A. J. (2011). Language teaching and learning from an intercultural perspective. In E. Hinkel (ed.), *Handbook of Research in Second Language Teaching and Learning*. New York: Routledge, pp. 837–855.

Liddicoat, A. J., & Scarino, A. (2013). *Intercultural Language Teaching and Learning*. New York: Wiley-Blackwell.

Maguire, D., Dale, L., & Pauli, M. (2020). *Learning and Teaching Reimagined: A New Dawn for Higher Education*. JISC. www.jisc.ac.uk/reports/learning-and-teaching-reimagined-a-new-dawn-for-higher-education.

McConachy, T. (2019). L2 pragmatics as 'intercultural pragmatics': Probing sociopragmatic aspects of pragmatic awareness. *Journal of Pragmatics*, 151, 167–176.

Spencer-Oatey, H., & Kádár, D. (2021). *Intercultural Politeness: Managing Relations across Cultures*. Cambridge: Cambridge University Press.

Thomas, J. (1983). Cross-cultural pragmatic failure. *Applied Linguistics*, 4(2), 91–112.

Wang, J., & Halenko, N. (2022). Developing the use of formulaic language for study abroad: A targeted instructional intervention. *The Language Learning Journal*.

Index

Milton Keynes UK
Ingram Content Group UK Ltd.
UKHW031444290224
438440UK00022B/170

9 781108 794930